AF885013

Environmental Law in Singapore

Environmental Law in Singapore

Fourth Edition

LYE Lin-Heng
Sean D. TSENG

This book was originally published as a monograph in the International Encyclopaedia of Laws/Environmental Law.

Founding Editor: Roger Blanpain†
General Editor: Frank Hendrickx
Volume Editor: Kurt Deketelaere

Wolters Kluwer

Published by:
Kluwer Law International B.V.
PO Box 316
2400 AH Alphen aan den Rijn
The Netherlands
E-mail: lrs-sales@wolterskluwer.com
Website: www.wolterskluwer.com/en/solutions/kluwerlawinternational

Sold and distributed by:
Wolters Kluwer Legal & Regulatory U.S.
920 Links Avenue
Landisville, PA 17538
United States of America
E-mail: customer.service@wolterskluwer.com

DISCLAIMER: The material in this volume is in the nature of general comment only. It is not offered as advice on any particular matter and should not be taken as such. The editor and the contributing authors expressly disclaim all liability to any person with regard to anything done or omitted to be done, and with respect to the consequences of anything done or omitted to be done wholly or partly in reliance upon the whole or any part of the contents of this volume. No reader should act or refrain from acting on the basis of any matter contained in this volume without first obtaining professional advice regarding the particular facts and circumstances at issue. Any and all opinions expressed herein are those of the particular author and are not necessarily those of the editor or publisher of this volume.

ISBN 978-94-035-5910-0

e-Book: ISBN 978-94-035-5920-9
web-PDF: ISBN 978-94-035-5930-8

This title is available on www.kluwerlawonline.com

© 2026 Kluwer Law International BV, The Netherlands, and/or subsidiaries, its licensors, and contributors. All rights are reserved, including those for text and data mining, AI training, and similar technologies.

No part of this publication may be reproduced, stored in a retrieval system, or transmitted in any form or by any means, electronic, mechanical, photocopying, recording, or otherwise, without written permission from the publisher.

Permission to use this content must be obtained from the copyright owner. More information can be found at: https://www.wolterskluwer.com/en/solutions/kluwerlawinternational/rights-and-permissions

Printed in the Netherlands.

The Authors

LYE Lin-Heng studied Law (LLB (Hons)) at the National University of Singapore (NUS), and at King's College, University of London (LLM), and Harvard University (LLM). She is an Advocate and Solicitor in Singapore and has taught Environmental Law and Property Law at the Law Faculty, NUS, for many years. She has now retired and is an Honorary Fellow at NUS. She was Director of the Faculty's Asia-Pacific Centre for Environmental Law (APCEL) from 2013 to 2018 and was instrumental in developing and chairing the university's multi-disciplinary MSc (Environmental Management) [MEM] programme (hosted by the School of Design & Environment) from its inception in 2001 to 2018. She was Visiting Associate Professor at Yale University's School of Forestry and Environmental Studies from 2003 to 2019. She was Vice-Chair of the IUCN Academy of Environmental Law and former co-chair of its Teaching and Capacity Building Committee. She was a member of the Board of Directors, WWF Singapore (2015–2021) and was Honorary Legal Advisor to the Nature Society, Singapore (NSS) for many years. She is now Honorary Advisor to both WWFS and NSS. She was a member of the Board of Directors of Singapore's public housing agency, the Housing & Development Board (HDB) (1998–2001). She is a member of the Strata Titles Board and was awarded Singapore's Public Service Medal (PBM) in 2016.

Sean D. TSENG studied Law (LLB (Hons)) at the undergraduate level at NUS and is qualified as an Advocate and Solicitor of the Singapore Supreme Court. He obtained his Master of Laws degree (LLM (Distinction)) from University College London (UCL) with an Environmental Law and Policy specialism. While at UCL, Sean won the Francis Taylor Building Prize for Best Overall Mark in Environmental Law & Policy, as well as the Maxi Alexander Prize for Research in Environmental Law & Policy for obtaining the highest mark for his dissertation. Sean taught Environmental Law at the Law Faculty of NUS for several years and has served as Adjunct Senior Research Fellow at APCEL since 2021. He is an award-winning essayist, winning the first prize for the CCS-ESS Essay Competition in 2022 (Environmental Sustainability: The Role of Competition and Consumer Protection Laws and Policies) in Singapore. He has contributed as a researcher and author to two United Nations reports, namely Regulating Air Quality: the First Global Assessment of Air Pollution Legislation (2021) and Environmental Courts and Tribunals – 2021: A Guide for Policy Makers (2022). He has also contributed as a leading author to the publication by the UN Global Compact Network Singapore and APCEL titled 'Putting Words into (Climate) Action: Ushering in Corporate Transition Plans'.

The law is stated as of 31 October 2025. For a full discussion on Environmental Law in Singapore, *see* Joseph Chun & Lye Lin Heng, *Environmental Law in Singapore* (2019), Academy Publishing, Singapore Academy of Law (xciii & 759 pp.).

Table of Contents

Table of Contents

Table of Contents

List of Abbreviations

AADMER	ASEAN Agreement on Disaster Management and Emergency Response
ABC	Active, Beautiful, Clean Waters
APCEL	Asia-Pacific Centre for Environmental Law
APEC	Asia-Pacific Economic Cooperation
APU	Anti-Pollution Unit
ARF	Additional Registration Fee
ARREST	Asia's Regional Response to Endangered Species Trafficking
ASEAN	Association of South East Asian Nations
ASTM	American Society for Testing and Materials
AVA	Agri-Food & Veterinary Authority
AWGNCB	ASEAN Working Group for Nature Conservation and Biodiversity
BAU	Business as Usual
BCA	Building and Construction Authority
BES	Bachelor in Environmental Studies
BESD	Building and Engineering Services Division
BOD	Biochemical Oxygen Demand
BSD	Business and Strategy Division
CAAS	Civil Aviation Authority of Singapore
CBD	Convention on Biological Diversity
CBPU	Central Building Plan Unit
CCCS	Competition and Consumer Commission of Singapore
CCRS	Centre for Climate Research Singapore
CDM	Clean Development Mechanism
CEA	Council for Estate Agencies
CEG	Clean Environment Group

List of Abbreviations

CEVS	Carbon Emissions-Based Vehicle Scheme
CFC	Chloroflourocarbon
CHM	Clearing-House Mechanism
CITES	Convention on International Trade in Endangered Species of Wild Fauna and Flora
CNG	Compressed Natural Gas
COD	Chemical Oxygen Demand
CPA	Carbon Pricing Act
CPPNM	Convention on Physical Protection of Nuclear Material
CRP	Centre for Radiation Protection
CRPNS	Centre for Radiation Protection and Nuclear Science
CSC	Certificate of Statutory Completion
CSG	Corporate Services Group
CVES	Commercial Vehicle Emissions Scheme
CWO	Corrective Work Order
DBS	Development Bank of Singapore
DCLD	Development Control and Licensing Division
DfE	Design for Efficiency Scheme
DG	Director-General
DGP	Development Guide Plans
DNA	Designated National Authority
DOE	Department of Environment, Johor, Malaysia
DOS	Department of Statistics
DSS	Department of Scientific Services
DTSS	Deep Tunnel Sewerage System
E2F	Energy Efficiency Fund
E2PO	Energy-Efficient Programme Office
EASe	Energy Efficiency Improvement Assistance Scheme
EB	Executive Board
ECA	Energy Conservation Act
EDB	Economic Development Board
EEAI	Electric Vehicle Early Adoption Incentive
EENP	Energy Efficiency National Partnership
EETD	Environmental Epidemiology and Toxicology Division
EHI	Environmental Health Institute
EIA	Environmental Impact Assessments

EMA	Energy Market Authority
EMMD	Environmental Monitoring and Modelling Division
EMS	Environmental Management System
ENMU	Environmental Noise Management Unit
EPCA	Environmental Pollution Control Act
EPD	Environmental Protection Division
EPHA	Environmental Public Health Act
EPHOG	Environmental Public Health Operations Group
EPM	Environmental Protection and Management
EPMA	Environmental Protection and Management Act
EPR	Extended Producer Responsibility
ERP	Environmental Robotics Programme
ES-ITM	Environmental Services Industry Transformation Map
ESA	Endangered Species (Import and Export) Act
ETD	Environment Technology Division
EV	Electric Vehicle
FASS	Faculty of Arts & Social Sciences
FDRS	Fire-Danger Rating System
FSSD	Fire Safety & Shelter Department
GDP	Gross Domestic Product
GFA	Gross Floor Area
GHG	Greenhouse Gas
GREET	Grant for Energy-Efficient Technologies
GRUAN	Global Climate Observing System Reference Upper Air Network
GVR	Green Vehicle Rebate
HAS	Health Sciences Authority
HBFC	Hydrobromoflourocarbon
HCFC	Hydrochloroflourocarbon
HCG	Hawker Centres Group
HDB	Housing and Development Board
HLB	Hotels Licensing Board
HRODD	Human Resources and Organisation Development Division
HSA	Health Sciences Authority
HSU	Hartridge Smoke Units
IAEA	International Atomic Energy Authority

List of Abbreviations

IBSS	International Basic Safety Standards
ICAO	International Civil Aviation Organization
ICRP	International Commission on Radiological Protection
IEG	Infrastructure and Engineering Group
IMCCC	Inter-Ministerial Committee on Climate Change
IMO	International Maritime Organisation
IPP	Interim PIC Procedure
JOTG	Joint Operations and Technology Group
JTC	Jurong Town Corporation
KPI	Key Performance Index
LEDS	Low-Emissions Development Strategy
LEEO	Law Enforcement Extension Office, ASEAN-WEN Program Coordination Unit
LETAS	Local Enterprises Technical Assistance Scheme
LNG	Liquefied Natural Gas
LoA	Letter of Approval
LTA	Land Transport Authority
MAS	Monetary Authority of Singapore
MEA	Multilateral Environmental Agreement
MELS	Mandatory Energy Labelling Scheme
MEM	Master of Science in Environmental Management
MEPS	Minimum Energy Performance Standard
MEWR	Ministry of Environment and Water Resources
MLW	Maximum Laden Weight
MMED	Microbiology and Molecular Epidemiology Division
MND	Ministry of National Development
MOM	Ministry of Manpower
MOSD	Meteorological Observations and Systems Division
MOT	Ministry of Transport
MPA	Maritime and Port Authority
MPs	Members of Parliament
MRI	Magnetic Resonance Imaging
MRT	Mass Rail Transit
MSD	Meteorological Services Division
MSE	Ministry of Sustainability and the Environment
MSJCE	Malaysia-Singapore Joint Committee on the Environment

MTI	Ministry of Trade and Industry
NBC	National Biodiversity Centre
NCCC	National Climate Change Committee
NCCS	National Climate Change Secretariat
NDC	Nationally Determined Contribution
NEA	National Environment Agency
NEEC	National Energy Efficiency Committee
NGO	Non-governmental Organisation
NHB	National Heritage Board
NIR	Non-ionising Radiation
NMPs	Nominated Members of Parliament
NParks	National Parks Board
NRF	National Research Foundation
NSS	Nature Society Singapore
NUS	National University of Singapore
NWP	Numerical Weather Prediction
ODS	Ozone Depleting Substances
OMV	Open Market Value
OSH	Occupational Safety & Health
PAP	People's Action Party
PCD	Pollution Control Department
PCU	Program Coordination Unit
PDD	Project Design Documentor
PEG	Public Engagement Group
PIN	Project Idea Note
PMA	Preservation of Monuments Act
PMB	Preservation of Monuments Board
PPSA	Prevention of Pollution of the Sea Act
PSA	Port of Singapore Authority
PSI	Pollutant Standard Index
PTA	Parks and Trees Act
QRA	Quantitative Risk Assessments
RCA	Regional Cooperative Agreement
RPI	Radiation Protection Inspectorate
RPNSD	Radiation Protection and Nuclear Science Division
RSA	Resource Sustainability Act

List of Abbreviations

RSAF	Republic of Singapore Air Force
RSG	Resource and Sustainability Group
SCD	Sanitation and Compliance Division
SCDF	Singapore Civil Defence Force
SCEM Training Grant	Singapore Certified Energy Manager Training Grant
SCP	Singapore Cooperation Programme
SDC	Sentosa Development Corporation
SDE	School of Design and Environment
SDS	Safety Data Sheets
SEAS	Sustainable Energy Association of Singapore
SEI	Singapore Environment Institute
SFA	Singapore Food Agency
SGP	Singapore Green Plan
SIAC	Singapore International Arbitration Centre
SLA	Singapore Land Authority
SME	Small and Medium-Sized Companies
SPPG	Strategic Planning and Policy Group (SPPG)
SSB	Sustainable Singapore Blueprint
TLD	Thermoluminescent Dosimeter
TOP	Temporary Occupation Permit
TSS	Total Suspended Solids
UNCLOS	UN Convention on the Law of the Sea
UNDP	United Nations Development Program
UNEP	United Nations Environment Programme
UNFCCC	United Nations Framework Convention on Climate Change
URA	Urban Redevelopment Authority
USAID	US Agency for International Development
VAP	Vientiane Action Program
VBCD	Vector Biology and Control Division
VCOD	Vector Control Operations Division
VES	Vehicular Emissions Scheme
WABA	Wild Animals and Birds Act
WCO	World Customs Organisation
WEF	World Economic Forum
WHO	World Health Organisation

WIED	Water Infrastructure and Engineering Division
WIOMD	Waste Infrastructure Operations and Management Division
WIPO	World Intellectual Property Organisation
WRMS	Waste Resource Management System
WRP	Water Reclamation Plant
WSD	Weather Services Division
WSHA	Workplace Safety and Health Act
WTE	Waste-to-Energy
WTO	World Trade Organisation

List of Abbreviations

General Introduction

§1. General Information

I. Geography and Population

A. Geography

1. The Republic of Singapore is a tiny tropical island comprising a main island and some sixty islets, totalling 736.3 sq. km with a coastline of 223 km.[1] It lies at the crossroads of Southeast Asia and the Asia-Pacific region,[2] situated just 137 km north of the Equator and immediately south of Peninsular Malaysia.[3] It is separated from Peninsular Malaysia by the Straits of Johor, and from the Indonesian islands to the south, by the Straits of Singapore. The island is linked to Peninsular Malaysia by two causeways: a 1.056 m (3/4 mile) causeway across the Straits of Johor, and a 1.9-km bridge at Tuas on the west.[4] The climate is tropical, hot and humid, with abundant rainfall. The daily temperature ranges from 25.0 to 31.6°C. The average daily humidity is 77.9%.[5] The long-term average annual rainfall is 2,113.3 mm.[6] With climate change, Singapore's annual mean surface temperature has risen at an average rate of 0.2°C–0.3°C per decade since the 1980s. Rainfall has also become more intense in recent years. The annual total rainfall for Singapore has increased at a rate of 83 mm per decade from 1980 to 2022.[7] There are two distinct monsoon seasons – the north-eastern monsoon from December to March, and the south-western monsoon from June to September. Afternoon showers are frequent, as are early evening thunderstorms. The terrain is largely lowland, with the highest point at only 163 m above sea level (Bukit Timah Hill). The central plateau is the water catchment area and a major nature reserve. Some 10% of the land is set aside for parks and nature reserves, of which 4.5% is legally protected, comprising four

1. https://tablebuilder.singstat.gov.sg/table/TS/M890621.
2. It is located between latitudes 1°09'N and 1°29' N and longitudes 103°36' E and 104°25' E – https://www.singstat.gov.sg/publications/reference/ebook/society/environment.
3. The land area has been added to from time to time, by reclamation. In the 1960s, its land area was 581.5 sq. km.
4. This was opened on 2 Jan. 1998.
5. https://www.singstat.gov.sg/publications/reference/ebook/society/environment.
6. *Ibid.*
7. https://www.nccs.gov.sg/singapores-climate-action/impact-of-climate-change-in-singapore/.

nature reserves and two national parks.[8] There are also twenty other administratively protected Nature Areas covering the majority of natural habitats within Singapore[9] and one marine park.

2. Despite its small land mass, Singapore has some 3,729 native vascular plant species, 96 mammal species, 157 reptile species and 30 different amphibian species, as well as some 404 species of birds and 335 species of butterflies. There are hundreds of fish species in the root systems of more than 31 true mangrove plant species. Seagrass meadows still remain, with 12 of the 23 Indo-Pacific species found within Singapore's waters. A total of 229 species of intertidal sponges have been recorded, and many more are likely to be observed in the subtidal areas, along with the 255 different species of hard corals.[10]

B. Population

3. Singapore is densely populated, with a population of some 6.11 million as of October 2025, up from 5.92 million in June 2023.[11] Of this, 77.4% live in government-subsidised public housing[12] in twenty-four towns and three estates built by the Housing Development Board (HDB).[13] Some 90% of Singaporeans own their own homes.[14] Singaporeans are mostly of three racial groups, comprising 75.6% Chinese, 15.1% Malay, 7.6% Indians and the rest, persons of other ethnic groups (1.7%).[15] Of the land area, 49.2% is used for residential, commercial and industrial purposes. At 8,300 persons per square km, Singapore has one of the highest population densities in the world.[16]

4. In 2024, the average life expectancy was 83.5 years (females at 85.6 years and males at 81.2 years),[17] and 63.1% of the residents were aged between 20 and 64 years. The total fertility rate is 0.97 children born per woman in 2025 (down from 1.14 in 2019).[18] The infant mortality rate is 2.3 per 1,000 live births. The literacy

---

8. *See Conserving our Biodiversity: Singapore's National Biodiversity Strategy and Action Plan* NParks Board 2009. *See also* NParks' Nature Conservation Master Plan (NCMP) 2015 (updated 20 May 2019), charting the course of Singapore's future biodiversity conservation efforts – https://www.nparks.gov.sg/biodiversity/our-national-plan-for-conservation/nature-conservation-masterplan; and https://www.nparks.gov.sg/-/media/nparks-real-content/biodiversity/national-plan/singapore_2009-nbsap_updated-may-2019_national-targets.ashx.
9. *See* Singapore 6th National Report to the Convention on Biological Diversity (2015–2018) National Parks Board Singapore 2015 at p. 1.
10. *See* Singapore 6th National Report to the Convention on Biological Diversity (2015–2018) National Parks Board Singapore 2020 at p. 61.
11. *See Population and Population Structure,* https://www.singstat.gov.sg/find-data/search-by-theme/population/population-and-population-structure/latest-data.
12. https://www.singstat.gov.sg/publications/reference/ebook/households/households.
13. https://www.hdb.gov.sg/cs/infoweb/about-us/history/hdb-towns-your-home.
14. https://www.statista.com/statistics/664518/home-ownership-rate-singapore/
15. https://www.population.gov.sg/files/media-centre/publications/Population_in_Brief_2024.pdf.
16. https://www.singstat.gov.sg/publications/reference/ebook/population/population.
17. *Ibid.*

rate in 2021 among residents aged 15 and above was 97.6% of which 36.1% of those aged 25 and above have university qualifications.[19]

II. Legal and Political Structure

A. General

5. Singapore is a republic with a written constitution that provides for its executive, legislative and judicial organs. Parliament is unicameral, comprising ninety-nine Members of Parliament (MPs)[20] with ninety-seven elected every five years by popular vote; two Non-Constituency MPs[21] and nine Nominated MPs (NMPs).[22] The Head of State is the President, elected by the people every six years. The Prime Minister is appointed by the President from the Members of Parliament.

B. Decision-Making Power and Competencies

6. The administration of the Government is vested in the Cabinet, which is constituted under Article 24 of the Constitution. It comprises the Prime Minister and other ministers and is collectively responsible to the Parliament. The Singapore government has the following Ministries:[23] Culture, Community and Youth; Defence; Digital Development and Information; Education; Finance; Foreign Affairs; Health; Home Affairs; Law; Manpower; National Development; Social and Family Development; Sustainability and the Environment; Trade and Industry; Transport; and the Prime Minister's Office.

III. Economic Characteristics

7. In the space of some forty years, Singapore has transformed from a poor Crown colony with polluted river basins and squatter colonies to a bustling modern metropolis. Largely dependent on exports, Singapore has a broad industrial base that has shifted from labour-intensive industries in the early 1960s to high-tech industries by the 1980s. Its three largest manufacturing sectors are electronics, refined

---

18. https://www.singstat.gov.sg/find-data/search-by-theme/population/births-and-fertility/visualising-data/fertility-dashboard.
19. https://www.singstat.gov.sg/modules/infographics/population.
20. https://www.parliament.gov.sg/about-us/structure/members-of-parliament.
21. Non-constituency MPs are opposition candidate who came closest to winning a seat and are appointed a 'non-constituency member'. *See* the Constitution of Singapore and the Parliamentary Elections Act at https://sso.agc.gov.sg/ – *see also* http://www.parliament.gov.sg.
22. The last election was held on 3 May 2025. The People's Action Party, the dominant party since independence, won 87 seats; the Workers' Party, the main opposition party, won ten. *See* https://www.channelnewsasia.com/singapore/ge2025-pap-secures-victory-seats-opposition-challenge-5107201.
23. https://www.sgdi.gov.sg/ministries.

petroleum products, and chemicals and chemical products. It has attracted major investments in pharmaceuticals and medical technology production as well as in renewable energy. It has a highly developed and successful free-market economy. It is an international business and financial centre served by excellent transportation and telecommunications networks. It is one of the world's busiest ports, an accolade achieved since 1986,[24] and Singapore's Port has been recognised thrice as an Asia-Pacific Economic Cooperation (APEC) Port Services Network (APSN) Green Port since it was launched in 2016, the accolade going to the Maritime and Port Authority of Singapore (MPA).[25] Singapore also has one of the world's best and busiest airports.[26] It is also the world's top bunkering port[27] and the third largest oil refining centre in the world, with four major oil companies (Shell, Caltex, BP and ExxonMobil) in operation with a combined refining capacity of 1.5 million barrels a day.[28]

8. Singapore ranked second globally (first in Asia-Pacific) in IMD's World Competitiveness Ranking 2025.[29] According to the WEF's Global Competitiveness Report 2019–2020, Singapore rose from 2nd to 1st place in the world among a list of 141 countries in terms of lack of corruption and high government efficiency. The WEF cited six contributing factors to the strong showing: government stability and its responsiveness to change, open economy, strong labour-employer relationships, strong intellectual property protection, good workforce diversity and healthy life expectancy.[30] As of April 2023, Singapore was reportedly the best place in the world to do business, as it had been for the 15th year running. Apart from its political stability and effective economic management, its strong points are its policy towards foreign investment and foreign trade and exchange controls, as well as its technological readiness.[31] Singapore's GDP per capita in 2024 was SGD 121,161 (USD 94,684).[32]

---

24. https://www.mpa.gov.sg/web/portal/home/about-mpa/awards.
25. https://www.apecpsn.org/apsn/GPASGREENPORTS/index.jhtml.
26. 'Since its opening in 1981, [Singapore's] Changi International Airport has made its mark in the aviation industry as a benchmark for service excellence, winning over 649 awards as at 2021. https://www.changiairport.com/corporate/about-us/awards-and-accolades.html.
27. https://www.a-star.edu.sg/enterprise/our-stories/connectivity-trade-logistics/singapore-as-the-world s-largest-bunkering-port; and https://www.manifoldtimes.com/news/ipec-2024-cpca- releases-lists-of-top-ten-global-bunkering-ports-and-marine-fuel-suppliers/.
28. The major oil refineries have the following capacities: ExxonMobil (605,000 bbl/d), Shell Eastern Petroleum (500,000) bbl/d) and Singapore Refining Co Ltd (290,000 bbl/d). *See* https://www.trade.gov/energy-resource-guide-singapore-oil-and-gas.
29. https://www.imd.org/centers/wcc/world-competitiveness-center/rankings/world-competitiveness-ranking/.
30. https://www.mfa.gov.sg/Overseas-Mission/Geneva/Speeches-and-Statements--Permanent-Mission-to-the-WTO-WIPO-and-WEF/2019/10/Singapore-Tops-the-World-Economic-Forum-Global-Competitiveness-Report-2019.
31. https://www.straitstimes.com/business/singapore-still-leads-the-way-as-the-world-s-best-place-to-do-business.
32. https://www.singstat.gov.sg/find-data/search-by-theme/economy/national-accounts/latest-data. The exchange rate was SGD 1.28 to USD 1.00 (USD 0.78 to SGD 1.00) as at 25 Jun. 2025. Hereafter, all references to fines etc. with $ rates are in Singapore dollars.

IV. Social and Cultural Characteristics

9. Singapore is a secular, multi-racial, multi-religious community of Chinese, Malays, Indians, and other races. Freedom of worship is guaranteed by the Constitution.[33] The main religions are Buddhism, Taoism, Christianity (including Catholicism), Hinduism, and Islam. There are four official languages: English, Malay, Tamil and Chinese (Mandarin). The national language is Malay, for historical reasons, but all schools teach in English, as English is the language of communication and of government. An exception is made for religious schools for Muslim students, called 'Madrasahs', where the medium of instruction is Malay and Arabic. A second language is compulsory for all students. The second language is generally assigned based on ethnicity; for instance, students of Chinese ancestry will study Mandarin as a second language. Students of mixed parentage can choose which language to study.[34]

10. Singapore has made full use of the law to control unsociable behaviour. It is well known for its draconian anti-litter policy. Littering is an offence that carries a penalty of a fine of up to SGD 2,000 for a first offence, SGD 4,000 for a second offence, and SGD 10,000 for a third or subsequent offence;[35] and the possibility of a Corrective Work Order (CWO).[36] The law even requires that buses provide litter bins.[37] It is the only country that has banned chewing gum[38] and imposes a fine for not flushing a public toilet after it has been used.[39] Acts of vandalism, where the damage to private or public property is done with an indelible substance, carry a

33. Article 15, Constitution of the Republic of Singapore, 1965. *See* http://statutes.agc.gov.sg/.
34. https://www.moe.gov.sg/primary/curriculum/mother-tongue-languages/learning-in-school.
35. Sections 17(1) and 21(1)(c) Environmental Public Health Act, 1987, 2020 Rev. Ed. as amended by Act 15 of 2014.
36. Section 21A to s. 21E Environmental Public Health Act and the Environmental Public Health (Corrective Work Order) Regulations 1 Nov. 1992. It is also an offence to spit (s. 17(1)(g) EPHA), which carries the same penalties as for littering.
37. Section 23 Environmental Public Health (Public Cleansing) Regulations 5 Feb. 1970, Reg. 3, GN No. S. 246/1970.
38. Chewing gum was first banned in 1992, with the passing of the Control of Export and Imports (Chewing Gum) Order. Singapore has now partially lifted this ban, as from 1 Jan. 2004, the sale of therapeutic chewing gum is allowed – *see* Regulation of Imports and Exports (Chewing Gum) Regulations, Reg. 4, GN No. S. 533/1995, amended by S. 632/2003, S. 407/2006 and S.525/2016. The Control of Manufacture Act, 1959, also prohibits the manufacture of chewing gum in Singapore insofar as it is not a 'health product categorised as an oral dental gum or a therapeutic product' – 2020 Rev. Ed. First Schedule para. 4.
39. Section 16, Environmental Public Health (Public Cleansing) Regulations (GN No. S 46/ 1970, as amended). This law also requires all public toilets to be provided with 'adequate toilet paper, soap or liquid detergent, litter bins, and clean towels or hand dryers.' S. 16A. *See Management Corporation Strata Title Plan No 641 v. Public Prosecutor* [1993] 1 SLR(R) 568; [1993] SGHC 76 at [22]–[24]. The then Chief Justice Yong Pung How held that the offence of not keeping a public toilet clean was one of strict liability as there was no requirement of *mens rea* in s. 52(8) EPHA. This was giving consideration to the fact that strict liability offences would be vital in promoting the objectives of the statute.

maximum fine of SGD 2,000 and imprisonment of up to three years, plus mandatory caning (three to eight strokes).[40] There are also laws to protect the natural environment. It is an offence to cut, collect or displace any plant or tree in any nature reserve, national park or public park,[41] or to kill, trap, take or keep any wild animal or bird.[42] All these offences, and many more, carry a fine of at least SGD 1,000. Some offences carry mandatory jail terms for a second or subsequent offence, such as illegal dumping or discharging a toxic substance into inland waters. Both offences carry a fine of up to SGD 50,000 for a first offence and/or a jail term of up to twelve months; doubling to SGD 100,000 for a second or subsequent offence plus mandatory jail (at least one month but not more than twelve months).[43] In the case of illegal dumping, the vehicle that was used may also be forfeited. These will be discussed in greater detail below.

V. The Environment

11. Despite its rapid industrialisation and high population density, Singapore has managed to keep its environment clean and green, with air and water pollution levels well within the standards for healthy living set by the World Health Organisation (WHO) and the United States Environmental Protection Agency (US-EPA). This has been achieved through an efficient administrative and legal system, effective land-use planning policies and a comprehensive environmental infrastructure to deal with air emissions, trade effluents, waste, sewerage, drainage, and public health.

12. All homes receive piped, potable water, streets are swept, and garbage is disposed of daily. Life expectancy averages 83.5 years, and infant mortality is low, at 2.3 for every 1,000 live births.[44] Its strict laws and their enforcement have ensured a low crime rate and provided a safe environment for its residents. Sound environmental management policies have secured a 'clean and green' physical environment. A 'clean' government[45] has ensured that funds are available for the building

---

40. Section 3 Vandalism Act, 1966, 2020 Rev. Ed. .
41. Section 8 Parks and Trees Act 2005, 2020 Rev. Ed. A 'public park' is defined to mean 'any State land, any land belonging to the Board or any other land, which is:
    a. utilized as a public park, recreation ground, playground, garden, public open space, walk, park connector or green verge; and
    b. managed or maintained by the Board or any management body designated under section 6A'. S. 2, Parks & Trees Act 2005, 2020 Rev. Ed.
42. Section 5C Wildlife Act, 1965, 2020 Rev. Ed.. It is also an offence to feed or keep pigeons (*see* the Animals and Birds (Pigeons) Rules, 1973) because pigeons may carry the salmonella bacteria.
43. Section 17, Environmental Protection and Management Act, Cap. 94A, Act 9 of 1999.
44. https://www.singstat.gov.sg/publications/reference/ebook/population/population.
45. *See* Lye Lin Heng, 'A Fine City in a Garden – Environmental Law and Governance in Singapore', [2008] SJLS 68-117; Lye Lin Heng, 'Environmental Law, Policy, Governance and Management for Cities: Getting It Right for a Sustainable Future – the Singapore Experience', chapter 9 in *Environmental Policies in Asia – Perspectives from Seven Asian Countries,* Jing Huang & Shreekant Gupta, eds. (2014) World Scientific, pp. 171–202.

of an excellent environmental infrastructure. Sound economic and land-use planning policies have ensured the preservation of green areas for nature conservation and recreation. Singapore's air and water quality are well within the US-EPA and WHO standards – water is safe to drink from the taps. Refuse is collected daily by licensed contractors, incinerated and the ash sent to an offshore landfill site. All inland waters support aquatic life, and the coastal waters meet recreational water standards. It has excellent transportation networks and telecommunication facilities.

13. Singapore's transport policies have resulted in a highly efficient public transport road and rail system. The use of private motor vehicles is discouraged by increasing the cost of motoring through innovative taxes, the vehicle quota system and electronic road pricing.[46]

14. In June 1992, Singapore's Green Plan was presented at the Earth Summit in Rio de Janeiro, Brazil. Prepared by the then Ministry of the Environment (ENV), it envisaged Singapore as a Model Green City and a regional centre for environmental technology by 2000. The Green Plan was complemented by the Green Plan Action Programmes (1993) and the recommendations of six Workgroups on Environmental Education, Environmental Technology, Resource Conservation, Clean Technologies, Nature Conservation and Environmental Noise. The Singapore Green Plan (SGP) was revised in 2000–2002, under four new Workgroups (Environmental Education, Nature Conservation, Resource Conservation and Waste Minimization, and Clean Technologies). The recommendations of these four groups were discussed and publicly debated and re-formulated into the Revised SGP 2012.[47] This was presented at the World Summit on Sustainable Development in Johannesburg, South Africa, in June 2002.

The Revised SGP 2012 had three Focus Groups (on air, water and clean land, nature and public health). Subsequently, an updated edition of the SGP 2012 was released – SGP 2012 (2006 Edition).[48] It covered six focus areas – Air and Climate Change, Water, Waste Management, Nature, Public Health, and International Environmental Relations. Arising from the review, four new targets have been added:

1. Reduce the ambient Particulate Matter 2.5 level to within an average of 15 $\mu g/m^3$ by 2014.
2. Improve carbon intensity (i.e., carbon dioxide emission per GDP dollar) by 25% from the 1990 level by 2012.

46. *See* Lye Lin-Heng, 'Transport-Based Air Pollution Management – The Singapore Experience' 6 *Asia-Pacific Journal of Environmental Law* (2001) Nos 3 & 4, 333–348; Lye Lin-Heng, 'Environmental Taxation in the Regulation of Traffic and the Control of Vehicular Pollution in Singapore', in *Critical Issues in Environmental Taxation: International and Comparative Perspectives* Vol. 1, Janet Milne, Kurt Deketelaere, Larry Kreiser, Hope Ashiabor, eds., 2003, Oxford University Press, pp. 387–405; Lye Lin-Heng, 'Environmental Taxation in the Management of Road Traffic in Singapore', in *Critical Issues in Environmental Taxation: International and Comparative Perspectives* Vol. VII, Lin-Heng Lye, Janet Milne, Hope Ashiabor, Lawrence Kreiser, Kurt Deketelaere, eds., Oxford University Press, pp. 205–225.
47. For the Singapore Green Plan 2012, *see* https://njgreenink.files.wordpress.com/2011/08/singapore-green-plan-2012.pdf.
48. https://www.cbd.int/doc/world/sg/sg-nbsap-v2-en.pdf.

3. Reduce Singapore's per capita domestic water consumption from 162 litres per day in 2004 to 155 litres per day by 2012.[49]
4. Partner with the 3P sectors (Public, Private, and People sectors) to generate greater awareness of the importance of conserving, valuing and enjoying water and develop a sense of shared ownership of our water resources.

In 2009, the Inter-Ministerial Committee on Sustainable Development (formed in January 2008) launched a new national framework to guide Singapore's Sustainable Development Efforts up to 2030. This was the first edition of the Sustainable Singapore Blueprint (SSB) titled 'A Lively and Liveable Singapore: Strategies for Sustainable Growth'.[50] It was jointly published by the Ministry of the Environment and Water Resources, as well as the Ministry of National Development (MND).

The SSB not only set higher targets than those in SGP 2012 (2006 edition) but also introduced new initiatives such as transforming Singapore into a 'City of Gardens', introducing minimum energy and water efficiency standards for more household appliances and establishing the Centre for Liveable Cities to host events such as the World Cities Summit and Singapore International Water Week.

The SSB has since been revised, with the latest edition being the SSB 2015 titled 'Our Home, Our Environment, Our Future'. New initiatives launched since the 2009 edition include: a new Maritime Singapore Green Initiative, more Active, Beautiful, Clean Waters (ABC) projects and renewed greening efforts to make Singapore a City in a Garden, among many other initiatives.[51]

15. On 10 February 2021, the government announced its *Singapore Green Plan 2030* (SGP 2030), a 'whole-of-nation' movement that charts the nation's targets for sustainability for the next ten years. It is headed by five ministries – the Ministries of Education; National Development; Sustainability and the Environment (formerly called the Ministry of Environment and Water Resources [MEWR]); Trade and Industry; and Transport.[52] It will be supported by the whole government, and it has five pillars:

i. City in Nature: to create a green, liveable and sustainable home for Singaporeans.
ii. Sustainable Living: to reduce carbon emissions, keep a clean environment, save resources and energy and make this a way of life in Singapore.
iii. Energy Reset: to use cleaner energy and increase energy efficiency to lower our carbon footprint.
iv. Green Economy: to seek green growth opportunities to create new jobs, transform our industries, and harness sustainability as a competitive advantage.

---

49. The 2030 Green Plan's target is to reduce household water consumption to 130 litres per capita per day.
50. https://www.nccs.gov.sg/files/docs/default-source/default-document-library/a-lively-and-liveable-singapore-strategies-for-sustainable-growth.pdf.
51. *See* https://www.clc.gov.sg/docs/default-source/books/ssbcombined-cover-text.pdf. *See also* http://www.greenfuture.sg/singapore-green-landscape-2020/key-reports/.
52. https://www.mnd.gov.sg/newsroom/press-releases/view/singapore-green-plan-2030-charts-ambitious-targets-for-next-10-years-to-catalyse-national-sustainability-movement-1.

v. Resilient Future: to build up Singapore's climate resilience and enhance its food security.

16. The realisation of these sustainability goals will require all parties to play their part. Thus, the SGP 2030 will be enabled by a Green Government led by the public sector, and a Green Citizenry with individuals, communities and businesses playing their part. To this end, the Ministry of Sustainability and the Environment (MSE) in 2022 established the position of Government Chief Sustainability Officer (GCSO) to drive the Government's sustainability efforts, including the SGP 2030.[53] These will be elaborated on below.

VI. Main Environmental Problems

17. As Singapore is highly industrialised, environmental pollution arising from energy generation, industrial operations and vehicular emissions continues to be a concern. Seasonal smoke haze resulting from forest fires in Indonesia is a major issue, as is the loss of nature areas due to development and urbanisation. Lack of water resources used to be a major concern, but this is largely resolved today, with water coming from four 'taps', namely, water from local catchments, imported water (from Malaysia), NEWater (reclaimed water), and desalinated water.[54] Marine pollution is a major concern, particularly as crude oil is transported by ships across the narrow Straits of Malacca and the Singapore Straits for refining and for the bunkering industry. Noise is also a concern, particularly from construction sites and stricter standards have been imposed from time to time. These will be discussed below.

§2. Historical Background

18. Founded by Stamford Raffles of the East India Company in 1819 as a trading port, Singapore came under the control of British India in 1826, as part of the Straits Settlements. It became a Crown Colony in 1867, fell to the Japanese in 1942, and resumed Crown Colony status in 1946. It obtained self-government in 1959 with the People's Action Party (PAP) taking the majority of votes. After a short-lived merger with Malaysia commencing on 16 September 1963, Singapore became a sovereign nation on 9 August 1965. Its Constitution was first promulgated on 3 June 1959, and amended in 1965 when it became a Republic.[55]

---

53. https://www.channelnewsasia.com/singapore/lim-tuang-liang-appointed-first-government-chief-sustainability-officer-jan-1-3174681.
54. https://www.pub.gov.sg/Public/WaterLoop/OurWaterStory.
55. Kevin YL Tan 'A Short Legal and Constitutional History of Singapore', Chapter 2, *The Singapore Legal System*, Kevin YL Tan ed.; 2nd ed. Singapore University Press, 1999, pp. 26–66; Kevin YL Tan, *An Introduction to Singapore's Constitution* (Talisman, 2005); Thio Li-Ann & Kevin YL Tan, *Constitutional Law in Malaysia and Singapore* (Lexis Nexis, 2010, 3rd ed.); Thio Li-Ann, *A Treatise on Singapore Constitutional Law* (Singapore Academy Publishing, 2012); Kevin YL Tan, *The*

19. A massive industrialisation programme was launched soon after independence, with the development of the Jurong Industrial Estate in the west. In 1968, the Economic Development Board (EDB) was reorganised, and the Jurong Town Corporation (JTC) and the Development Bank of Singapore (DBS) were established. The Monetary Authority of Singapore (MAS) was established in 1970 to formulate and implement Singapore's monetary policies. This heralded a programme of economic restructuring and social engineering to educate the workforce, curb population growth, and provide jobs as well as housing for the growing population.

20. Since its first general election, Singapore has been governed by the same political party, the PAP. This has provided political stability and ensured the continuity and follow-through of various governmental policies at all levels. Mr Lee Kuan Yew was the first Prime Minister in 1959. He was succeeded by Mr Goh Chok Tong in 1990, who was then succeeded in 2004 by Mr Lee Hsien Loong, the son of the first Prime Minister Lee. In May 2025, Mr Lawrence Wong took over as the fourth Prime Minister and continues to hold the post today.

21. Population control policies implemented in the early years have proven so effective that today, the fertility rate is only 0.97 children per woman, so Singapore has to woo migrants with relevant talents. Government policies in various areas, including economy, finance, education, land-use planning, transportation, urban development, law, and foreign policy, have been carefully considered, administered, and implemented by able civil servants and an educated and industrious workforce, and have brought prosperity to the nation.

22. In terms of its physical environment, Singapore in its early years faced the same problems that beset developing countries today. These include the lack of proper sewage disposal facilities, highly polluted rivers and river basins, indiscriminate waste disposal leading to land pollution and water pollution, poor health management systems leading to outbreaks of typhoid and cholera, polluted air from old and inefficient power plants and motor vehicles, and frequent floods due to poor drainage. Singapore's success in managing its environment stems from the fact that a clean and green environment was part of Prime Minister Lee Kuan Yew's strategy in wooing investors in the early years.[56] It has proven to be the right strategy. A healthy and pleasant living environment continues to play an important role in ensuring that Singapore remains an attractive place for investors, for talented migrants, and for its own citizens.

Constitution of Singapore: A Contextual Analysis, (2015) Bloomsbury Publishing. *See also* https://www.sal.org.sg/Resources-Tools/Legal-Heritage/Legal-and-Constitutional-History-of-Singapore.

56. 'We have built. We have progressed. But there is no hallmark of our success more distinctive and more meaningful than achieving the position as the cleanest and greenest city in South-east Asia.' Per Lee Kuan Yew, Prime Minister, Singapore, at the launching ceremony of the 'Keep Singapore Clean' campaign, 1 Oct. 1968.

§3. LEGAL STRUCTURE

I. Sources of Law

23. Singapore has two sources of law. The first source is English common law as developed in England and imported into Singapore; the second comprises laws passed by Parliament (Acts), as well as subsidiary legislation (rules, regulations, orders and notifications made by the relevant Ministers under enabling legislation).[57]

A. *English Common Law*

24. The Second Charter of Justice was issued on 27 November 1826, and imported English law as it stood in England on that date, subject to local customs and religions and local legislation. Thus, English case law, English statutes, and the common law principles of contract and tort were imported into Singapore.

In 1878, the Civil Law Ordinance was passed, in which section 6 (later re-enacted as section 5, Civil Law Act) directed local courts to apply English laws in all mercantile issues. This provision was plagued with uncertainties. It was amended in 1979 and finally repealed in November 1993 with the passage of the Application of English Law Act.[58] This Act lists those English imperial and commercial statutes that apply in Singapore and specifies their applicability. It incorporates specific provisions (particularly from pre-1826 English statutes) relating to property, trusts, succession and insurance into the relevant local statutes. It also specifies that common law and equity, so far as they were part of Singapore law immediately before the commencement of the Act, would continue to be part of Singapore law, so far as they were applicable to the circumstances of Singapore and subject to such modifications as local circumstances might require.[59]

B. *Statutory Laws*

25. Local legislation comprises Acts of Parliament ('primary legislation') and regulations, rules, orders and notifications ('subsidiary legislation').[60]

---

57. *See* Helena HM Chan, *The Legal System of Singapore* (Butterworths Asia, 1995); *The Singapore Legal System, supra* n. 55; *The Legal System of Singapore: Institutions, Principles and Practices* Gary Chan, Jack Lee, LexisNexis 2015, Chapter 1 'History of the Singapore Legal System'.
58. Act 35 of 1993, 2020 Rev. Ed.
59. *See* Walter Woon, 'The Applicability of English Law in Singapore', Chapter 6, *The Singapore Legal System, supra* n. 55, pp. 230–248.
60. Primary and subsidiary laws may be found at https://sso.agc.gov.sg/. They may also be found on the website of the relevant enforcement authority, such as the NEA at https://www.nea.gov.sg/corporate-functions/resources/legislation-international-law/legislation or the National Parks Board at https://www.nparks.gov.sg/who-we-are#laws. *See also* https://www.lawnet.sg/lawnet/group/lawnet/legal-research/basic-search.

Primary laws in Singapore are first introduced as a Bill (i.e., a statute in draft form) by a government minister in Parliament. A Bill goes through three readings before being put to the vote. Upon receiving the President's assent, it becomes law on the date prescribed. Proposed laws which are controversial or may require further examination are referred to a Select Committee, usually chaired by the Speaker of Parliament. Informed members of the public, experts and interested parties are invited to appear before the Committee to present their views. Citizens may also make representations on the proposed law before the Committee. The proposed law may then be re-drafted based on this feedback and re-presented before Parliament.[61]

Subsidiary legislation is passed according to the procedure spelt out in the parent Act. Generally, they are passed on to publication by the relevant Minister in the Government Gazette.

C. *Sources of Environmental Law*

26. Environmental law in Singapore comprises statutory law as well as common law principles of tort, which serve as constraints on a landowner's use of his land. There are also 'soft laws' such as guidelines, codes of practice and directions issued by the National Environment Agency (NEA), a statutory board under the Ministry of Sustainability and the Environment (MSE), as well as other ministries such as the Ministries of National Development, Law, and Manpower.

The 'soft laws' issued by the NEA include Codes of Practice on Pollution Control and on Environmental Health, as well as the Revised Singapore Green Plan (SGP) presented in 2002 and revised again in 2006.[62] Subsequently, the Sustainable Singapore Blueprint (SSB) was launched in 2009 and revised in 2015, 2016 and 2019. Today, the 2030 SGP involves several government ministries (MSE, MND, Education, Transport, Trade and Industry) as it is a 'whole of government' approach and guides the country towards achieving its sustainable development goals.[63]

27. The Constitution does not contain any provisions relating to the environment or environmental rights. While the common law tort actions of nuisance, negligence, trespass and the rule in *Rylands v. Fletcher* continue to apply, comprehensive statutory laws and an efficient environmental management system (EMS) incorporating sound land-use planning have resulted in a clean and green environment with pollution largely under control. The government has taken initiatives towards sustainable development,[64] and many of its laws embody the polluter pays principle.

---

61. *See* Kevin YL Tan 'Parliament and the Making of Law in Singapore', Chapter 4 in *The Singapore Legal System, supra* n. 55, pp. 123–159; *see also* http://www.parliament.gov.sg/.
62. *See* text, paras 14 to 16.
63. *See* https://www.greenplan.gov.sg.
64. 'Due to the constraints our island-state face, we had no choice but to regard environmental protection seriously. It is the only way we can keep our country liveable. As such, we have based our environmental policies and programmes on the principle of balancing development and environment. We have embodied the spirit of Agenda 21 in our philosophies and policies in environmental protection

II. Judicial System

A. *The Judiciary*

28. The Judiciary comprises the Supreme Court (composed of the General Division of the High Court, the Appellate Division of the High Court and the Court of Appeal); the State Courts (comprising the District Courts, Magistrates' Courts, Coroner's Court, the Small Claims Tribunal, Employment Claims Tribunals, Community Dispute Resolution Tribunals); and the Family Justice Courts (comprising the Family Division of the High Court, Family Courts and Youth Courts).[65] The Chief Justice is appointed by the President with the advice of the Prime Minister; other judges are appointed by the President with the advice of the Chief Justice and the Prime Minister. Appeals to the Judicial Committee of the Privy Council were abolished in 1994. The jury system was abolished in 1970. A Presidential Council for Minority Rights is established under Part VII of the Constitution.

Judges of the Supreme Court enjoy security of tenure and can only be removed in the circumstances set out in the Constitution (Article 98). Judicial Commissioners may be appointed to exercise the functions of a judge for short periods of time (Articles 94(7), 95).

29. Jurisdiction for the different courts varies depending, in criminal cases, on the maximum sentence for the particular offence, and in civil cases, on the amount of the claim. District and Magistrates' Courts have original criminal and civil jurisdiction. District Courts try civil cases for claims up to SGD 250,000, and criminal cases for which the maximum term of imprisonment does not exceed ten years.[66] Magistrates' Courts try civil cases for claims up to SGD 60,000, and criminal cases for which the maximum term of imprisonment does not exceed five years.[67] They also conduct preliminary inquiries into offences with a view to committal for trial by the High Court. The Youth Courts deal with offences allegedly committed by children under the age of 14 years or young persons aged between 14 and 16 years.

30. The High Court has unlimited jurisdiction in both civil and criminal cases, but all criminal cases carrying the death penalty must be tried by the High Court.

---

and management. We have also incorporated the strategies in Agenda 21 in our development programmes to achieve environmental sustainability' Ministry of Foreign Affairs First Secretary Ms Foo Teow Lee on Singapore's Implementation of Agenda 21, 2001 at http://app.mfa.gov.sg/pr/read_content.asp?View,1084; *see also* https://www.nea.gov.sg/docs/default-source/envision/chapter-2-safeguard-a-place-to-live.pdf.

65. Constitution of the Republic of Singapore, Part VIII – The Judiciary, Articles 93–101; *see also* https://www.judiciary.gov.sg/; the Supreme Court of Judicature Act, 1969, 2020 Rev. Ed.; the State Courts Act, 1970, 2020 Rev. Ed; and the Family Justice Act, 2014, 2020 Rev. Ed. The State Courts used to be called the Subordinate Courts – *see* Yeo Tiong Min, 'Jurisdiction of the Singapore Courts'. Chapter 7, *The Singapore Legal System*, *supra* n. 55, 249–296; Walter Woon, 'The Doctrine of Judicial Precedent', Chapter 8, *The Singapore Legal System*, *ibid.*, 297–323. Lye Lin Heng 'The Judiciary and Environmental Governance in Singapore', *Journal of Court Innovation*: *The Role of the Environmental Judiciary (NY)*, Vol. 3 No. 1, Winter 2010, pp. 133–155.
66. The State Courts (Variation of District Court Limit) Order 1, 1997, GN S 333/97; S 153/2014).
67. The State Courts (Variation of Magistrate Court Limit) Order 2 1999, GN S 263/99; S 154/2014.

The Court of Appeal is the final appellate court of Singapore. It hears appeals, both civil and criminal, from the High Court and determines questions of law reserved for its decision by the High Court.

31. As the laws that protect the environment usually carry fines not exceeding SGD 50,000 and imprisonment not exceeding two years, infringements of these laws are heard by the Magistrates' Courts. Fines of up to SGD 100,000 can be imposed for serious breaches of the law. These cases will be heard by District Courts (e.g., section 17 Environmental Protection and Management Act (EPMA) – discharge of toxic substances into water courses). Hefty fines of up to SGD 1 million can be imposed on cases involving pollution of the marine environment by oil under the Prevention of Pollution of the Sea Act, 1990 (PPSA).[68] Offences carrying such heavy penalties would normally be heard by the High Court, but section 32 of the PPSA expressly empowers District and Magistrates' Courts to try these offences.

B. The Syariah Court and Muslim Law

32. The Muslim community is governed by a separate system of law in relation to family matters, administered by separate courts and judicial officers under the Administration of Muslim Law Act. This Act establishes the Syariah Court and its Appeal Board. The Syariah Court is presided over by a President and is essentially a family court, hearing issues relating to inheritance, marriage, divorce, betrothals, nullity of marriage or judicial separation, the disposition or division of property on divorce, the payment of maintenance and consolatory gifts.[69]

C. Other Tribunals

33. There are also specific tribunals such as the Community Disputes Resolution Tribunal,[70] the Employment Claims Tribunal,[71] the Industrial Arbitration Court,[72] the Appeals Board (Land Acquisition),[73] the Strata Titles Board[74] and the Copyright Tribunals.[75] However, there is no special court for cases that involve the environment.

---

68. Act 18 of 1990, 2020 Rev. Ed. And s. 7(1)(a) Criminal Procedure Code 2010, 2020 Rev Ed.
69. The Administration of Muslim Law Act, 1966, 2020 Rev. Ed. *See also* https://www.syariahcourt.gov.sg/.
70. *See* https://www.judiciary.gov.sg/civil/file-neighbour-dispute-claim.
71. *See* https://www.judiciary.gov.sg/civil/employment-claims.
72. *See* http://www.iac.gov.sg/.
73. *See* https://ab.mlaw.gov.sg/.
74. *See* https://www.stratatb.gov.sg/.
75. *See* https://www.ipos.gov.sg/about-ip/copyright/copyright-tribunals.

The Singapore International Arbitration Centre (SIAC)[76] commenced operations on 1 July 1991. It provides facilities for international and domestic commercial arbitration and conciliation and aims to promote arbitration and conciliation as alternatives to litigation for the settlement of disputes. The SIAC Rules are based largely on the UNCITRAL Arbitration Rules and the Rules of the London Court of International Arbitration with some modifications.

The *Singapore Mediation Centre*[77] was launched on 16 August 1997, following a successful pilot project on Commercial Mediation. It is the flagship mediation centre in Singapore and provides a range of comprehensive mediation services for civil disputes of all natures. Mediation is actively encouraged in Singapore, as one of the first options in dispute resolution, with litigation as a last resort.

§4. Institutional Structure and Governance

34. There is no one ministry that solely handles matters relating to the environment. The Ministry of Sustainability and the Environment (MSE) takes charge of all matters relating to pollution, public health, food security and water. The Ministry of National Development (MND) takes charge of nature conservation, land-use planning, urban renewal and development. The Ministry of Manpower (MOM) is responsible for matters relating to environmental health and safety of workers. The Maritime and Port Authority (MPA) handles marine pollution.

I. The Ministry of Sustainability and the Environment (MSE)

35. The MSE[78] oversees three statutory boards:[79] the National Environment Agency (NEA),[80] the Public Utilities Board (PUB)[81] and the Singapore Food Agency (SFA).[82] The NEA broadly takes charge of pollution and public health. The PUB is responsible for the supply of water to the whole island, for the development of the country's water resources and the operation and maintenance of the water

76. *See* http://www.siac.org.sg/.
77. *See* http://www.mediation.com.sg/.
78. This was first called the Ministry of Environment (ENV), established in 1972. *See Singapore – My Clean and Green Home*, Ministry of the Environment, 1997. It became the Ministry of Environment and Water Resources (MEWR) in 2004, and was renamed Ministry of Sustainability and Environment (MSE) on 25 Jul. 2020. *See* https://www.mse.gov.sg/.
79. Statutory boards are organisations created by the Government of Singapore to serve specific functions. They have some degree of autonomy, such as in operations and hiring, but must operate in line with government policy direction and maintain standards of governance.
80. NEA was formed on 1 Jul. 2002 'to focus on the implementation of environmental policies'. Its mission today is 'To ensure a clean and sustainable environment for Singapore, together with our partners and the community.' It seeks to maintaining a high standard of public health; improving and sustain a clean environment; provide up-to-date and reliable weather information services and promote resource efficiency and conservation, in collaboration with our partners and community. *See* https://www.nea.gov.sg/corporate-functions/who-we-are.
81. *See* https://www.pub.gov.sg/AboutUs.
82. https://www.sfa.gov.sg/about-sfa.

supply system.[83] The SFA was formed on 1 April 2019 to oversee food safety and security, taking over the food-related functions carried out by the former Agri-Food & Veterinary Authority of Singapore (AVA), NEA and the Health Sciences Authority (HSA). Together with its three statutory boards, the MSE works towards ensuring a clean, sustainable environment and the safe supply of water and food for Singapore.

36. It is significant that while the Ministry of Environment (ENV) was formed in 1972, the Anti-Pollution Unit (APU) was established two years earlier, in 1970, and brought under the control of the Prime Minister's office. It was not until 1986 that the APU was merged with ENV. This clearly indicates the importance that the first Prime Minister Lee Kuan Yew placed on pollution control. On 1 July 2002, ENV was renamed the Ministry of the Environment and Water Resources (MEWR), with two statutory boards, the National Environment Agency (NEA) and the Public Utilities Board (PUB). Its vision then was 'A clean environment. Water for all. Together, a sustainable Singapore' and its two statutory boards had a joint mission: 'To deliver and sustain a clean and healthy environment and water resources for all in Singapore.' It was renamed the Ministry of Sustainability and the Environment (MSE) on 27 July 2020.[84]

37. Today, its vision is stated as a commitment to 'a clean and sustainable environment with resilient supplies of safe food and water'.[85] Its three strategic directions include economic resilience, resource resilience and climate resilience:

> *Climate Resilience*: to address existential threats of climate change, especially rising sea levels and cope with rising temperatures and changing rainfall patterns to sustain a liveable environment.
> *Economic Resilience*: to ensure the future Singapore economy remains competitive by overcoming carbon & resource constraints, and to rally stakeholders towards sustainable economic growth.
> *Resource Resilience*: to ensure safe and secure supply of critical resources, i.e., water and food, and to overcome global resource constraints by maximising resource efficiency and closing our resource loops.

A. *The National Environment Agency (NEA)*

38. The NEA was formed under MSE on 1 July 2002 to focus on the implementation of environmental policies. It is 'responsible for ensuring a clean and green environment, and the sustainable development of Singapore. Its key roles are to protect Singapore's resources from pollution, maintain a high level of public health and provide timely meteorological information'.[86]

---

83. *See* https://www.mse.gov.sg/about-us/our-history/.
84. *Ibid.*
85. https://www.mse.gov.sg/about-us/.
86. https://www.nea.gov.sg/corporate-functions/who-we-are.

It has articulated its vision as 'A clean environment, towards a liveable and sustainable Singapore'; and its mission as 'To ensure a clean and sustainable environment for Singapore, together with our partners and the community.' Its roles are stated as:

- Maintaining a high standard of public health.
- Improving and sustaining a clean environment.
- Providing up-to-date and reliable weather information services.
- Promoting resource efficiency and conservation, in collaboration with our partners and community.[87]

It comprises six divisions, namely:[88]

1. Environmental Protection.
2. Public Health.
3. Meteorological Services.
4. Policy, Corporate and Technology.
5. Internal Audit.
6. Legal.

1. *The Environmental Protection Division (EPD)*
   The EPD implements programmes to monitor, reduce and prevent environmental pollution. It is also responsible for the operation of the four waste-to-energy (WTE) incineration plants and the offshore Semakau sanitary landfill in Singapore. In order to conserve energy resources and landfill space, this Division implements programmes to minimise waste generation and maximise recycling and energy conservation.
   EPD has four groups/divisions:
   i. Clean Environment Group (CEG) – The CEG is responsible for pollution control, from front-end development control and licensing work to downstream environmental monitoring and hazardous substance control. It comprises the Development Control and Licensing Division (DCLD); Environmental Monitoring and Modelling Division (EMMD); and two Pollution Control Divisions.
   ii. Infrastructure and Engineering Group (IEG) – The IEG is responsible for all infrastructure planning and development in NEA and serves as NEA's engineering centre of excellence for waste management facilities, hawker centres and after-death facilities. It comprises the Building and Engineering Services Division (BESD); Water Infrastructure and Engineering Division (WIED); and Waste Infrastructure Operations and Management Division (WIOMD).

87. https://www.nea.gov.sg/corporate-functions/who-we-are/our-purpose.
88. https://www.nea.gov.sg/corporate-functions/who-we-are/groups-and-divisions/environmental-protection-groups-and-divisions.

iii. Resource and Sustainability Group (RSG) – The RSG is responsible for promoting environmental sustainability. The divisions under RSG implement regulations, programmes and incentives that serve to mitigate greenhouse gas (GHG) emissions, ensure a sustainable waste-to-resource management system, and enhance resource efficiency in the people, public and private sectors. It comprises the Carbon Mitigation Division, Sustainability Division, and Waste Management Division.

2. *The Public Health Division (EPHD)* is responsible for public health and overall cleanliness in Singapore. It ensures a high standard of hygiene in the food retail industry and enhances the living environment through programmes such as the upgrading of hawker centres and food courts, and the clean public toilets programme. It comprises two groups and three divisions:
   i. The Environmental Health Institute (EHI) conducts research, surveillance, and risk assessment to acquire knowledge on environmental issues affecting public health. Its key thrust is to develop evidence-based, cost-effective tools and strategies to safeguard a healthy environment. EHI's work falls under five transdisciplinary programmes: Mosquito-Borne Diseases, Zoonotic Diseases, Indoor Air Quality, Environmental Surveillance, and Chemical Pollutants. The EHI includes the Environmental Epidemiology and Toxicology Division (EETD), Microbiology and Molecular Epidemiology Division (MMED), and the Vector Biology and Control Division) (VBCD).
   ii. The Environmental Public Health Operations Group (EPHOG) is responsible for vector control, sanitation, littering, environmental hygiene, enforcement of anti-smoking regulations, port health, malaria surveillance, and management of public feedback. It has a Central Regional Office that oversees two specialist sections – the Rat Control Section and the Port Health Section; an Eastern Regional Office that oversees the Malaria Surveillance Section – a specialist section for the surveillance of malaria vectors in Singapore; and a Western Regional Office that oversees two specialist sections (Enforcement Section & Video Surveillance Section) which manage strategic enforcement operations on littering, including high rise littering, and smoking prohibitions across the island. EPOG also has a Sanitation and Compliance Division (SCD) and a Vector Control Operations Division (VCOD). The SCD manages the operations, enforcement and compliance in the areas of sanitation, littering, smoking and environmental hygiene. It handles the enforcement administration for the operational departments across NEA, including the execution of Warrant of Arrests. SCD also coordinates the contingency response plans for the Group (EPHOG). The VCOD works with the Regional Offices to implement and perform the critical work needed to prevent, detect and respond to public health emergencies posed by vector-borne diseases.

   The three divisions of the EPHD are:
   i. Division of Public Cleanliness (DPC): The DPC provides cleaning services for public areas such as public roads, pavements, drains, and other

public areas not under the maintenance of Town Councils. It also manages the clean up of public places after emergency events such as road spillage, coastal oil spills, floods, tsunamis, volcanic ash fallout and disinfection of premises during outbreaks of infectious diseases.

ii. Memorial Facilities and Planning Division (MFPD): The MFPD is responsible for the planning and delivery of after-death facilities and services to ensure timely, adequate and sustainable provision of after-death facilities, supported by a professional funerary industry.

iii. Public Health Operational Policy Division (PHOPD) seeks to strengthen policies, processes and operational capabilities in the areas of vector control and sanitation to meet current and future challenges.

3. *The Meteorological Services Singapore (MSS)* provides information on the weather and issues alerts on air pollution, such as from transboundary haze caused by the burning of forests. It also provides vital meteorological services to the aviation and maritime communities and the military. It has the Centre for Climate Research Singapore (CCRS) and three divisions:
   i. Weather Services Division (WSD).
   ii. Meteorological Observations and Systems Division (MOSD).
   iii. Business and Strategy Division (BSD).

   The CCRS undertakes research to advance scientific understanding of tropical climate variability and changes affecting Singapore and the wider Southeast Asia region.

   The WSD delivers national weather assessments, forecasts, warnings, and hazard monitoring services for civil aviation, military, maritime, government agencies, businesses and the general public. The MOSD implements and maintains a comprehensive network of specialised meteorological observing systems and applications to support operational weather forecasting and the provision of meteorological services. The BSD manages corporate affairs and provides strategic support for MSD. It is responsible for strategic planning, international relations and partnerships, customer relationship management, including contracts, facility management, outreach and events.

   The Radiation Protection and Nuclear Science Group (RPNSG) is the national authority for radiation protection in Singapore and serves to protect the public, radiation workers and the environment from the harmful effects of radiation. It administers and enforces the Radiation Protection Act and Regulations through a system of licensing and inspections.

4. *The Policy, Corporate and Technology Group* first comprises a Corporate Services Group (CSG) which includes a Finance Division (FD), Human Resources and Organisation Development Division (HRODD), Procurement Policy and Services Division and the Singapore Environment Institute (SEI). Next comes the Hawker Centres Group (HCG); a Joint Operations and Technology Group (JOTG); Public Engagement Group (PEG); and the Strategic Planning and Policy Group (SPPG).

   The SPPG is responsible for corporate planning, key performance index (KPI) and risk management, research and statistics, strategic and longer-term policy planning and formulation, as well as safeguarding and advancing Singapore's international environmental interests. It comprises a Policy Division and a Strategic Research Division.

5. *The Singapore Environment Institute (SEI)*[89] was established in February 2003 as the training and knowledge management division of the NEA. It is responsible for delivering in-house training to build an agile, resourceful and resilient NEA workforce. SEI also oversees NEA's knowledge management initiatives and records management practices. SEI works with institutes of higher learning to develop training programmes for local environmental services industry. The Institute also conducts capacity-building workshops for selected foreign government officials.

B. The Public Utilities Board (PUB)

39. PUB is a statutory board under the MSE.[90] It is the national water agency that manages Singapore's water supply, water catchment and used water in an integrated way. Singapore has built a robust, diversified and sustainable water supply from four water sources known as the 'Four National Taps' – water from local catchment, imported water,[91] high-grade reclaimed water known as NEWater and desalinated water.[92] The PUB is responsible for the collection, production, distribution and reclamation of water in Singapore:

Collection – Rainwater is collected through rivers, streams, canals and drains and stored in seventeen reservoirs.[93] With the pipelines linking the various reservoirs, the excess water can be pumped from one reservoir to another, thus optimising storage capacity.

Production – Raw water is piped to the waterworks for treatment.

Distribution – After treatment, the water is stored in covered reservoirs before distribution to *customers*.

Reclamation – Water that has been used by households and industries is collected through an extensive sewerage system and treated at water reclamation plants (WRPs). Treated used water is further purified using a three-step process involving: (1) microfiltration/ultrafiltration, (2) reverse osmosis with advanced membrane technology, and (3) ultraviolet disinfection to produce high-grade reclaimed water,

89. *See* https://www.nea.gov.sg/programmes-grants/courses/sei.
90. https://www.pub.gov.sg/AboutUs.
91. Singapore has a 1962 Water Agreement with Johor, a state in Malaysia under which Singapore can draw up to 250 million gallons of water a day from the Linggiu Reservoir, Johor River, and Singapore is obliged to provide Johor with treated water up to 2% of the water it imports. The 1962 Water Agreement will expire in 2061. Thus, there is an urgent need for Singapore to be self-sufficient in water. *See* https://www.pub.gov.sg/Public/WaterLoop/OurWaterStory/ImportedWater.
92. https://www.pub.gov.sg/watersupply/fournationaltaps.
See PUB Publication *Our Water, Our Future* (2016) Rev Ed 2017; also 'Active, Beautiful, Clean Waters' at https://www.pub.gov.sg/abcwaters.
93. https://www.pub.gov.sg/Public/WaterLoop/OurWaterStory/Local-Catchment-Water.

branded as NEWater.[94] As it is ultra-clean, NEWater is used mainly for industrial and air-con cooling purposes at wafer fabrication plants, industrial estates and commercial buildings. The biggest users of NEWater are wafer fabrication plants, which require water quality that is even more stringent than water for drinking. NEWater is delivered to industrial customers via a dedicated pipe network. During dry periods, NEWater is added to the reservoirs to blend with raw water. The raw water from the reservoir is treated at the waterworks before it is supplied to consumers as tap water. Twice a year, NEWater is audited by an external audit panel comprising international experts in engineering, water chemistry, toxicology and microbiology, and it has consistently exceeded international standards.

Singapore is 100% served by modern sanitation today. Used water is collected through a network of sewers that leads to the WRPs. Currently, there are four WRPs serving a population of over 5 million.[95] Singapore has a Deep Tunnel Sewerage System (DTSS) built by PUB for long-term sustainability. The DTSS channels used water to a centralised WRP for treatment. The treated water will then be discharged into the sea or further purified into NEWater.[96] Singapore has five desalination plants. The latest was opened on 17 April 2022.[97]

Singapore's 2030 Green Plan has the following targets for PUB in relation to efficiency and energy consumption:

1. By 2021, PUB should generate sufficient solar energy from floating solar panels to power 100% of Singapore's waterworks.[98]
2. By 2025:
   i. energy consumption for desalination should be reduced from the current 3.5 kWh/m3 to 2 kWh/m3;
   ii. Singapore's first integrated used water treatment facility at Tuas Nexus should be 100% energy sufficient.
3. 2030 & beyond – reduce energy desalination to 1 kWh/m^3. This will be done through investments in desalination and used water technologies, e.g., electrochemical desalination and step-feed membrane technology.

---

94. Today, there are four NEWater plants supplying up to 40% of Singapore's current water needs. By 2060, NEWater is expected to meet up to 55% of Singapore's future water demand. *See* https://www.pub.gov.sg/Public/WaterLoop/OurWaterStory/NEWater.
95. https://www.pub.gov.sg/Professionals/Requirements/Used-Water.
96. https://www.pub.gov.sg/Professionals/Requirements/Used-Water/DTSS.
97. https://www.pub.gov.sg/Public/WaterLoop/OurWaterStory/DesalinatedWater. *See also* https://www.channelnewsasia.com/singapore/singapore-5th-desalination-plant-jurong-island-energy-efficient-2630546.
98. This target has been met. The Sembcorp Tengeh Floating Solar Farm opened on 14 July 2021, at Tengeh Reservoir. With 122,000 solar panels spanning across 45 hectares, the 60 MWp photovoltaic farm is sufficient to power Singapore's five local water treatment plants. *See* https://www.pub.gov.sg/news/pressreleases/2021PR013.

C. The Singapore Food Agency (SFA)

40. The SFA was formed as a statutory board under the Ministry of Sustainability & the Environment on 1 April 2019 to oversee food safety and food security from farm-to-fork. The SFA brings together food-related functions carried out by the former Agri-Food & Veterinary Authority of Singapore (AVA), the NEA and the HSA.[99] As the lead agency for food-related matters, SFA's mission is to ensure and secure a supply of safe food for Singapore.

41. Singapore is making greater efforts to be more self-sufficient in food production. Under the 2030 Singapore Green Plan (SGP), the top decks of suitable multi-storied car parks will be converted into urban farms and community gardens.

II. The Ministry of National Development (MND)

42. MSE's work is complemented by the MND as well as the Ministry of Trade and Industry (MTI). The MND is responsible for national land-use planning and the physical development of Singapore.[100] Its portfolios include land-use planning, urban redevelopment and building conservation, public housing, the construction industry, and parks and greenery. Its vision is 'An Endearing Home, A Distinctive Global City', and aims to achieve this 'by developing world-class infrastructure, creating a vibrant and sustainable living environment and building rooted and cohesive communities'. Singapore's lack of physical space necessitates careful, well-conceived plans and policies on land-use planning and infrastructural development.

43. MND oversees five statutory boards – the Urban Redevelopment Authority (URA), the Housing and Development Board (HDB), the National Parks Board (NParks), the Council for Estate Agencies (CEA) and the Building and Construction Authority (BCA). NParks manages nature areas, URA is in charge of land-use planning, and the HDB manages public housing.

A. The Urban Redevelopment Authority (URA)

44. The URA is Singapore's national land-use planning authority. Its mission is 'to make Singapore a great city to live, work and play in'.[101] URA prepares long-term strategic plans and detailed local area plans for physical development and coordinates efforts to bring these plans to reality. Prudent land-use planning has enabled

---

99. https://www.sfa.gov.sg/about-sfa/who-we-are.
100. 'We guide Singapore's land use planning, urban redevelopment and building conservation, deliver affordable and quality public housing, develop an efficient construction industry to ensure a safe, quality and sustainable built environment, provide and manage parks, open spaces and the conservation of nature areas, maintain a high standard of animal and plant health, as well as protect consumer interest by raising the professionalism in the real estate agent industry.' *See* https://www.mnd.gov.sg/who-we-are/introduction.
101. *See* https://www.ura.gov.sg/Corporate/About-Us.

Singapore to enjoy strong economic growth and social cohesion and ensures that sufficient land is safeguarded to support continued economic progress and future development.[102]

B. The Housing and Development Board (HDB)

45. The Housing and Development Board (HDB) is Singapore's public housing authority.[103] It was established in 1960, when only 9% of the population lived in public housing. Today, some 80% of the population live in high-rise apartments built by HDB, of whom around 90% own their own home.[104] These apartments are purchased by Singaporean citizens or permanent residents and held on 99-year leases. Short-term rental flats are for the very poor and are not encouraged, as home ownership for all is a national aspiration that continues to play a significant role in nation-building.

C. The National Parks Board (NParks)

46. NParks is responsible for providing and enhancing the concept of Singapore as a Garden City.[105] It manages four nature reserves, two national parks, and some four hundred parks, as well as the park connector network, the lush roadside greenery in Singapore, and one marine park. As Singapore's scientific authority on nature conservation, NParks monitors and coordinates measures to ensure the health of designated nature areas. It is also the lead agency in the efforts to continually upgrade the Landscape and Horticulture Industry in Singapore. It administers and implements the Parks and Trees Act, Wildlife Act, Endangered Species (Import and Export) Act and their subsidiary laws.

III. Other Ministries and Statutory Boards

47. The Ministry of Trade and Industry (MTI) aims 'To promote economic growth and create good jobs, to enable Singaporeans to improve their lives. Together with our statutory boards, we will ensure that Singapore's economy continues to be competitive, is able to attract investments, and nurture a deeper base of global Singapore enterprises.'[106] MTI oversees nine statutory boards and one government department.

---

102. *See*. https://www.ura.gov.sg/Corporate/About-Us/What-We-Do.
103. *See* https://www.hdb.gov.sg/cs/infoweb/about-us.
104. https://www.hdb.gov.sg/cs/infoweb/about-us. HDB's tallest project is the 50 storeys project at Duxton Plain, called 'The Pinnacle@Duxton', with its seven towers collectively the world's tallest public residential buildings. https://www.visitsingapore.com/see-do-singapore/architecture/modern/pinnacle-at-duxton/.
105. *See* https://www.nparks.gov.sg/who-we-are/mission-history.
106. https://www.mti.gov.sg/About-Us/About-MTI.

48. The statutory boards are: Agency for Science, Technology and Research (A*STAR), Economic Development Board (EDB), Enterprise Singapore, Jurong Town Corporation (JTC), Singapore Tourism Board (STB), Competition and Consumer Commission of Singapore (CCCS), Energy Market Authority (EMA), Hotels Licensing Board (HLB), Sentosa Development Corporation (SDC) and the Singapore Department of Statistics (DOS) which delivers statistics and statistical services to empower decision-making.[107]

49. The EDB was established in 1962 to promote industrial development by encouraging and facilitating foreign investors to locate their industries in Singapore. Today, its mission is 'to create sustainable economic growth, with vibrant business and good job opportunities for Singapore'. EDB continues to be responsible for strategies that enhance Singapore's position as a global centre for business, innovation, and talent. EDB informs foreign investors of all regulations and works closely with MSE, JTC and A*STAR to ensure coordination in attracting the type of industries that Singapore is seeking.[108] Besides facilitating investments, EDB also engages Singapore's existing base of companies to transform their operations and boost productivity and to generate growth in adjacent and disruptive areas by growing new businesses out of Singapore.

50. JTC is responsible for the planning, construction and operation of industrial estates in Singapore, taking over from the EDB on 1 June 1968.[109] JTC handles all applications for industrial premises and works closely with the NEA. Applications for new factories are screened by NEA's Pollution Control Department (PCD), which will ensure that environmental requirements are adhered to, such as installing pollution control equipment and treatment facilities.

51. Other government ministries and departments are also involved in aspects of environmental management. The Ministry of Manpower (MOM)'s Occupational Safety & Health Division (OSH) administers provisions in the Workplace Safety and Health Act (WSHA) (which replaced the Factories Act) to ensure a safe and healthy environment for workers.[110] The Ministry of Transport (MOT)[111] comprises four statutory boards – the Civil Aviation Authority of Singapore (CAAS), the Maritime and Port Authority (MPA), the Land Transport Authority (LTA) and the Public Transport Council (PTC).

107. https://www.mti.gov.sg/About-Us/MTI-Family.
108. https://www.edb.gov.sg/en/about-edb/who-we-are.html.
109. https://www.jtc.gov.sg/about-us/Pages/default.aspx.
110. https://www.mom.gov.sg/about-us/divisions-and-statutory-boards/occupational-safety-and-health-division.
111. *See* https://www.mot.gov.sg/.

§5. Environmental Policy

I. Domestic Environmental Policy

52. Environmental policy in Singapore is led by the government through a largely top-down approach. In the areas of pollution control and environmental health, this has proven to be very effective, as there is long-term planning for environmental infrastructure and swift implementation. In pollution control, the government is proactive in seeking the best technology to resolve problems such as waste disposal and the supply of clean water. Laws are reviewed and amended when necessary and innovative ways are devised for enforcement. Nature conservation laws have also seen substantial amendments in recent times, although considerable inadequacies remain.[112] These will be discussed below.

II. International Conventions/Treaties

53. Singapore has signed and ratified a number of multilateral environmental agreements (MEAs), such as the Convention on International Trade in Endangered Species of Wild Flora and Fauna (CITES), the Convention on Marine Pollution (MARPOL), the Vienna Convention on Ozone Depleting Substances (ODS), the Convention on Biological Diversity (CBD), and the United Nations Framework Convention on Climate Change (UNFCCC). Singapore ratified the Kyoto Protocol on 12 April 2006 and also ratified the Paris Agreement on Climate Change on 21 September 2016, becoming one of the first few countries to do so.

54. As a general rule, Singapore takes its international obligations seriously, such that implementing legislation at the national level is usually passed soon after ratification of or accession to an international agreement. These MEAs guide domestic policy, as long as they are not contrary to national objectives. Officials from the relevant Ministries attend all Meetings of the Parties to these Conventions and amendments to the laws are passed where necessary to ensure compliance.

III. Regional Cooperation: ASEAN

55. Singapore is a member of the Association of Southeast Asian Nations (ASEAN). ASEAN was established on 8 August 1967 by five countries (Indonesia,

112. *See* Lye Lin-Heng, 'A Fine City in a Garden: Environmental Law and Governance in Singapore', [2008] SJLS 68–117; Douglas L. Tookey 'Singapore's Environmental Management System: Strengths and Weaknesses and Recommendations for the Years Ahead' (1998) 23 Wm & Mary Envtl L & Pol'y Rev. 169–270. *See also* Lye Lin-Heng, 'Land Law and the Environment: Re-examining the Concept of Ownership and Forging New Rights and Obligations in a Changed World' (2010) 22 SAcLJ 189–228; Lye Lin-Heng 'Environmental Law, Policy, Governance and Management for Cities: Getting it Right for a Sustainable Future – The Singapore Story', Chapter 7 in *Environmental Policies in Asia – Perspectives from Seven Asian Countries*, Jing Huang, Shreekant Gupta, eds (2014) World Scientific pp. 171–202.

Malaysia, the Philippines, Singapore and Thailand). It now comprises eleven states, with the inclusion of Brunei, Vietnam, Laos, Cambodia, Myanmar,[113] and now most recently, Timor-Leste, having joined in October 2025.[114] While occupying only 3% of the world's total land area, the region is renowned for its rich biological heritage, comprising the three mega biodiversity countries, namely Indonesia, Malaysia and the Philippines, which together represent around 80% of global biological diversity. The ASEAN region is home to around 60% of the world's tropical peatlands and 42% of the world's mangrove forests. Total forest cover in ASEAN is 211,172,100 hectares, and protected areas in ASEAN account for 14% of the total land area. ASEAN has the highest proportion of endemic bird (9%) and mammal (11%) species and the second highest proportion of endemic vascular plant species (25%).[115] More than 2,000 species have been discovered in the ASEAN region over the past two decades.[116]

56. ASEAN cooperation on the environment began in 1978 with the formation of the ASEAN Experts Group on the Environment (now the ASEAN Senior Officials on the Environment). The ASEAN Environmental Ministers also hold regular meetings at least once a year. Three working groups have been established: on Nature Conservation and Biodiversity, on Marine and Coastal Zone Management and on Multilateral Environmental Agreements (MEAs). ASEAN policy on the environment aims at an integrated approach towards an ASEAN conservation strategy, to harmonise environmental quality standards as well as to prevent and abate transboundary pollution.

57. Since 1978, there have been three ASEAN Environment Programmes, for the periods 1978–1982, 1983–1987, and 1988–1992. After the UN Conference at Rio in 1992, the *ASEAN Strategic Plan of Action for the Environment* was formulated for the period 1994–1998. This Plan comprised ten strategies. It was soon followed by the *Hanoi Plan of Action* for 1999–2004 with fifteen very specific objectives, including the carrying out of the ASEAN Cooperation Plan on Transboundary Pollution (June 1995) with emphasis on the Regional Haze Action Plan

113. *See* the ASEAN website at https://asean.org/. ASEAN hard and soft law instruments can be found in this site – http://www.asean.org/resources. They can also be found on the website of the Centre for International Law at the Law Faculty, National University of Singapore – *see* 'Documents Database' at https://cil.nus.edu.sg/database-cil/. *See also* Koh Kheng-Lian, *ASEAN Environmental Law, Policy and Governance: Selected Documents*, Vol. I (2009) and II (2012), World Scientific; Koh KL, 'Transboundary and Global Environmental Issues: The Role of ASEAN in Transnational Environmental Law', *Vol. 1(1), Transnational Environmental Law,* 1, pp. 1–16 (Cambridge University Press: 2012); Koh, KL 'The Discourse of Environmental Security in the ASEAN Context', Chapter 9 in Jessup B & Rubenstein K. (eds) *Environmental Discourses in Public and International Law* (Cambridge University Press: 2012), pp. 218–237; Koh, KL, Robinson, Nicholas A, Lye, LH, *ASEAN Environmental Legal Integration: Sustainable Goals* (Cambridge University Press, 2016).
114. *See* https://asean.org/forging-a-new-era-timor-leste-admitted-into-asean/.
115. *See* https://asean.org/wp-content/uploads/2024/04/APMS-2-Apr-Web.pdf.
116. *See* 'Overview of ASEAN Cooperation on the Environment' at https://asean.org/our-communities/asean-socio-cultural-community/environment/.

(December 1997).[117] ASEAN cooperation on the environment focuses on transboundary pollution, and an integrated approach to nature conservation and biodiversity, coastal and marine environment, and MEAs. It also emphasises public awareness and environmental education and the harmonisation of environmental laws and standards in the region.

58. The Hanoi Plan has benchmarks based on set time frames and targets, such as developing a framework and improving regional coordination for the integrated protection and management of coastal zones by 2001; strengthening institutional and legal capacities to carry out Agenda 21 and other international environmental agreements by 2001; harmonising the environmental databases of member countries by 2001; carrying out a regional water conservation programme by 2001; establishing a regional centre or network to promote environmentally sound technologies by 2004; drawing up and adoption of an ASEAN Protocol on access to genetic resources; and developing a Regional Action Plan for the Protection of the Marine Environment from Land-based and Sea-based Activities.

59. At the 9th ASEAN Bali Summit in October 2003, the ASEAN leaders reaffirmed the broad vision for ASEAN 2020. They agreed to establish an ASEAN Community that would be supported by the three pillars of 'political and security cooperation', 'economic cooperation', and 'socio-cultural cooperation'. To this end, a framework was adopted to achieve this ASEAN Community through the ASEAN Security Community, ASEAN Economic Community and ASEAN Socio-Cultural Community (ASCC). In November 2004, the *Vientiane Action Program (VAP)* was signed. It is a six-year plan building up to the realisation of the end goal of ASEAN and the Declaration of ASEAN Concord II of establishing an ASEAN Community in 2020.

Part 3.3 of VAP provides for the promotion of environmental sustainability. It states that the ASCC promotes a clean and green ASEAN with fully established mechanisms for sustainable development to ensure the protection of the Region's environment, the sustainability of its natural resources and the high quality of life of its people. The medium-term strategies and milestones in pursuit of this goal are to focus on environmental management and resource management. The former includes the prevention of transboundary haze pollution via the *ASEAN Agreement on Transboundary Haze Pollution*, aiming for zero waste and minimal impact on the environment, promoting business opportunities in environmental goods and services through relevant environmentally sound technologies; ensuring cities/urban areas in ASEAN are environmentally sustainable while meeting the social and economic needs of the people; and striving for harmonisation of environmental policies, legislation, regulations, standards and databases, taking into account the

117. The Regional Haze Action Plan (RHAP) was adopted in December 1997 and updated in July 1999 by the ASEAN Environment Ministers. It has three priority areas: prevention of land and forest fires through better management policies and enforcement; establishing operational mechanisms for monitoring; and strengthening regional land and forest fire-fighting capability. A Haze Technical Task Force was established.

national circumstances of Member Countries, to support the integration of the environmental, social and economic goals of the region. The latter includes taking care of ASEAN's coastal and marine environment, its biological diversity and 'promoting the sustainability of water resources to ensure sufficient water quantity of acceptable quality to meet the needs of the people of ASEAN in terms of health, food security, the economy and the environment, taking into consideration the strong linkage between water, health and poverty'.

60. The *ASEAN Agreement on Transboundary Haze Pollution* was concluded in 2002. This was followed by the Yangon Resolution on Sustainable Development on 18 December 2003, and the *ASEAN Declaration on Heritage Parks* on the same date. Singapore's Sungei Buloh Wetlands Reserve and Bukit Timah Nature Reserve have been declared ASEAN Heritage Parks.

The ASEAN Statement on CITES was signed in October 2004, following which the ASEAN Wildlife Enforcement Network (ASEAN-WEN) was established[118] to combat illegal trade in wildlife. In 2016, ASEAN-WEN was merged with the ASEAN Expert Group on CITES to form the ASEAN Working Group on CITES and Wildlife Enforcement.[119]

The Cebu Resolution on Sustainable Development was passed in November 2006.

61. The *ASEAN Agreement on Disaster Management and Emergency Response (AADMER)* was signed in July 2005 and entered into force on 24 December 2009. It proved to be very helpful when floods devastated much of Thailand in 2011, claiming more than 500 lives, disrupting the lives of 8.8 million others and displacing more than 200,000 from their homes.[120] On 15 October 2011, the ASEAN-Emergency Rapid Assessment Team (ASEAN-ERAT) was dispatched to Thailand to assess flood-affected areas and determine the basic and immediate needs of the affected population.[121] When Typhoon Bopha hit the Mindanao region in the Philippines on 3 December 2012, more than 5 million people were affected, with 906 dead, 2,660 injured, and 932 missing. The ASEAN Coordinating Centre for Humanitarian Assistance on Disaster Management (AHA Centre) deployed the ASEAN-ERAT to assess needs and quickly provide necessary aid to disaster-affected areas.[122] Member States also sent aid and deployed a response team to assist in planning and preparation in these areas. Following the disaster, the AHA Centre launched a Disaster Emergency Logistics System for ASEAN to 'provide

118. *See* https://cites.org/eng/news/sundry/2005/ASEAN-WEN.shtml.

119. http://awgciteswe.org/.

120. 'Thailand latest Southeast Asia nation hit hard by floods,' [online] *CNN*, Published 7 Oct. 2011 Available at https://edition.cnn.com/2011/10/07/world/asia/southeast-asia-floods/index.html.

121. *See* https://asean.org/the-asean-emergency-rapid-assessment-team-dispatched-to-respond-to-floods-in-thailand/.

122. Association of Southeast Asian Nations, ASEAN Supports the Typhoon Affected Communities in The Philippines [online] Available at https://asean.org/asean-supports-the-typhoon-affected-communities-in-the-philippines/.

rapid delivery of relief items in times of disaster emergencies'.[123] AADMER is further enhanced by the AADMER Work Programme. This programme lays the mechanisms for joint response and disaster reduction at the regional level through programmes such as enhanced risk assessment, improving risk awareness, building resilience into essential infrastructures and services for the ASEAN Community to thrive despite disaster and climate impacts, and intensifying ASEAN's institutional and logistical capacity to deliver regional response.

62. ASEAN continues to engage in regional projects. In 2022, ASEAN and the UN Office for Project Services (UNOPS) signed an agreement to combat marine plastic pollution in the region, implementing a five-year project with support from UNOPS and the World Bank.[124] In 2023, ASEAN launched a regional river management project, aimed at establishing integrated river basin management (IRBM) systems and sharing knowledge between member states.[125]

A. *The ASEAN Charter, 2007*

63. On 20 November 2007, the ASEAN Declaration on Environmental Sustainability was signed at the 13th ASEAN Summit. The key theme of discussions at the Summit was 'Energy, Environment, Climate Change and Sustainable Development'. That same day, on the 40th Anniversary of the founding of ASEAN, the *ASEAN Charter* was signed in Singapore. The next day, on 21 November 2007, the Singapore Declaration on Climate Change, Energy and the Environment was signed at the Third East Asia Summit. The ASEAN Charter entered into force on 15 December 2008, providing a legal status and institutional framework for ASEAN, aiming to turn it into a more effective and cohesive organisation. The Charter resolves, *inter alia,* 'to ensure sustainable development for the benefit of present and future generations and to place the well-being, livelihood and welfare of the peoples at the centre of the ASEAN community building process'. It also preserves the principles of sovereignty and non-interference in the internal affairs of Member States and enhances consultation on matters affecting the common interests of ASEAN.

64. Since then, various declarations, statements and other instruments have been agreed upon, including the following:[126]

- ASEAN Declaration on the 13th session of the Conference of the Parties to the UNFCCC and the 3rd session of the CMP to the Kyoto Protocol (2007).
- Singapore Resolution on Environmental Sustainability and Climate Change (11th AMME, 2009).

---

123. *Ibid.*
124. *See* https://environment.asean.org/news/detail/joint-media-release-asean-and-unops-sign-agreement-to-combat-marine-plastic-pollution-in-southeast-asia.
125. *See* https://environment.asean.org/news/detail/asean-integrated-river-management-project-launched-in-manila.
126. *See* https://asean.org/wp-content/uploads/2018/02/50.-December-2017-ASEAN-Cooperation-on-Environment-At-A-Glance.pdf.

- ASEAN Joint Statement on Climate Change to COP-15 to the UNFCCC and CMP-5 to the Kyoto Protocol (15th ASEAN Summit, 2009).
- ASEAN Leaders' Statement on Joint Response to Climate Change (16th ASEAN Summit, 2010).
- ASEAN Leaders' Statement on Climate Change to COP-17 to the UNFCCC and CMP-7 to the Kyoto Protocol (19th ASEAN Summit, 2011).
- Joint Statement of ASEAN Environment Ministers for the Eleventh Meeting of the Conference of the Parties to the CBD (2012).
- New Delhi ASEAN-India Ministerial Statement on Biodiversity (2012).
- Bangkok Resolution on ASEAN Environmental Cooperation (2012).
- ASEAN Joint Statement on Climate Change, (2014).
- Statement by the ASEAN Environment Ministers for the 12th Meeting of the Conference of the Parties to the CBD (2014).
- ASEAN Joint Statement on Climate Change (2015).
- Declaration on ASEAN Post 2015 Environmental Sustainability and Climate Change Agenda (2015).
- ASEAN Joint Statement, 13th Meeting of the Conference of the Parties, CBD (CBD COP 13) (2016).
- ASEAN Joint Statement on Climate Change, 22nd Conference of the Parties (COP 22), UNFCCC (2016).
- ASEAN Joint Statement on Climate Change, 23rd Session of the Conference of the Parties, UNFCCC (2017).
- ASEAN Joint Declaration on Hazardous Chemicals and Wastes Management (Adopted by ASEAN Environment Ministers) (2017).
- ASEAN Joint Statement on Climate Change, 2018 24th Session of the Conference of the Parties, UNFCCC (COP-24).
- ASEAN Joint Statement, 14th Meeting of the Conference of the Parties, CBD (CBD COP 14) (2018).
- ASEAN State of Climate Change Report, 12 October 2021.[127]
- ASEAN Joint Statement on Climate Change, 26th session of the Conference of the Parties (COP 26), 2021.[128]
- ASEAN Joint Statement on Climate Change, 27th session of the Conference of the Parties (COP 27).[129]
- ASEAN Joint Statement on Climate Change, 28th session of the Conference of the Parties (COP 28).[130]
- ASEAN Joint Statement on Climate Change, 28th session of the Conference of the Parties (COP 29).[131]

---

127. https://asean.org/wp-content/uploads/2021/10/ASCCR-e-publication-Final-12-Oct-2021.pdf.
128. https://asean.org/wp-content/uploads/2021/10/10.-ASEAN-Joint-Statement-to-COP26.pdf.
129. https://asean.org/asean-joint-statement-on-climate-change-to-the-27th-session-of-the-conference-of-the-parties-to-the-united-nations-framework-convention-on-climate-change-unfccc-cop-27/.
130. https://environment.asean.org/news/detail/asean-joint-statement-on-climate-change-to-the-28th-session-of-the-conference-of-the-parties-to-the-united-nations-framework-convention-on-climate-change-unfccc-cop-28.
131. https://asean.org/asean-joint-statement-on-climate-change-to-the-29th-session-of-the-conference-of-the-parties-to-the-united-nations-framework-convention-on-climate-change-unfccc-cop-29/.

65. ASEAN environmental cooperation priority areas of importance are reflected in the Blueprint for the ASEAN Socio-Cultural Community (ASCC Blueprint). The ASCC Blueprint was developed to ensure that concrete actions were undertaken to promote establishment of an ASCC. The first edition, ASCC Blueprint 2009–2015, was signed in Singapore at the 13th ASEAN Summit in 2007. It was updated as the ASCC Blueprint 2025[132] and adopted by ASEAN Leaders at the 27th ASEAN Summit in 2015 in Kuala Lumpur, Malaysia. Key areas of priority for environmental sustainability are provided in the ASCC Blueprint as follows:

- Section C. 'Sustainable'

C.1. Conservation and Sustainable Management of Biodiversity and Natural Resources

C.2. Environmentally Sustainable Cities

C.3. Sustainable Climate

C.4. Sustainable Consumption and Production

In moving towards the realisation of the overarching goals of an ASEAN Community 2025, the ASCC envisions the achievement of a sustainable environment in the face of social changes and economic development. Its objective is to promote and ensure balanced social development and sustainable environment that meet the needs of the people at all times.

An ASEAN Strategic Plan on Environment (ASPEN) 2016-2025 was developed to translate the ASCC Blueprint 2025 into a more detailed plan of action, serving as a guiding document for ASEAN in promoting ASEAN cooperation on environment until 2025.[133] The ASEAN nations now look towards making progress in developing the Post-2025 ASPEN, which aims to enhance regional cooperation and coordination on emerging and cross-cutting issues such as plastic pollution, circular economy, blue and green economy, nature-based solutions, and air pollution, in alignment with the ASCC Strategic Plan for the ASEAN Community Vision 2045 and global development agenda.[134]

66. While the efforts at regional cooperation on the environment are laudable, in practice, the crisis of the Indonesian forest fires has shown that the culture of musyawarah or 'seeking consensus' and non-interference is still predominant in the region and has proven to be a formidable obstacle to the swift resolution of transboundary environmental problems.[135] Various action plans involving the three

---

132. https://www.asean.org/wp-content/uploads/2012/05/8.-March-2016-ASCC-Blueprint-2025.pdf.
133. https://asean.org/wp-content/uploads/2016/10/RFP-ASPEN-.pdf; *see also* https://www.asean.org/wp-content/uploads/2012/05/8.-March-2016-ASCC-Blueprint-2025.pdf.
134. *See* https://asean.org/18th-asean-ministerial-meeting-on-the-environment-and-the-20th-meeting-of-the-conference-of-the-parties-to-the-asean-agreement-on-transboundary-haze-pollution/.
135. *See* Koh Kheng Lian & Nicholas A. Robinson, 'Regional Environmental Governance "Examining the Association of Southeast Asian Nations (ASEAN)"', in *Global Environmental Governance – Options & Opportunities,* Daniel C. Esty & Maria H. Ivanova, eds, 101–120; Koh Kheng Lian and Nicholas A. Robinson 'Strengthening Sustainable Development in Regional Inter-governmental Governance: Lessons from the 'ASEAN Way', (2002) 6 Sing. JICL 640–682; Robinson Nicholas A. 'Forest Fires as a Common International Concern: Precedents for the Progressive Development of International Environmental Law', 18 Pace Env LR [2000–2001].

ASEAN nations of Singapore, Malaysia, and Indonesia have been undertaken to resolve this transboundary haze problem, but have thus far not proven particularly effective.[136]

136. *See* paras 118 to 120.

Part I. Pollution Control

Chapter 1. General Law and Policy

§1. Introduction

67. Two main statutes control land-based pollution in Singapore – the Environment Protection and Management Act 1999 (EPMA) and the Environmental Public Health Act 1987 (EPHA).

68. The EPHA relates to environmental public health issues, including, *inter alia*, public cleanliness, waste management, and sanitation. The EPMA relates to, *inter alia*, air, water, land, and noise pollution, hazardous substances, and greenhouse gases.[137]

§2. Singapore's Environmental Management System (EMS) for Pollution Control

69. Singapore's success in managing the environment stems from sound environmental management policies and effective implementation. This translates to an effective environmental management system (EMS). In relation to pollution control, Singapore's EMS comprises four integrated strategies, as follows:

1. Prevention.
2. Monitoring.
3. Enforcement.
4. Public education.

I. Prevention: Land-Use Planning

70. The prevention of pollution starts with careful land-use planning and identification of the kinds of industries that can or should be allowed, and where they

137. Prior to 2008, the EPHA was known as the Environmental Pollution Control Act (EPCA) before it was renamed: Environmental Pollution Control (Amendment) Act 2007.

should be located.[138] Singapore has been guided by a number of different land-use plans, which include the Master Plans of 1958, 1980, 2003, 2008, and 2014;[139] as well as the Concept Plans for 1971, 1991, 2001, and 2011.[140] The latest Master Plan (2019) was gazetted on 27 November 2019.[141] It comprises a Written Statement and fifty-five Development Guide Plans, the latter specifying in detail the land use for fifty-five areas covering all of Singapore. A Draft Master Plan was later released in June 2025.[142] The Master Plan is reviewed every five years. It guides Singapore's development in the medium term, over the next ten to fifteen years, translating the broad, long-term strategies set out in the Long-Term Plan (Formerly known as the Concept Plan), into detailed implementable plans for Singapore.[143] The Long-Term Plan is a strategic land-use plan that will guide Singapore's development over the next forty to fifty years, ensuring there is sufficient land to meet Singapore's economic growth while providing a good quality living environment. It is reviewed every ten years. The latest review of the Long-Term Plan was carried out from 2021 to 2022.[144] The previous review was carried out from 2011 to 2013, and led up to the release of the Land-Use Plan 2030 by the Ministry of National Development (MND).[145] The Land-Use Plan is a conceptual plan that outlines the strategies to provide the physical capacity to sustain a high-quality living environment for a possible population range of 6.5 to 6.9 million by 2030. The Land-Use Plan also sets aside land to meet national needs beyond 2030, so that future generations have options and room for future growth.

71. While the Economic Development Board (EDB)[146] identifies the kinds of industries that Singapore should attract, there are close consultations with other ministries to ensure that environmental considerations are incorporated at the land-use planning, development control and planning stages, so as to minimise the

---

138. It is fitting that NEA's Code of Practice on Pollution Control (Singapore Standards 593 (2013)) starts with 'Judicious Siting of Industries'. *See* https://www.scribd.com/doc/274971651/SS-593-Code-of-Practice-for-Pollution-Control.
139. *See* https://www.ura.gov.sg/Corporate/Planning/Master-Plan/Previous-Master-Plans. *See* below at Part II, Ch. 5, Zoning and Land-Use PLanning.
140. For a detailed assessment of the role of land-use planning in the Singapore environmental context, *see* Lye Lin Heng, 'Land-Use Planning, Environmental Management and the Garden City as an Urban Development Approach in Singapore', in *Land Use Law for Sustainable Development,* Nathalie J. Chalifour, Patricia Kameri-Mbote, Lye Lin Heng, John Nolon eds., Cambridge University Press, 2007, pp. 374–397. *See also* Lye Lin Heng, 'Landscape Protection Laws in the Evolution of Modern Singapore'. *Landscape, Nature and Law*, ed. Antonio Herman Benjamin (2005), Sao Paolo, Brazil: Laws for a Green Planet Institute, pp. 119–134.
141. *See* https://www.ura.gov.sg/Corporate/Planning/Master-Plan.
142. https://www.channelnewsasia.com/singapore/ura-draft-master-plan-unveils-proposals-new-homes-orchard-and-newton-5200016.
143. Lye Lin Heng, 'Singapore: Long Term Environmental Policies' in *Cities of the Pacific Rim – Diversity & Sustainability*, PECC Sustainable Cities Taskforce, Genevieve Dubois-Taine, Christian Henriot, Eds., 2001 PUCA, pp. 155–168.
144. https://www.ura.gov.sg/Corporate/Planning/Long-Term-Plan-Review.
145. *Ibid.*
146. https://www.edb.gov.sg/en/about-edb/who-we-are.html.

impact of pollution on the surrounding land use.[147] Discussions are held with officers from the Ministry of Sustainability and Environment (MSE)'s National Environment Agency (NEA) to see if the pollution that ensues from new industries can be controlled; with planners from the MND's Urban Redevelopment Authority (URA) to establish the possible sites for these industries; with the Jurong Town Corporation (JTC), the largest landlord of industrial premises, with private industrial estate developers and with Singapore's public housing agency, the Housing and Development Board (HDB) to discuss the physical logistics of location for these factories; and with the Ministry of Manpower (MOM) to ascertain the impacts of these new industries on the workforce.

72. Planners from the URA will check with NEA's PCD on the siting of these new industries or development projects to ensure their compatibility with the surrounding land use.[148] This is part of the planning process, to ensure that pollutive industries are located in specially designated areas such as Jurong Island[149] with measures to control, manage and minimise pollution as well as to maximise industrial and technological synergies. In particular, PCD will examine measures to control air, water and noise pollution, the management of hazardous substances, and the treatment and disposal of toxic wastes.

73. To guide land-use planning and to assist industrialists in the selection of suitable industrial premises, industries are classified into four categories: clean, light, general and special industries, based on the impact of residual emissions of fumes, dust, and noise on surrounding land use.[150] Buffer zones are prescribed for each of these categories except for clean industries. Special industries require a buffer zone of at least 500 m between the boundaries of a factory and the nearest industrial building. Special industries that can potentially cause serious pollution, such as oil refineries, petrochemical and chemical plants, toxic industrial waste treatment facilities, and sewage treatment works, require a buffer zone of at least 1 km from the nearest residential building. Special industries which handle large quantities of hazardous substances are sited on offshore islands (e.g., Jurong Island) or industrial estates which are located away from residential estates.

Industrial premises that are located close to residential areas and within the water catchment areas may only be occupied by clean or light industries.[151] Food industries are also classified into light, general or special categories, depending on their

147. *See* the annual reports of the National Environment Agency – https://www.nea.gov.sg/corporate-functions/resources/publications/annual-reportshttps://www.nea.gov.sg/integrated-sustainability-report-2020-2021.
148. http://www.ura.gov.sg/.
149. Jurong Island is an amalgamation of several small islands to form a specialised complex for the petrochemical and energy industries. *See* https://www.jtc.gov.sg/jurongisland.
150. *See* examples of these categories in the Code of Practice on Pollution Control, Singapore Standard 593 (2013).
151. *See* the NEA's Code of Practice on Pollution Control *(ibid)* for examples of these classifications – *supra* n. 138.

scale of operations and pollutive capacity. In order to prevent cross-contamination, food industries are sited in industrial premises in areas designated as food zones or in areas with compatible industrial uses.

74. Before a proposed development can be built, the developer is required to submit Building Plans of the proposed works to the Building Plan and Management Division of the Building and Construction Authority (BCA) for approval.[152] These Building Plans must also be submitted to and approved by various authorities, including the Fire Safety Bureau, the National Parks Board (NParks) and NEA's Central Building Plan Unit (CBPU). The CBPU examines all building plans to ensure they comply with sewerage, drainage, environmental health and pollution control requirements. In particular, CBPU will screen prospective industries to ensure that they:

- are sited in designated industrial estates and are compatible with the surrounding land use;
- adopt clean technology to minimise the use of hazardous chemicals and the generation of wastes;
- adopt processes which facilitate the recycling, reuse and recovery of wastes;
- do not pose unmanageable health and safety hazards and pollution problems;
- install pollution control equipment to comply with discharge or emission standards.

When the factory building is completed, inspectors from CBPU will inspect the premises to check if the structure has been built in compliance with the requirements of the Sewerage, Drainage, Environmental Health and PCD. Only when this is approved will the factory be given a Temporary Occupation Permit (TOP) or a Certificate of Statutory Completion (CSC).

II. Monitoring and Enforcement

75. Singapore's second strategy in pollution control is monitoring air and water quality, which is constantly monitored.[153]

The main sources of air pollution in Singapore are emissions from industries and motor vehicles and, from time to time, transboundary smoke haze from land and forest fires in the region. The ambient air in Singapore is continuously monitored through a network of air monitoring sensors located in different parts of Singapore. They measure the level of six air pollutants – sulphur dioxide (SO_2), nitrogen dioxide (NO_2), ozone (O_3), carbon monoxide (CO), particulate matter (PM10), and fine particulate matter (PM 2.5). The concentrations of these are used to compute the Pollutant Standards Index (PSI) over a twenty-four-hour period across various

152. *See* Building Control Act, 1989, 2020 Rev. Ed. ; https://www1.bca.gov.sg/.

153. *See* Chapter 2 (Air Pollution) and chapter 3 (Water Pollution) below. *See also* https://www.nea.gov.sg/corporate-functions/resources/publications/annual-reports.

regions of Singapore.[154] The PSI, an indicator of air quality developed by the US-EPA, is made available to members of the public on an hourly basis on the NEA website, haze microsite and myENV app, via the internet.[155] NEA also continuously measures various volatile organic compounds (VOCs), including benzene, toluene, xylene (BRX) and ground-level ozone.[156]

NEA embarked on a collaboration with the United Kingdom's Meteorological Office from 2013 to 2018 to develop SINGV – NEA's convective-scale Numerical Weather Prediction (NWP) system. In 2019, SINGV was operationalised in NEA's Central Forecast Office to provide additional guidance in the provision of the weather forecast and warning services for Singapore and the surrounding region.[157] SINGV was upgraded in December 2023 and has improved rainfall forecast accuracy in the year since.[158] In May 2019, NEA's Upper Air Observatory was certified as a Global Climate Observing System Reference Upper Air Network (GRUAN) station.[159] GRUAN stations aim to ensure that high-quality measurements of the upper atmosphere are consistently collected. The data is used to determine climatic trends in the upper atmosphere, calibrate data from satellites, and study atmospheric processes.[160] With the certification, NEA is the first certified GRUAN station located in the equatorial region, forming part of a global network of fifteen certified stations.[161]

76. Singapore's inland waters are monitored by the NEA's Environmental Pollution Department (PCD) from forty-eight streams and ponds in the water catchment areas. The water quality of the fifteen reservoirs within the water catchment areas is jointly monitored by PCD and the Public Utilities Board (PUB) every quarter. The water is analysed for pH levels, dissolved oxygen, Biochemical Oxygen Demand (BOD), Total Suspended Solids (TSS) and other properties. The sixteen rivers and streams in non-water catchment areas are also monitored quarterly. Samples of trade effluent may also be collected by the PCD for analysis. Coastal water quality is continuously monitored from a network of eight buoy-based water quality monitoring stations along the Straits of Johor and the Straits of Singapore to assess if the water quality has been affected by oil spills, eutrophication of seawater, and algae blooms, which may affect the fish farms located in the coastal waters. Samples are also taken to analyse additional water quality parameters such as heavy metals and VOCs.[162] NEA's PCD also monitors coastal waters monthly from thirty-six sampling points along the Straits of Johor and twelve sampling points along the

154. https://www.nea.gov.sg/our-services/pollution-control/air-pollution/air-quality. *See also* https://www.nea.gov.sg/our-services/pollution-control/air-and-coastal-water-quality-monitoring.
155. *See* https://www.haze.gov.sg/resources/historical-readings;https://www.haze.gov.sg/resources/1-hr-pm2.5-readings; and https://www.haze.gov.sg/resources/readings-over-the-last-24-hours.
156. *See supra* n. 154.
157. *See* https://ccrs.weather.gov.sg/singv-%E2%94%80-a-tropical-convective-scale-nwpnowcasting-capability-for-singapore/.
158. *See* https://file.go.gov.sg/ccrs-newsletter7.pdf.
159. *See* https://www.nea.gov.sg/docs/default-source/resource/publications/annual-report/nea-integrated-sustainability-report-2019-2020-(lores).pdf.
160. https://www.gruan.org/network/sites/singapore.
161. *See* https://www.gruan.org/network/sites.
162. https://www.nea.gov.sg/our-services/pollution-control/air-and-coastal-water-quality-monitoring.

Straits of Singapore. NEA also monitors the water quality of seven recreational beaches (Sentosa Island, Seletar Island, Sembawang Park, Changi, East Coast Park, Pasir Ris, and Punggol) based on the WHO's guidelines of Enterococcus counts not exceeding 200 counts per 100 ml for 95% of the samples.[163] In 2024, six out of the seven beaches had their water quality graded as 'Good', with Sembawang Park graded as 'Fair'.[164]

77. Coastal waters are monitored monthly by the PCD from thirty-six sampling points along the Straits of Johor and twelve sampling points along the Straits of Singapore. These samples are subject to physical, chemical and microbiological examinations. In 2014, a real-time, continuous water quality monitoring system for coastal waters of Singapore was commissioned. The system comprises eight buoy-based monitoring stations with sensors for water quality parameters.

III. Penalties for Breach

78. Singapore's environmental laws draw on three measures for effective implementation: administrative measures, criminal sanctions, and civil sanctions. The criminal sanctions include fines, imprisonment, forfeiture, confiscation, and, in the case of littering, a Corrective Work Order (CWO).[165] The administrative measures include the issuance of licences and permits and the mandatory keeping of records. Owners or occupiers may also be required to execute certain works, failing which they may be ordered to do so, or the works may be executed by a government authority and the costs recovered from the owner/occupier. A person may also be ordered to comply with the requirements, standards or conditions laid down by a particular statute, failing which a Notice or Order may be issued, requiring him to comply with the requirements. Failure to comply entails pecuniary penalties which may include a fine, compensation, damages and costs, as well as payment for all expenses incurred in the execution of works to comply with the Notice or Order.[166]

IV. Liability Questions

79. As Singapore inherited the common law from England, a polluting act may be both an offence under statutory law, as well as a tort (i.e., a civil wrong). Where the act is a breach of a statutory law, prosecutions will be brought either by officers from the relevant Ministry or the Public Prosecutor. However, an individual who has suffered harm and seeks compensation will have to bring a private action in tort using the common law private actions of nuisance, negligence, trespass, or the rule in *Rylands v. Fletcher* against the polluter. He may also ask for an injunction to stop

163. *Ibid.*; https://www.nea.gov.sg/our-services/pollution-control/water-quality/recreational-beaches.
164. https://www.nea.gov.sg/our-services/pollution-control/water-quality/recreational-beaches.
165. Foo Kim Boon 'Environmental Criminal Law in Singapore' (1997) 9 SAcLJ 294–309. *See also*, by the same author, 'Control of Pollution in Singapore' (1993) 5 SAcLJ 81–101.
166. For example, *see* s. 41 EPMA – Default in compliance with notice or order.

the wrongful act. Defendants who are insured may pass liability on to the insurer. In the case of pollution by bulk oil tankers, civil liability is imposed under the Merchant Shipping (Civil Liability and Compensation for Oil Pollution) Act, 1998.

80. All courts have jurisdiction to hear civil as well as criminal cases. Civil claims for up to SGD 60,000 are tried in the Magistrates' Courts,[167] while claims for up to SGD 250,000 are tried in the District Courts.[168] The usual requirements as to standing apply, requiring the plaintiff to show that he has *locus standi* to apply to court for the remedy requested. So far, no actions have been brought before the courts by non-government organisations and there has been no public interest litigation relating to the environment.

81. It should be noted that a nuisance would be a tort in common law, but may also be a public nuisance and a crime under statutory laws. Under the Environmental Public Health Act 1987 (EPHA),[169] a nuisance is defined broadly in section 2 as 'any act, omission or thing occasioning or likely to occasion injury, offence, harm, danger or damage to the sense of sight, smell or hearing, or which is likely to be injurious or dangerous to health or property'. Section 44(a) to (n) lists various kinds of public nuisances, which can be dealt with summarily by the Director-General (DG) of Public Health by issuing a nuisance order.[170] The penalties for committing a nuisance are a fine of SGD 1,000 for the first conviction, SGD 2,000 for the second conviction, and SGD 5,000 for a third and subsequent convictions.[171] Nuisances may also fall under the Miscellaneous Offences (Public Order and Nuisance) Act 1906, for which the fine is SGD 1,000 unless a Magistrate's Order is sought, whereupon the fine is doubled to SGD 2,000.

82. Prosecutions under the various statutory laws are usually brought by prosecutors from the relevant Ministry, with advice from the Attorney General's chambers when necessary. More difficult cases may be prosecuted by the Attorney General's chambers. Some laws stipulate that prosecutions can only be instituted with the written consent of the Attorney General.[172]

§3. ENVIRONMENTAL IMPACT ASSESSMENTS (EIA)

83. There are no specific laws or regulations that legislate environmental impact assessment (EIA) studies as being mandatory. Instead, governmental agencies adopt

---

167. State Courts (Variation of Magistrate's Court Limit) Order, GN S 263/1999, amended by GN S 154/2014 and GN S 263/2019.
168. The State Courts (Variation of District Court Limit) Order, 1997, GN S. 333/97; amended by GN S S 333/1999 and GN S 153/2014.
169. Act No. 14 of 1987, 2020 Rev. Ed.
170. Section 45 EPHA.
171. Section 21(2) EPHA.
172. For example, discharging toxic substances or hazardous substances into inland waters (Section 17(6) Environmental Protection and Management Act).

an EIA framework in evaluating the environmental impacts of developing proposals, with approvals only granted when regulatory standards are met.[173] Proposed development projects near sensitive areas (e.g., nature reserves, marine and coastal areas, areas of significant biodiversity or ecological sensitivity, and areas with potential transboundary impact) are subject to greater scrutiny, and more thorough studies may be required by regulatory agencies.[174] The EIA framework has been strengthened in recent years. In 2024, NParks revised its guidelines for Biodiversity Impact Assessments (BIA), the biodiversity component of EIAs and one especially applicable to the abovementioned sensitive areas.[175] Transparency has improved, and all environmental study reports (except those with security considerations) are published online.[176] EIAs are now centralised, with consultants carrying out EIAs managed by NParks instead of individual developers.[177]

84. In terms of enforcement, agencies are empowered by various laws to issue requirements and directions to developers and take direct enforcement action.[178] Under the Planning Act, statutory permissions and conditions can be imposed for the conduct of environmental studies.[179] More broadly, the Director-General (DG) of Environmental Protection is empowered under the EPMA to require the owner or occupier of hazardous installations to carry out impact analysis studies.[180] These are called Quantitative Risk Assessments (QRA) and are controlled by the PCD.[181] The DG may also, by notice in writing, require any person intending to carry out any activity likely to cause substantial pollution of the environment or increase the level of such pollution:

a. to carry out a study on environmental pollution control and related matters;
b. to submit for the DG's approval, within a specified time, a proposal to implement measures for the prevention, reduction or control of pollution of the environment; and
c. to implement such measures for the prevention, reduction or control of pollution of the environment as the DG may approve or specify.

173. *See* https://www.ura.gov.sg/Corporate/Planning/Our-Planning-Process/Bringing-plans-to-Reality/Environmental-Impact-Assessment. A list of past reports is available on the same website for illustration.
174. *Ibid.*
175. https://www.nparks.gov.sg/nature/enhancing-biodiversity-guidelines-resources. These guidelines were first introduced in 2020.
176. https://www.straitstimes.com/singapore/environment/development-works-in-singapore-to-be-more-sensitive-to-wildlife-under-changes.
177. https://www.straitstimes.com/singapore/environment/nparks-to-centralise-environmental-impact-assessment-of-development-works.
178. https://www.straitstimes.com/singapore/environment/development-works-in-singapore-to-be-more-sensitive-to-wildlife-under-changes.
179. https://www.straitstimes.com/singapore/environment/environmental-impact-assessments-to-be-further-strengthened-desmond-lee.
180. Section 26 EPMA.
181. *See* the revised Quantitative Risk Assessment (QRA) guidelines: QRA Technical Guidance, Revision No 4 (1 Jul. 2024); QRA Criteria Guidelines, Revision No 2 (11 Jul. 2024). https://www.nea.gov.sg/our-services/development-control/overview. *See* https://www.nea.gov.sg/docs/default-source/our-services/qra-technical-guidance_nov16.pdf.

Failure to comply is an offence.[182]

§4. The Right to a Healthy Environment

85. There is no specific provision for the right to a healthy environment contained in the Constitution of Singapore or any other written law. The right to a clean and healthy environment has also not been tested in any Singapore court of law, although in other common law jurisdictions, the constitutional right to life (Article 9) has been held to include the right to a healthy environment.[183]

86. At a regional level, ASEAN is set to adopt the ASEAN Declaration on the Right to a Safe, Clean, Healthy, and Sustainable Environment.[184] A draft version of the Declaration sets out, amongst other rights, the right of every person to 'a safe, clean, healthy and sustainable environment, which includes clean air, a safe and stable climate, healthy ecosystems and biodiversity, safe and sufficient water and adequate sanitation, healthy and sustainably produced food, and non-toxic environments'.[185] Such a Declaration may well provide a blueprint to guide member states such as Singapore to advance this right at the national level.

§5. Environmental Management Within Corporations

87. There is no specific law on the organisation of environmental management within companies. Pollution laws extend liability to directors, officers, and members of corporations, as well as to partners of partnerships and officers and members of unincorporated associations.[186] The laws also shift the onus of proof onto the corporation, partnership or association should there be an environmental mishap.[187] While there is no requirement for ISO 14001 certification,[188] the government

182. Section 36 EPMA.
183. *See* 'Emerging Trends in National Environmental Legislation in Developing Countries' UNEP's New Way Forward, Environmental Law and Sustainable Development, UNEP, reproduced in Capacity Building for Environmental Law in the Asian and Pacific Region, Vol. 1 2002, Donna Craig, Koh Kheng-Lian &Nicholas A Robinson, eds. ADB pp. 173–186; also, 'Judicial Decisions and Alternative Dispute Resolution' *ibid.*, Chapter 11; Dr Parvez Hassan & Azim Azfar 'Securing Environmental Rights through Public Interest Litigation in Southeast Asia', 22 Va. Envtl. L. J. 215 [2003–2004].
184. *See* https://asean.org/joint-press-release-of-aichr-asoen-interface-consultation-on-the-proposed-asean-declaration-on-the-right-to-a-safe-clean-healthy-and-sustainable-environment/.
185. https://www.unescap.org/sites/default/d8files/event-documents/AER%20WG_3M_3_Add1%20Draft%20ASEAN%20declaration%20on%20environmental%20rights.pdf.
186. Section 71 EPMA. Similar provisions appear in other statutes, including s. 67 the Sewerage and Drainage Act 1999, and s. 42 of the Hazardous Waste (Control of Export, Import and Transit) Act, 1997, which implements the Basel Convention on the Control of Transboundary Movements of Hazardous Wastes and their Disposal.
187. E.g. Section 17(5) EPMA.
188. ISO 14001 is an internationally recognised standard for environmental management systems (EMS): https://www.iso.org/standard/60857.html.

encourages it and offers funding support for companies seeking to embark on sustainability standards adoption projects.[189]

88. The Workplace Safety and Health Act, 2006 (WSHA) and its predecessor, the Factories Act, require factories with fifty or more employees to set up a Safety Committee. Corporations are encouraged and sometimes mandated to obtain green labels for their products. The Singapore Green Labelling Scheme was created in 1992 in line with the ISO 14024 standard, and serves to identify products that reach high environmental standards.[190] The NEA administers the Mandatory Energy Labelling Scheme (MELS) and sets Minimum Energy Performance Standards (MEPS) for certain types of household appliances, including air-conditioners, refrigerators, clothes dryers, and lighting.[191] The MELS makes energy labelling compulsory and aims to help consumers make informed purchasing decisions, while the MEPS aims to raise energy efficiency of appliances across the market; both schemes are continually revised and updated. A corporation's overall environmental awareness and initiatives can be rewarded with the Singapore Environmental Achievement Award, initiated by the Singapore Environment Council and supported by the NEA.[192] There is also an annual Singapore President's Award for the Environment, administered by the Ministry of Sustainability and the Environment (MSE), which is 'the highest environmental accolade for individuals, organisations and companies that have made significant contributions towards environmental and water resource sustainability in Singapore'.[193]

189. Through the Enterprise Sustainability Programme: https://www.enterprisesg.gov.sg/resources/blog/green-standards-global-markets-how-singapore-companies-can-thrive-through-adopting-sustainability-standards/.
190. *See* https://sgls.sec.org.sg/cms.php?cms_id=3.
191. *See* https://www.nea.gov.sg/our-services/climate-change-energy-efficiency/energy-efficiency/household-sector/about-mandatory-energy-labelling-and-minimum-energy-performance-standards.
192. *See* https://web.sec.org.sg/seaa/.
193. *See* https://www.mse.gov.sg/take-action/pae/overview.

Chapter 2. Air Pollution

§1. General

89. While Singapore's air quality is relatively better than other major cities, it has not met the standards set out by the global air quality guidelines issued by the World Health Organisation (WHO) as revised in 2021. As such, air pollution continues to be a concern and air quality is constantly monitored.[194] The main sources of air pollution are industries, motor vehicles and the seasonal burning of forests in the region. Pollution is generated from the burning of fossil fuels for heat generation in industries, electricity generation and transportation.[195] The main air pollutants are sulphur dioxide, oxides of nitrogen, carbon monoxide, ozone, lead, hydrocarbons and particulates. There are increasing concerns about fine particulates (PM 2.5), as more than 50% of fine particles come from emissions of diesel engines. Steps have been taken to ensure cleaner diesel fuel and vehicles.[196]

90. To control the emissions generated by motor vehicles, NEA regulates the type and quality of fuel that can be used in Singapore and also sets minimum exhaust emission standards for all vehicles. Regulation 19 of the EPM (Vehicular Emissions) Regulations makes it an offence for any person to use or permit the use of any smoky vehicle on the road. With effect from 1 July 2012, the EPM (Off-Road Diesel Engine Emissions) Regulations require all off-road diesel engines, whether new or old, to be imported for use in Singapore, to comply with the EU Stage II, US Tier II or Japan Tier I off-road diesel engine emission standards.[197] This regulation includes those with engine power above 560 kW. The engine or off-road diesel equipment can be sent to an overseas or Singapore-accredited laboratory for an emissions test according to the ISO 8178 standards. For new off-road diesel engines, NEA will accept common emissions test reports for each make and model. For a used off-road diesel engine, NEA requires an emissions test to be conducted on each and every unit before it can be allowed for use in Singapore (*see* paragraphs 106–120 below on 'Emissions from Vehicular Sources').

194. Singapore's PSI remained in the 'good' and 'moderate' range for most of 2023. *See* https://www.singstat.gov.sg/publications/reference/ebook/society/environment. *See* also paragraph 40 of this book and https://www.nea.gov.sg/our-services/pollution-control/air-pollution/air-quality.
195. http://app.nea.gov.sg/cms/htdocs/category_sub.asp?cid=29.
196. *See* below, under 'vehicular emissions'.
197. Off-road diesel engines are any equipment or machinery that is equipped with diesel engines as the main or auxiliary prime mover and not registered with the Land Transport Authority (LTA) for use on public roads. Examples of off-road diesel engines include construction equipment such as cranes, excavators, forklifts and power generators. Diesel engines used in ships, railways, locomotives and aircraft *do not fall* under this regulation.

91. To encourage changes to cleaner technology, the Income Tax Act grants a 100% allowance on capital expenditure for the installation of any 'efficient pollution control equipment or device', any 'certified energy-efficient equipment', 'certified energy-saving equipment', or 'certified machine, equipment or system which reduces or eliminates exposure to chemical risk'.[198]

§2. Legislation

92. The Environmental Protection and Management Act (EPMA) (formerly the Environmental Pollution Control Act, EPCA) controls air pollution from stationary sources, mobile sources, and other sources of burning, such as waste, joss sticks, and candles. The use of open fires to dispose of waste has been banned since 1973 under the Clean Air (Prohibition on the Use of Open Fires) Order. On 1 April 1999, this was replaced by the EPM (Prohibition on the Use of Open Fires) Order. The burning of joss sticks and candles is also regulated – only joss sticks and candles of certain sizes are allowed.[199] Emission of smoke, fumes, gases, or smells that are a nuisance or injurious or dangerous to health may constitute a public nuisance under the EPHA.[200] Factories in breach of these laws will be required to install odour control equipment.

I. Ambient Air Quality Standards

A. *Emissions from Stationary Sources*

1. Air Emission Standards

93. Emissions standards were first set in the 1970s by the Clean Air (Standards) Regulations. This was replaced in 2001 by the Environmental Protection and Management (Air Impurities) Regulations (EPM (Air Impurities) Regulations), which continues to be the applicable law today. These emissions standards were tightened in 2015 to reflect higher international standards, cleaner fuel, and technological advancements.[201] These new standards were finalised after feedback from industries. Existing industries were given a grace period until 2018 and 2023 (for different pollutants) to comply with the revised standards.[202]

---

198. Section 19A (5), (6), (7), (8) of Income Tax Act. These terms are defined in S. 19A (15).
199. Environmental Public Health (Burning of Joss Sticks and Candles) Regulations, Cap. 95, GN S. 76/1998, Reg. 1.
200. Sections 44, 45, EPHA, Cap. 94.
201. Environmental Protection and Management (Air Impurities) (Amendment) Regulations 2015.
202. EPM (Air Impurities) (Amendment) Regulations, reg. 5; https://www.businesstimes.com.sg/singapore/economy-policy/new-industrial-plants-must-meet-tighter-emissions-standards-july-1-nea.

2. Dark Smoke and Impurities

94. The EPM (Air Impurities) Regulations prohibit the emission of dark smoke from chimneys (defined as darker than shade No. 1 on the Ringlemann Chart). Emissions of air impurities must conform to the emission standards prescribed in these Regulations. Standards are prescribed for some twenty-three types of pollutants, including gaseous emissions and solid particles.

95. The Director-General (DG) of Environmental Protection has wide powers where emissions are not within prescribed limits, e.g., he may require that certain equipment (including monitoring equipment) be installed or altered, specify the type of fuel to be used, or require that the height of chimneys be altered.[203] The occupier must keep proper records, carry out tests on emissions if required,[204] keep all equipment properly maintained, allow ready access to and coöperate with inspectors. NEA conducts regular inspections to ensure pollution control equipment is maintained and operated properly.[205] Under the NEA's Source Emission Test Scheme, industries must conduct source emission tests on their own or engage accredited laboratories to do so for them, and take measures to ensure compliance with the prescribed emissions standards.[206]

3. Control of Fuel Quality

96. The DG may also control the type of fuel that may be used. Industries located in designated industrial estates must use fuel oil containing not more than 1% sulphur by weight. Cleaner fuel with a lower sulphur content is required for industries located nearer urban areas. Occupiers of industrial or trade premises on which fuel-burning equipment is situated shall (provided the DG requires) install an instrument, equipment, or device that would enable the ready ascertainment of whether smoke is being discharged from any chimney. This could include a smoke density indicator, providing an indication in the boiler room, furnace room, or control room of the density of smoke being discharged from the chimney.[207]

4. Permission Required to Use Certain Premises

97. Permission is required to occupy or use premises that have the potential to cause serious air pollution or which store large quantities of hazardous substances. These premises are designated as 'Scheduled Premises' in the Schedule to the EPMA and must be sited in designated industrial sites, sufficiently far away from residential areas. They fall into three categories:

---

203. Section 13 EPMA.
204. Section 13(1)(g) EPMA.
205. https://www.mse.gov.sg/policies/clean-air.
206. https://www.mse.gov.sg/resources/faq.
207. Regulation 3, Environmental Pollution Control (Air Impurities) Regulations 2001.

1. Premises engaged in highly pollutive industrial activities (fourteen activities are listed – cement works, concrete works, asphalt works, ceramic works, chemical works, coke or charcoal works, ferrous and non-ferrous metal works, gas works, crushing, grinding and milling works, petroleum works, scrap metal recovery works, primary metallurgical works, pulping works and abrasive blasting works).
2. Premises that use high-capacity polluting equipment, such as boilers/steam generators, large incinerators or furnaces.
3. Premises that store large quantities of highly toxic or highly flammable chemicals, chemical products, hydrocarbons or hydrocarbon products.

Applications for such licences must give details of the type of industry or manufacturing process and the methods undertaken to control air pollution and manage hazardous and toxic substances. The licence may be granted subject to various conditions, such as the installation or alteration of certain plant or equipment, alteration of methods or processes, erection or alteration of chimney heights, and the use of cleaner fuel. Alterations thereafter require permission.

5. Offences and Penalties

98. The following constitute offences for air pollution under the EPMA:

- occupying or using scheduled premises without a licence (section 6);
- failing to maintain any fuel-burning equipment and any air pollution control equipment (section 10);
- emitting dark smoke from a chimney (section 11);
- emitting air impurities in excess of the prescribed limits (section 12);
- contravening an order prohibiting the use of combustible materials, fuel-burning equipment or industrial plants in designated areas and at designated times (section 14).

The penalties for the above offences are:

- on the first conviction: a fine not exceeding SGD 20,000 and if the offence is continuing, a further daily fine not exceeding SGD 1,000;
- on a second or subsequent conviction, a fine not exceeding SGD 50,000 and in the case of a continuing offence, a further daily fine not exceeding SGD 2,000.[208]

99. The court may, in addition to such fine, order the person to pay for any expenses incurred in the execution of any work. Offences may be compounded by the DG by accepting from the person reasonably suspected of having committed the offence a sum not exceeding either SGD 15,000 or half of the prescribed maximum

208. *See* s. 67, EPMA.

fine, whichever is lower.[209] Offences are brought before the District or the Magistrates' Courts.[210] Prosecutions are instituted by officers from NEA.[211]

6. Liability

100. Liability generally falls on the owner or occupier of the industrial or trade premises. Where the owner or occupier is a body corporate, partnership, or unincorporated association, liability can be extended to its officers or members if the offence was committed with their consent or connivance, or was attributable to their act or default.[212]

B. Emissions from Vehicular Sources

101. Singapore is one of the first countries to implement congestion pricing based on the 'polluter pays principle' in relation to vehicular pollution. All motor vehicles are subject to various taxes to ensure that the costs of owning and operating a car are prohibitive. The number of cars that are allowed is also controlled under a 'vehicle quota' system.[213] Road taxes increase with the engine capacity and age of the car. To ensure that vehicles are kept in good condition, cars are subject to mandatory checks when they are three years old, and thereafter they must be inspected every two years for exhaust emissions and roadworthiness.[214] Singapore is also a pioneer in road congestion pricing, being the first city in the world to implement congestion pricing for a restricted area (here, the city centre).[215] These policies help reduce road congestion as well as pollution from vehicular emissions.[216]

---

209. Section 72 EPMA.
210. Section 73 EPMA.
211. *See Public Prosecutor v. Grit Blasting Pte Ltd* [2006] SGDC 4 – fine SGD 5,000 for spray painting outside designated premises. *See also C & A Aviation (Pte) Ltd and ors v. Fokker Service Asia Pte Ltd* [2001] SGDC 313, [2002] SGHC 37 – spray painting of vehicles – claim in nuisance failed.
212. Section 71 EPMA.
213. *See* Winston TH Koh & David KC Lee, 'The Vehicle Quota System in Singapore: An Assessment' in Transportation Research Part A, Jan 1994, Vol. 28, issue 1, pp 31-47.
214. Sections 90, 91, Road Traffic Act 1961, 2020 Rev. ed. ; Road Traffic (Motor Vehicles, Compulsory Inspection) Rules, Cap. 276, Rule 26 (1985), amended S 562/2003; https://onemotoring.lta.gov.sg/content/onemotoring/home/owning/ongoing-car-costs/inspection.html.
215. https://www.straitstimes.com/life/made-in-singapore-erp-and-the-polarising-traffic-solution-pioneered-by-the-republic.
216. For a detailed account of these measures and the laws that apply, *see* the author's papers 'Environmental Taxation in the Regulation of Traffic and the Control of Vehicular Pollution in Singapore', *Critical Issues in Environmental Taxation – International and Comparative Perspectives,* Vol. 1, 2002, Janet Milne and Ors, eds., Richmond; and 'Environmental Taxation in the Management of Traffic in Singapore', Lin-Heng Lye and Ors, eds., *Critical Issues in Environmental Taxation – International and Comparative Perspectives,* Vol. VII, 2009, Oxford University Press, pp. 205–225. *See also* the Land Transport Authority at http://www.lta.gov.sg/ and https://www.onemotoring.com.sg/content/onemotoring/home.html.

102. Vehicles are constantly monitored for roadworthiness. Compulsory inspections also test for exhaust emissions. Cars that exceed emission standards are given a short time for remediation, failing which they will not be able to obtain a renewal of the road tax and will therefore not be allowed on the roads.[217] Diesel-driven vehicles are required to undergo mandatory inspections every six months, where they are required to pass the smoke emission test.

103. As diesel vehicles contribute about 50% of the total PM 2.5 emissions, a number of measures have been instituted to reduce pollution from these sources. A system of certification has been implemented to ensure that only motor workshops with trained mechanics, proper equipment and procedures are accredited for the maintenance of diesel-driven vehicles.[218] A more stringent smoke test for diesel vehicles caught emitting black smoke was imposed from 1 September 2000. All diesel-driven vehicles must undergo the Chassis Dynometer Smoke Test (CDST) to ensure their emissions are within bounds.

1. Emission Standards

104. The EPMA empowers the NEA to prescribe emission standards from any source of air pollution, including motor vehicles. Emissions standards for vehicles are prescribed by the EPM (Vehicular Emissions) Regulations, with effect from 1 July 1999.[219] These Regulations prescribe emission standards for exhaust and noise emissions for various categories of vehicles, including motor vehicles, diesel vehicles, motorcycles and scooters. There is a general prohibition on the emission of any smoke or visible vapour from any motor vehicle, whether petrol or diesel-driven, when in use.[220] All new petrol-driven motor vehicles must be capable of running on unleaded petrol. A certificate from the vehicle's manufacturer may be accepted as prima facie evidence that a vehicle registered after 1 July 1999 conforms to the prescribed standard.

105. All new petrol and diesel vehicles must comply with the Euro IV exhaust emission standard as specified in the EC Directive 98/69/EC-B(2005) for passenger cars and light duty vehicles with MLW of 3,500 kg or less and EC Directive 1999/96/EC-B1(2005) for heavy vehicles with MLW of more than 3,500 kg before these vehicles. Vehicles that fail to comply cannot be registered for use in Singapore.

106. Motorcycles/scooters registered between 1 October 1991 and 30 June 2003 are required to comply with the US 40 CFR 86.410-80 Emission Standard. With

217. Section 91, Road Traffic Act.
218. PCD initiated the formation of an industry-led Motor-Industry Certification Board (MICB) – Motor Workshops may apply for certification under this scheme, which started on 1 Sep. 2000. Some 30 workshops have been registered.
219. GN S 291/99, Reg. 6, 2001 Rev. Ed.
220. Fifth Schedule para. 5.

effect from 1 July 2003, all motorcycles/scooters must comply with the exhaust emission standard as specified in the European Directive 97/24/EC before they can be registered for use in Singapore.

107. All off-road diesel engines (ORDEs) imported since 1 July 2012 for use in Singapore must comply with EU Stage II, US Tier II or Japan Tier I emissions standards under the EPM (Off-Road Diesel Engine Emissions) Regulations 2012. ORDEs are defined as internal combustion engines which operate by burning diesel except those for the propulsion of aircraft, railway locomotives, vessels and road-going vehicles. Examples of ORDEs covered by the Regulations include cranes, excavators, forklifts and power generators, but not diesel engines used in vessels, railway locomotives, and aircraft. An emission test must be submitted showing conformance to emissions standards before the ORDE can be approved for use.[221]

108. From 1 September 2017, all new petrol vehicles will have to meet the Euro VI emission standards, while all new diesel vehicles will have to meet the Euro VI emission standards from 1 January 2018. Test standards for existing diesel vehicles have been tightened from 50 Hartridge Smoke Units (HSU) to 40 HSU to reduce air pollution brought about by smoky diesel vehicles.[222] From April 2026 onwards, foreign commercial diesel vehicles exceeding 50 HSU will be denied entry into Singapore (a tightening of the current standard of 60 HSU).[223]

109. Tighter emission standards will also apply to motorcycles, which will have standards raised to Euro IV for three-wheeled and large motorcycles with an engine capacity of more than 200cc by 1 January 2018. For smaller motorcycles with an engine capacity of 200cc and below, the Euro VI standard will be implemented from 1 January 2020.[224] As of 6 April 2023, NEA will tighten the in-use emission standards for local motorcycles registered before 1 July 2003. These motorcycles can continue to be used until 30 June 2028, as long as they meet the tightened in-use emission standards.[225]

2. Control of Fuel Quality

110. Petrol or diesel used by motor vehicles must conform to the standards prescribed in the EPM (Vehicular Emissions) Regulations.[226] To reduce lead emissions, unleaded petrol was introduced in 1991 and leaded petrol was phased out in

---

221. EPM (Off-Road Diesel Engine Emissions) Regulations, regs 8–9; https://www.nea.gov.sg/our-services/pollution-control/air-pollution/air-pollution-regulations.
222. EPM (Vehicular Emissions) Regulations, Fifth Schedule, para. 4.
223. https://www.nea.gov.sg/docs/default-source/asr/fy2024/nea-annual-sustainability-report-2024-2025.pdf.
224. *See* https://www.nea.gov.sg/our-services/pollution-control/air-pollution/air-quality.
225. *See* https://www.nea.gov.sg/media/news/news/index/in-use-emission-standards-for-older-motorcycles-and-noise-standards-for-all-vehicles-will-be-tightened-in-april-2023.
226. EPM (Vehicular Emissions) Regulations, s. 11A. Eighth Schedule; https://www.nea.gov.sg/our-services/pollution-control/air-pollution.

1998.[227] To reduce sulphur emissions, the sulphur content of petrol and diesel has been lowered over the years; today, petrol and diesel must have sulphur content lower than 0.001%.[228]

3. Owners of Motor Fleets

111. There are special provisions for the owners of motor vehicle fleets.[229] The DG may require such persons to carry out various measures to ensure that every vehicle conforms to the prescribed standards, including the carrying out of regular servicing and repair, and the keeping of full and accurate records of such servicing and repair.[230]

4. Offences

112. Under Part V of the EPM (Vehicular Emissions) Regulations, it is an offence to drive a smoky vehicle or a vehicle that makes excessive noise. It is also an offence to keep the engine running, if the vehicle is stationary on the road.[231] The penalty for a breach of any of these regulations is a fine not exceeding SGD 2,000, or a fine not exceeding SGD 5,000 for second or subsequent offences. Prosecutions are instituted by officers from NEA. NEA works closely with the Land Transport Authority (LTA) and the Traffic Police to control vehicular pollution.

5. Green Vehicles

113. The Green Vehicle Rebate (GVR) Scheme was introduced in 2001 to encourage the uptake of green vehicles by giving rebates on electric, hybrid, and compressed natural gas (CNG) vehicles. The GVR was then replaced by the Carbon Emissions-Based Vehicle Scheme (CEVS) in 2013,[232] which was in turn replaced by the two emissions schemes in effect today, the Vehicular Emissions Scheme (VES) and the Commercial Vehicle Emissions Scheme (CVES). The NEA

227. https://www.nea.gov.sg/docs/default-source/resource/publications/environmental-protection-division-annual-report/epd-2004.pdf.
228. https://www.nea.gov.sg/our-services/pollution-control/air-pollution/air-quality.
229. Defined to mean a person who is the owner or who has under his control or possession three or more public service vehicles (other than trishaws) for the purposes of his trade or business generally, or as a manufacturer or dealer of motor vehicles, or for the transporting of goods or cargo (EPM (Vehicular Emissions) Regulations, Part III, s. 291/99).
230. EPM (Vehicular Emissions) Regulations, reg. 11.
231. EPM (Vehicule Emissions) Regulations, reg. 21.
232. https://www.nccs.gov.sg/media/press-release/new-carbon-emissions-based-vehicle-scheme-(cevs)-from-1-january-2013/.

introduced the VES in 2018, which levies either a rebate or a surcharge onto car buyers depending on the emissions levels of the car – cleaner cars earn a rebate, while more pollutive cars incur a surcharge. The CVES was introduced in 2021, with a similar effect for light commercial vehicles.[233]

114. Under the Commercial Vehicle Emissions Scheme (CVES), most, if not all, diesel models will fall into the surcharge band and be liable for a SGD 10,000 surcharge. This makes a diesel model's price at least SGD 20,000 more than that of the petrol version. Automobile retailers note that the price gap can go up to SGD 25,000, which amounts to almost 25%-30% of the selling price of a vehicle. Additionally, enhanced incentives are offered to car owners for replacing their older diesel models with petrol or electric variants – enabling them to save up to SGD 50,000 in upfront cost.[234]

115. Separately, the Early Turnover Scheme (ETS) incentivises owners of older diesel commercial vehicles to replace them with newer, cleaner models, but this scheme is set to cease in 2025.[235] Furthermore, no new diesel car and taxi registrations will be allowed from 2025 onwards.[236]

In recent years, there has been an increasing push towards adoption of electric vehicles (EVs). Compared to cars with internal combustion engines, EVs are reportedly less pollutive and quieter, and have a much lower carbon footprint.[237] To encourage uptake, the government offers rebates to purchasers (the EV Early Adoption Incentive (EEAI), for newly registered electric cars) and grants to build vehicle chargers in private premises.[238] By 2030 (and in line with its Green Plan 2030 goals), the government also aims to ramp up EV charging infrastructure to 60,000 charging points and have all new car registrations be of cleaner-energy models.[239]

116. Beyond private cars, the government also intends to continue encouraging other modes of transport. As part of Green Plan 2030, it aims to, by 2030, expand the rail network from some 240 km now to 360 km, triple the cycling path network, and achieve 75% rail and bus model share. The government will also only purchase cleaner-energy public buses going forward.[240]

---

233. https://www.nea.gov.sg/our-services/pollution-control/air-pollution/air-pollution-regulations.
234. *See* https://www.straitstimes.com/singapore/transport/end-of-the-road-for-diesel-vans-and-light-trucks (3 Feb. 2021).
235. https://www.nea.gov.sg/our-services/pollution-control/air-pollution/air-pollution-regulations.
236. https://www.lta.gov.sg/content/ltagov/en/industry_innovations/technologies/electric_vehicles/transitioning_to_evs.html.
237. https://www.mot.gov.sg/what-we-do/green-transport/electric-vehicles.
238. https://www.lta.gov.sg/content/ltagov/en/industry_innovations/technologies/electric_vehicles/transitioning_to_evs.html.
239. https://www.greenplan.gov.sg/targets/.
240. https://www.greenplan.gov.sg/files/media-release-annex.pdf.

C. Emissions from Other Sources

1. Open Burning

117. The open burning of trade and industrial refuse such as construction wastes is prohibited under the Environmental Protection and Management (Prohibition on the Use of Open Fires) Order, 1999.[241] The only open fires allowed in trade and industrial premises are those for fire-fighting practices or for the disposal of tail gases from industrial plants. Factories that emit odorous smells are required to install odour control equipment. There are also restrictions on the burning of joss sticks or candles that exceed a certain height or diameter.[242]

2. Transboundary Pollution

118. A major source of air pollution in Singapore comes from the large-scale burning of forests in Indonesia. Efforts at resolving this are predominantly at the regional level and reflected in the ASEAN Agreement on Transboundary Haze Pollution. This Agreement was signed by the governments of all ten ASEAN countries on 10 June 2002 in Kuala Lumpur, Malaysia. This Agreement is the first regional arrangement in the world that binds a group of contiguous states to tackle transboundary haze pollution resulting from land and forest fires. It has also been regarded as a global role model for tackling transboundary issues. Parties to the Agreement are required to:

i. cooperate in developing and implementing measures to prevent, monitor, and mitigate transboundary haze pollution by controlling sources of land and/or forest fires; develop monitoring, assessment and early warning systems, exchange information and technology; and provide mutual assistance;
ii. respond promptly to a request for relevant information sought by a State or States that are or may be affected by such transboundary haze pollution, with a view to minimising the consequences of the transboundary haze pollution; and
iii. take legal, administrative and/ or other measures to implement their obligations under the Agreement.

The Agreement established an ASEAN Coordinating Centre for Transboundary Haze Pollution Control to facilitate cooperation and coordination in managing the impact of land and forest fires, in particular haze pollution arising from such fires.

This Agreement failed to prevent the annual return of the haze from 2004 to 2015. Indonesia, the country primarily responsible for transboundary pollution arising from its forest fires, only ratified this 2002 Agreement in September 2014, the last

241. GN S 161/99 (2008 Rev Ed), Order 2. This ban has been in place since 1973, under the predecessor Clean Air (Prohibition on the Use of Open Fires) Order.
242. Environmental Public Health (Burning of Joss Sticks and Candles) Regulations, GN S 76/98 (2200 Rev Ed), Cap. 93.

Member State to do so.[243] However, some practical steps were taken in the early years when there was an agreement between Singapore and Indonesia to collaborate with the Jambi Provincial Government and Indonesia's State Ministry of Environment (*Kementerian Negara Lingkungan Hidup* or KLH in short) to develop a Master Plan to deal with land and forest fires in the Muaro Jambi Regency. The aim was to encourage sustainable practices by Indonesian farmers and minimise the haze problem over time by tackling it at its root.[244] Since January 2007, Singapore has sent a team of MEWR/NEA officers to Jambi on several fact-finding trips to understand the ground conditions, laws and technical capabilities to prevent and mitigate land and forest fires. Singapore has also organised a Workshop involving officials from the KLH and Jambi Province to jointly develop the Master Plan in Singapore in March 2007. The Master Plan is an overarching framework for land clearing without the use of fire, and prevention and mitigation of peatland fires, covering the following five areas:

1. Fire prevention.
2. Fire suppression.
3. Legislation and Enforcement.
4. Early Warning and Monitoring.
5. International and Regional Assistance and Collaboration.

119. The key focus of the Master Plan was on Fire Prevention. The Jambi Project sought to establish Jambi as a model for sustainable 'land clearing' practices in Indonesia, which could be replicated in other regencies or sub-districts in Jambi and other fire-prone districts. The Jambi Provincial Government will own the Master Plan. The Master Plan, if successfully implemented, can be used as a model for other fire-prone districts in Indonesia. Under the Letter of Intent, Singapore will offer technical assistance to implement some specific action programmes. Some programmes are long-term, while others may be implemented within one to two years. Singapore will implement selected action programmes jointly with Jambi. A sum of about SGD 1 million was set aside for the implementation of these action programmes. Among the action programmes identified for joint implementation by

---

243. Alan Khee-Jin Tan, 'The ASEAN Agreement on Transboundary Haze Pollution: Prospects for Compliance and Effectiveness in Post-Suharto Indonesia', 13 NYU Envtl. L J 647 (2005); Simon S.C. Tay, 'Southeast Asian Fires: The Challenge for International Environmental Law and Sustainable Development'. 11 Geo. Int'l Envtl. L. Rev. 241 (1998–1999); Alan Khee-Jin Tan, 'Forest Fires or Indonesia: State Responsibility and International Liability, 48 Int'l & Comp. L.Q. 826 (1999); Alan KJ Tan, 'Can't We Even Share Our Maps? Co-operative and Unilateral Mechanisms to Combat Forest Fires and Transboundary "Haze" in Southeast Asia' in S. Jayakumar, Tommy Koh, Robert Beckman and Hao Duy Phan eds, *Transboundary Pollution: Evolving Issues of International Law and Policy* (Edward Elgar Publishing, 2015) 327–361. *See also* Indonesia's Parliament Agrees to ratify ASEAN Haze Pact [online] Jakarta, 16 Sep. 2014, Available at https://www.straitstimes.com/asia/se-asia/indonesias-parliament-agrees-to-ratify-asean-haze-pact.

244. Joint Statement by State Ministry of Environment, Indonesia and Ministry of the Environment and Water Resources, Singapore, 3rd Indonesia-Singapore Environmental Partnership Meeting and Signing of Letter of Intent (LOI) for the Joint Development of a Master Plan and the Implementation of Agreed Activities to deal with Land and Forest Fires in Muaro Jambi Regency, Jambi Singapore, 7 Nov. 2007, MEWR News Release 51/2007.

Jambi and Singapore are two programmes on the 'Development of a Fire-Danger Rating System (FDRS) for Muaro Jambi Regency' and 'Developing the Capacity of Jambi Officers in Reading and Interpreting Satellite Pictures for Hotspot Information'.[245] Subsequent to the development of the Master Plan, the Singapore and Indonesian government further collaborated in implementing actions under the Master Plan. Capacity building workshops were held throughout 2009 for the Jambi community as part of the action plan on 'Enhancement of Aquaculture Expertise in Jambi'.[246] However, this Plan has since lapsed.

In 2013, very severe pollution from forest fires in Indonesia was experienced in Singapore, Malaysia and also Southern Thailand. Singapore's PSI was an extremely hazardous 401. Singapore's offers to revive the cooperation with Jambi provide a haze assistance plan that includes aircraft for cloud seeding, satellite imagery, and hotspot coordination and extension to other provinces were not accepted.[247]

120. Thereafter, Singapore passed its Transboundary Haze Pollution Act, 2014 (THPA) after extensive public consultation and debate.[248] This law allows the prosecution of errant companies, partnerships or individuals in Singapore that have links to plantations in Indonesia by holding them responsible for a particular haze episode in Singapore if satellite and other images show that there is burning from their property in Indonesia. This is facilitated by a series of presumptions that help establish a causal link to enable the entity to be charged.[249]

The THPA is notable for its extra-territorial criminal[250] and civil liability[251] regime for entities responsible for conduct which causes, contributes to, or condones haze pollution in Singapore. An entity engaging in such conduct may be found guilty of an offence and liable to a fine of up to SGD 100,000 per day, up to SGD 2,000,000 in aggregate.[252] An entity can also be found to be guilty of an offence even if it is not directly responsible for any conduct but is found to have participated in the management of another entity (which owns or occupies land situated outside of Singapore) responsible for the illegal conduct.[253] The same offences

---

245. *See* http://haze.asean.org/?wpfb_dl=137 'Indonesia-Singapore Collaboration to deal with the land and forest fires in Jambi province'.
246. *See* Eighth Meeting of the Sub-Regional Ministerial Steering Committee (MSC) on Transboundary Haze Pollution Singapore, 19 Aug. 2009 at https://www.asean.org/wp-content/uploads/images/archive/PR-8th-MSC-Transboundary-Haze-Pollution.pdf.
247. *See* https://www.mlaw.gov.sg/news/parliamentary-speeches/oral-answer-pqs-on-haze (8 Jul. 2013); and https://www.eco-business.com/news/singapore-funded-efforts-fight-haze-face-challenges-ground/ (Straits Times, July 1, 2013). *See also* Barry Desker 'The Trouble with Indonesia-Singapore Relations', 21 Oct. 2015, https://thediplomat.com/2015/10/the-trouble-with-indonesia-singapore-relations/.
248. *See* https://sso.agc.gov.sg/Act/THPA2014; 2020 Rev. Ed.
249. *See* Lye Lin Heng, *Country Report – Singapore* (2015) IUCN Academy of Environmental Law Journal, pp. 360–368; https://www.iucnael.org/en/e-journal/previous-issues/86-journal/issue/615-issue-2015.
250. Section 5, TPHA.
251. Section 6, TPHA.
252. Section 5(2), TPHA.
253. Section 5(3), TPHA.

can also give rise to civil liability if the entity is found to have breached its duty, and in consequence of that breach, any person in Singapore sustains personal injury, physical damage, or economic loss.[254]

Most importantly, the THPA raises certain presumptions. Section 8(1) creates a presumption of causation which requires the defendant to prove that haze pollution is not caused by the fire on its land, even if at or about the same time, there are land or forest fires in any other part of the world. In turn, section 8(2) also creates a presumption of responsibility through ownership or occupation if the fire found on the defendant's land causes haze pollution in Singapore. This means that the onus is on the defendant to prove that they did not cause or condone the land or forest fires which caused the haze pollution in Singapore. Additionally, section 8(3) raises the presumption of responsibility through participation in management, and section 8(4) raises the presumption of ownership or occupation through any of the maps recognised by the Act.

The Director-General is also empowered by the THPA to issue Preventive Measures Notices[255] to any entity that, in his opinion, is directly or indirectly involved in any conduct which is causing or contributing to, or is likely to cause or contribute to, any haze pollution in Singapore. An entity which fails to comply with the notice shall be liable on conviction to a fine not exceeding SGD 5,000 or to imprisonment for a term not exceeding one month or to both.[256]

II. Indoor Air Quality

A. General

121. For indoor air quality (IAQ), general guidelines can be found in the 2023 'Updated Guidance on Improving Ventilation and Indoor Air Quality in Buildings for a Healthy Indoor Environment.'[257] It applies to non-residential premises, including both air-conditioned and naturally ventilated premises, with the exception of certain specialised premises (which will be discussed below). The Guidance provides recommended measures to enhance indoor ventilation and air quality, including installing and maintaining ventilation systems, using air filters and cleaners, and preventing air leakage. IAQ should be closely monitored and maintained according to Singapore Standard SS554:2016 (Code of Practice for Indoor Air Quality for Air-Conditioned Buildings), and air-conditioning and mechanical ventilation (ACMV)

254. Section 6(3), THPA.
255. Section 9(1), TPHA.
256. Section 10(g), TPHA. *See* Lye Lin Heng, *Country Report—Singapore,* (2015*)* IUCN Academy of Environmental Law Journal, pp. 360–368 which examines this new law – at https://www.iucnael.org/en/e-journal/previous-issues/86-journal/issue/615-issue-2015.
257. https://www.nea.gov.sg/our-services/public-cleanliness/environmental-cleaning-guidelines/advisories/guidance-on-improving-ventilation-and-indoor-air-quality-in-buildings-for-a-healthy-indoor-environment.

systems should conform to SS553:2016 (Code of Practice for Air-Conditioning and Mechanical Ventilation in Buildings).

122. The Workplace Safety and Health (WSH) Council (under the Ministry of Manpower) has also issued guidelines for the management of IAQ in air-conditioned workplaces. This set of guidelines works in tandem with the other guidance and provides recommendations for establishing a systematic IAQ management programme suitable for most organisations.[258]

123. Under the EPHA, publicly accessible buildings must be kept clean and free of conditions that may endanger users' lives or health.[259] Where publicly accessible premises are air-conditioned, the DG of Public Health may prescribe temperature and humidity controls and require the installation of devices to record temperature and humidity.[260]

B. Factory Air Quality and Safety

124. Indoor air quality in factories and other industrial premises is regulated under the Workplace Safety and Health Act, 2006 (WSHA).[261] It imposes duties on various persons who are in a factory – occupiers, employers, self-employed persons, principals, persons at work, manufacturers and suppliers of machinery, equipment or hazardous substances used at work, persons who erect, install or modify machinery or equipment, as well as persons in control of machinery.[262]

125. Under the WSHA and subsidiary legislation, it is the duty of occupiers and employers to ensure the safety and health of persons in the workplace.[263] It is the duty of occupiers to ensure adequate ventilation that can render harmless gases and vapours that may be injurious to health.[264] Measures must be taken to protect persons from toxic dust, fumes, and other contaminants.[265] The legislation specifies maximum permissible exposure levels (PEL) to toxic substances that a worker may be exposed to, over the short term (a fifteen-minute period) and long term (an eight-hour working day and a forty-hour work week).[266]

258. https://www.tal.sg/wshc/resources/publications/wsh-guidelines/wsh-guidelines-management-of-indoor-air-quality-in-air-conditioned-workplaces.
259. Section 60, EPHA.
260. Section 60(3), EPHA.
261. Act 7 of 2006, (2020 Rev Ed), repealing the Factories Act.
262. Part 4, WSHA.
263. Sections 11, 12 WSHA.
264. Reg. 5, Workplace Safety and Health (General Provisions) Regulations (WSH(GP)R).
265. Reg. 39, WSH(GP)R.
266. Reg. 40, WSH(GP)R.

C. Prohibition Against Smoking in Public Places

126. To protect non-smokers from the harmful effects of second-hand tobacco smoke, smoking is prohibited in numerous public spaces.[267] 'Smoking' includes the holding of any cigarette or other tobacco product which is alight or emitting smoke.[268] The smoking ban has been extended over the years, and today covers indoor areas generally (whether air-conditioned or not), and a large number of outdoor areas such as parks, schools, and bus stops.[269] Smoking is generally banned within buildings, save for designated smoking areas. The ban extends to common areas of residential buildings such as common corridors, staircases, stairwells, void decks and multi-purpose halls, and in public areas such as covered walkways and link ways, all pedestrian bridges, 5 m from the edge of bus stops and hospital outdoor compounds. In addition, a large section of the Orchard Road precinct has been designated as a No Smoking Zone. The penalty for contravening the ban is a fine not exceeding SGD 1,000.[270]

127. The responsibility of enforcing the smoking ban is distributed throughout the community. If a person smokes in a prohibited space, the manager of the premises must stop them from smoking or request them to leave, failing which the manager must seek police assistance. If the manager fails to do so or fails to investigate a complaint of a person smoking, they are liable to a fine. A person hindering a manager in carrying out their duties is also liable to a fine and/or imprisonment.[271] The manager of a prohibited space must display sufficient no-smoking notices, failing which they are liable to a fine.[272]

D. Office Air Quality

128. The Environmental Public Health Act (EPHA) requires that all buildings to which the public has access be kept clean (section 60). Where the premises are air-conditioned, the Director-General of Public Health may, by written notice, prescribe temperature and humidity controls and require the owner to install automatic devices for recording the temperature and humidity of the building (section 60(3)).

129. In October 1996, NEA's Institute of Environmental Epidemiology published its Guidelines for Good Indoor Air Quality in Office Premises,[273] which addresses carbon dioxide, carbon monoxide, formaldehyde, ozone, volatile organic

267. The smoking prohibition is largely governed by the Smoking (Prohibition in Certain Places) Act 1992, the Smoking (Prohibition in Certain Places) Regulations 2018, and the Smoking (Prohibition in Certain Places) (Composition of Offences) Regulations 2020.
268. Section 2, Smoking (Prohibition in Certain Places) Act 1992.
269. https://www.nea.gov.sg/our-services/smoking-prohibition/overview.
270. Section 3, Smoking (Prohibition in Certain Places) Act 1992.
271. Section 6, Smoking (Prohibition in Certain Places) Act 1992.
272. Section 5, Smoking (Prohibition in Certain Places) Act 1992.
273. *See* http://www.bca.gov.sg/greenmark/others/NEA_Office_IAQ_Guidelines.pdf.

chemicals, total bacterial counts, total fungal counts, suspended particulate matter, air temperature, relative humidity, and air movement in all buildings, new and existing, which are used as office premises.

Guideline maximum concentrations for acceptable indoor air quality are specified for carbon dioxide, carbon monoxide, formaldehyde, and ozone, based on their known health effects. Recommended maximum concentrations for acceptable indoor air quality are specified for suspended particulate matter, volatile organic chemicals, bacteria and fungi based on their effects on health. Guidelines are also specified for indoor air temperature, relative humidity, and air movement.

E. Legionnaire's Disease: Cooling Towers and Water Fountains

130. The Environmental Public Health (Registrable Aerosol-generating Systems) Regulations took effect from 2021 and are aimed at controlling Legionnaire's disease,[274] a form of pneumonia caused by the Legionella bacteria breathed in from water droplets. Under these Regulations, owners and occupiers of buildings must clean and disinfect all registrable aerosol-generating systems (including cooling towers) at least once every six months and carry out Legionella bacteria testing at least every three months. Failing to do so entails a fine not exceeding SGD 5,000 for the first offence, and a fine not exceeding SGD 10,000 for subsequent offences. Prosecutions are instituted by the NEA.

274. These Regulations replaced the previous Environmental Public Health (Cooling Towers and Water Fountains) Regulations (Rg 7) enacted in 2001. *See also* https://www.nea.gov.sg/our-services/pollution-control/water-quality/aerosol-generating-systems.

Chapter 3. Water Pollution

131. As a city-state, the main sources of water pollution in Singapore are domestic wastewater, sewage and sullage, and industrial effluent. Pollution may also come from solid wastes, if not properly disposed of.

132. Water pollution is controlled in Singapore by: first, a comprehensive sewerage infrastructure and solid waste management systems that aim to prevent pollution at source; by requiring industries to pre-treat their trade effluent to prescribed standards before discharge into the sewerage system; third, by careful siting of industries that use or store large quantities of chemicals away from water catchment areas. The water quality of both inland water bodies and coastal areas is regularly monitored. For inland water bodies, the parameters monitored include pH, dissolved oxygen, BOD, total suspended solids (TSS), ammonia and sulphide. Coastal water samples are analysed for metals, total organic carbon and other physical, chemical and bacteriological parameters.[275]

§1. Sewage and Drainage Systems

133. Singapore is served by a modern sanitation system consisting of separate sewerage and drainage systems. The drainage system consists of rivers, canals, and drains, and conveys collected rainwater to one of Singapore's seventeen freshwater reservoirs.[276] The sewerage system collects used water through a network of sewers and conveys it to water reclamation plants (WRPs) for treatment. A portion of this treated water is further purified to produce NEWater,[277] while the remainder is sent to the waterways and the sea. The public sewerage system serves all industrial estates and almost all residences, and is managed and regulated by the Public Utilities Board (PUB).[278]

I. Trade Effluent

134. The provision, operation and maintenance of the sewerage system are governed by the Sewerage and Drainage Act (SDA).[279] All wastewater must be discharged into the public sewerage system. Industrial wastewater must be treated to specified standards before discharge, and industries which generate large quantities of acidic effluent must install systems to prevent its discharge into public sewers.[280]

275. *See* https://www.nea.gov.sg/our-services/pollution-control/water-quality/keeping-our-water-clean.
276. https://www.pub.gov.sg/Resources/News-Room/PressReleases/2024/11/Amendments-to-Sewerage-and-Drainage-Act.
277. https://www.pub.gov.sg/Resources/News-Room/PressReleases/2024/12/From-waste-to-resource---Managing-trade-effluent-discharge.
278. https://www.nea.gov.sg/our-services/pollution-control/water-quality.
279. Act 10 of 1999, 2020 Rev. Ed.; amended by Act 10 of 2012.
280. https://www.nea.gov.sg/our-services/pollution-control/water-quality.

Trade effluent can only be discharged into the public sewerage system with the written approval of PUB.[281] Approval will only be granted if the trade effluent meets discharge limits as specified in the Sewerage and Drainage (Trade Effluent) Regulations (SDTER).[282] Trade effluent to be discharged must also not contain any dangerous or hazardous substances[283] or any of the substances specified in Regulation 9 SDTER.[284]

135. If public sewers are not available, industries may apply to NEA for permission to discharge trade effluent into the watercourses (e.g., drains, canals, and rivers, i.e. the drainage system). The discharge of wastewater into watercourses is regulated under the EPMA and the Environmental Protection and Management (Trade Effluent) Regulations (EPMTER), and administered by NEA.[285] Trade effluent can only be discharged into waterways or land with the written permission of the DG of Environmental Protection.[286] Approval will only be granted if the trade effluent meets discharge limits as specified in Regulation 10 EPMTER.[287] Trade effluent to be discharged must also not contain any toxic or hazardous substances.[288]

136. Industries can apply to PUB for permission to discharge trade effluent containing biodegradable pollutants directly into public sewers, for a tariff payment. The tariff is calculated based on how much the Biochemical Oxygen Demand (BOD) and Total Suspended Solids (TSS) loading exceeds allowable standards, and seeks to recover the additional cost for treating this higher pollution load at sewage treatment works, and for repairing the sewerage system.[289]

A. *Offences*

137. Under the SDA, it is an offence to discharge trade effluent into the public sewerage system without prior approval. For a first conviction, the penalty is a fine of SGD 4,000–20,000 and/or imprisonment up to three months and a daily fine of

281. Section 16, Sewerage and Drainage Act; *see also* https://www.pub.gov.sg/Professionals/Requirements/Used-Water/TradeEffluent.
282. Reg. 10, Second and Third Schedules.
283. Section 16A, Sewerage and Drainage Act.
284. Reg. 9 covers a wide range of substances, including toxic industrial waste, inflammable substances, certain specified organic compounds, radioactive materials, pesticides, and blood and infectious wastes.
285. https://www.nea.gov.sg/our-services/pollution-control/water-quality.
286. Section 15, EPMA.
287. These standards are significantly stricter than those in the SDTER for the sewerage system, as befits the 'cleaner' nature of the waterways. There are also different standards for controlled and uncontrolled watercourses, with those for controlled watercourses being stricter. Controlled watercourses are those watercourses from which water supplied by PUB under the Public Utilities Act is obtained.
288. Section 17, EPMA.
289. SD(TE)R reg. 11(6), Fourth and Fifth Schedules; https://www.nea.gov.sg/our-services/pollution-control/water-quality.

up to SGD 1,000 per day if the offence continues; for subsequent convictions, the fine increases to SGD 10,000–50,000 and the daily fine increases to up to SGD 2,000 (the length of imprisonment remains the same).[290] It is also an offence to discharge dangerous or hazardous substances without approval, the penalty being a fine and/or imprisonment (and which is harsher for repeat offenders).[291] These penalties (among others) were increased from 2025 onwards to strengthen deterrence against illegal discharge and better reflect the impact illegal discharge can have on Singapore's water resources.[292]

138. Under the EPMA, it is an offence to discharge trade effluent, oil, chemical, sewage or other polluting matter into any drain or land without a licence (section 15). The penalty is a fine of up to SGD 20,000 on a first conviction and a daily fine of SGD 1,000 if the offence continues.[293] The guilty party may also be ordered to pay compensation for expenses incurred by the execution of any works.[294] The fine increases to SGD 50,000 for a subsequent offence, with a daily fine of SGD 2,000 if the offence continues. The person who discharges such polluting matter must inform the Director-General (DG). Failure to inform is an offence, carrying a fine of up to SGD 5,000. These offences may be compounded for a sum not exceeding SGD 5,000 (section 72). It is also an offence to discharge trade effluent without treating it in the prescribed manner (section 16). The penalty is similar to that for discharging without a permit. Prosecutions are brought by the NEA.

Under the EPMA, where the owner or occupier is a body corporate, partnership, or unincorporated association, liability can be extended to its officers or members if the offence was committed with their consent or connivance, or was attributable to their act or default.[295] Similarly, under the SDA, liability can be extended to such directors, managers, secretaries, or similar officers of the organisation.[296]

B. Deep Tunnel Sewerage System (DTSS)

139. A new wastewater conveyance, treatment and disposal system will eventually replace the existing system. Called the DTSS (Phase 1 & 2), this project consists of two large, deep tunnels criss-crossing the island, two centralised water reclamation plants (WRP), deep sea outfall pipes and a link sewer network. The link sewers intercept flows from existing sewers upstream of the existing sewage treatment works. These flows will be channeled by gravity via deep tunnels to two centralised wastewater treatment plants strategically located in the southern coastal

---

290. Section 16 SDA.
291. Section 16A SDA.
292. https://www.pub.gov.sg/Resources/News-Room/PressReleases/2024/11/Amendments-to-Sewerage-and-Drainage-Act.
293. Section 67 EPMA – this is a general penalty provision where no penalty is prescribed under the Act.
294. Section 67(2) EPMA.
295. Section 71 EPMA.
296. Section 67 SDA.

areas, with the treated effluent discharged through deep-sea outfalls. The entire DTSS project will be developed in two phases over the next twenty years.

140. Phase 1, the North Tunnel, was completed at the end of 2008, comprising a 48-km-long deep sewer tunnel running from Kranji to Changi, a centralised WRP at Changi, two 5-km-long deep sea outfall pipes and 60 km of link sewers. The heart of the DTSS, the Changi WRP, is a state-of-the-art used water plant capable of treating 900,000 cubic m (202 million gallons) or 320 Olympic-size swimming pools of used water a day to international standards. The treated used water is then discharged into the sea through deep-sea outfall pipes or channelled to the Changi NEWater factory on the rooftop of the reclamation plant, where it is further purified through advanced membrane technologies into NEWater, Singapore's own brand of reclaimed water. This project was awarded 'Water Project of the Year' at the Global Water Awards 2009 in Zurich, Switzerland, on 28 April 2009, as the water project with the most significant contribution to water technology and environmental protection.[297]

Phase 2 will comprise the South Tunnel and its network of link sewers leading to a WRP at Tuas and another deep-sea outfall. It uses the deep tunnels to convey used water entirely by gravity to three centralised water treatment plants strategically located in coastal areas. Treated used water is then reclaimed, with excess effluent discharged to the sea in an environmentally responsible manner. It is expected to be completed before 2030. When the entire DTSS is completely, existing intermediate pumping stations and conventional WRPs will be phased out, freeing up land.[298]

C. Toxic Substances

141. It is an offence to discharge toxic substances into inland waters.[299] The penalty is a maximum fine of SGD 50,000 or twelve months imprisonment or both; a second conviction carries a mandatory imprisonment of not less than one month but not more than one year, in addition to a fine of up to SGD 100,000. A third offence may result in an order for the stoppage of work.[300] Under section 71, liability may be extended to members or officers of a company, as well as partners or members of unincorporated associations, if the offence was committed intentionally or negligently. However, prosecutions under section 17 EPMA require the written consent of the Public Prosecutor.[301]

Where the owner or occupier is a body corporate, partnership or unincorporated association, liability can be extended to its officers or members if the offence was committed with their consent or connivance, or was attributable to their act or default.[302]

---

297. *See* https://www.pub.gov.sg/dtss/about and https://www.pub.gov.sg/dtss/phase1.
298. https://www.pub.gov.sg/dtss/phase2.
299. section 17(1) EPMA.
300. Section 17(2) EPMA.
301. section 17(6) EPMA.
302. Section 71 EPMA.

D. Silt and Suspended Solids

142. The Sewerage and Drainage (Surface Water Drainage) Regulations[303] prohibit the discharge of silt and other suspended solids into the storm water drainage system. Discharge with Total Suspended Solids in concentrations greater than 50 mg/L is prohibited.[304] Persons carrying out earthworks or construction works must maintain earth control measures in accordance with the Code of Practice on Surface Water Drainage issued by the PUB.[305] The penalty for both offences is a fine not exceeding SGD 5,000, and a daily fine of SGD 500 for continuing contravention.[306]

E. Clean-Up

143. The DG may require a person who has discharged or spilt any toxic substance, trade effluent, oil, chemical, sewage, hazardous substances, or other polluting matter into any drain, land or sea, to remove and clean up the substance within a specified time. Failure to comply is an offence carrying a fine of up to SGD 50,000 (section 18 EPMA).

II. Drinking Water

144. The quality of drinking water is regulated by the Environmental Public Health (EPH) (Water Suitable for Drinking) (No. 2) Regulations 2019,[307] complemented by the Singapore Food Agency (SFA)'s Code of Practice on Drinking Water Sampling and Safety Plans.[308] Drinking water standards set out under EPH Regulations are based on the WHO Guidelines for Drinking Water Quality.[309] It specifies the standards for water suitable for drinking – the microbial, physico-chemical, radiological and chemical parameters (*see* Schedule Part I to Part IV). Water providers must prepare and implement a water safety plan and a water sampling plan to ensure that the drinking water they supply complies with the standards specified in the Schedule.[310] The water safety and water sampling plans must be prepared in accordance with the Code of Practice and submitted to the Director-General of Public Health (DG) for approval before being implemented.[311]

303. GN S. 169/1999 (2007 Rev Ed).
304. Reg. 4(1) Sewerage and Drainage (Surface Water Drainage) Regulations.
305. Reg. 4(2), *ibid.*
306. Reg. 6, *ibid.*
307. GN S. 274/2019. The previous EPH (Quality of Piped Drinking Water) Regulations 2008 and the EPH (Water Suitable for Drinking) 2019 Regulations (GN 156/2019) are revoked (*see* r. 13).
308. https://www.sfa.gov.sg/docs/default-source/legislation/environmental-public-health-act/code-of-practice-on-drinking-water-sampling-and-safety-plans-sfa-apr-2019.pdf.
309. https://www.pub.gov.sg/Public/WaterLoop/Water-Quality/Drinking-Water.
310. Regs 6, 7, EPH (Water Suitable for Drinking) (No. 2) Regulations 2019.
311. *Ibid.*

The EPH (Water Suitable for Drinking) (No. 2) Regulations are complemented by the Singapore Food Agency (SFA)'s Code of Practice on Drinking Water Sampling and Safety Plans (issued on 1 April 2019).[312] Every supplier is also required at least once a year to conduct a review of his water safety plan. This review must be conducted in accordance with the relevant code of practice and a report of the review submitted to the DG by 31 December of the year in which the review is conducted or such later time that the DG may allow in any particular case (R 5). Where the DG is of the opinion that a supplier has not conducted the review of his water safety plan in accordance with the relevant code of practice or in an otherwise satisfactory manner, the DG may direct the supplier to conduct a further review of the water safety plan and submit a further report or an amended report (R 8).

145. The supplier is also required to: (a) monitor the quality of the drinking water being supplied by him and ensure that the drinking water is sampled, tested and analysed in accordance with the water sampling plan approved by the DG under regulation 6; (b) ensure that adequate measures are put in place to prevent the contamination or adulteration of the samples taken for testing and analysis; and (c) test the samples in a testing laboratory accredited by the Singapore Accreditation Council to conduct the required test or any other place allowed by the DG. (R 6)

312. https://www.sfa.gov.sg/docs/default-source/food-retailing/practices-and-guidelines/code-of-practice-on-drinking-water-sampling-and-safety-plans-sfa-apr-2019.pdf. (1 Apr. 2019).

Chapter 4. Hazardous Substances

§1. Background and Laws

146. The NEA's PCD controls environmentally hazardous chemicals under the EPMA and the EPM (Hazardous Substances) Regulations and the EPM (Ozone Depleting Substances) (ODS) Regulations.[313] These laws control hazardous substances that may pose a mass-disaster potential, are highly toxic and pollutive and/or generate toxic wastes that can only be disposed of with considerable difficulties. Flammable petroleum products in Singapore are controlled under Part VI of the Fire Safety Act, 1993,[314] by the Fire Safety & Shelter Department (FSSD) of the Singapore Civil Defence Force (SCDF). Radioactive substances are controlled by the NEA's Centre for Radiation Protection and Nuclear Science (CRPNS). A list of some fifteen explosive precursors is controlled under the Guns, Explosives and Weapons Control Act 2021, most of which were previously listed in the EPMA.[315] A list of chemicals with potential uses in chemical weapons is controlled by Singapore Customs, pursuant to Singapore's obligations under the international Chemical Weapons Convention.[316]

§2. Import, Export, Sale, Storage and Use of Hazardous Substances

147. Part VII of the EPMA (sections 21–27) governs the importation, manufacture, sale, storage, and use of hazardous substances. Any person who wishes to import, sell or export any hazardous substance must obtain a Hazardous Substances Licence.[317] Any person who wishes to purchase, store and/or use any hazardous substance must obtain a Hazardous Substances Permit.[318] The NEA prescribes storage requirements, including requirements for the storage area, containers and tanks,

313. GN S 604/2000; EPMA 2008 Rev. ed. R. 9.
314. Act 39 of 1993, (Rev. Ed. 2000), amended by Act 7 of 2004, Act 14 of 2013, Act 10 of 2015, Act 22 of 2019.
315. The Guns, Explosives and Weapons Control Act 2021 is administered by the Ministry of Home Affairs, and came into force on 1 July 2025, replacing (inter alia) the Arms and Explosives Act 1913. Previously, these explosive precursors were controlled under the Arms and Explosives Act (https://www.mha.gov.sg/mediaroom/press-releases/commencement-of-the-guns-explosives-and-weapons-control-act/).
316. https://www.customs.gov.sg/businesses/chemical-weapons-convention/controlled-chemicals/. The applicable legislation is the Chemical Weapons (Prohibition) Act 2000.
317. https://www.nea.gov.sg/our-services/pollution-control/chemical-safety/hazardous-substances/management-of-hazardous-substances. The licence is valid for either one year or three months, and costs SGD 525 or SGD 135 respectively: https://www.gobusiness.gov.sg/browse-all-licences/national-environment-agency-(nea)/hazardous-substances-(hs)-licence.
318. https://www.nea.gov.sg/our-services/pollution-control/chemical-safety/hazardous-substances/management-of-hazardous-substances. The permit is valid for one year, and costs SGD 160. (https://www.gobusiness.gov.sg/browse-all-licences/national-environment-agency-(nea)/hazardous-substances-(hs)-permit).

emergency plans, and safety audits.[319] The DG can require the removal of hazardous substances from any premises.[320] The DG can also require the owner or occupier of hazardous installations to carry out impact analysis studies.[321]

In workplaces, a person who manufactures or supplies any hazardous substance for use at work must ensure it is safe for use, and that information about its safe use (e.g., hazards and precautions) is available to anyone using it.[322] Hazardous substances must be under the control of a competent person with adequate knowledge of their properties and dangers, and must be stored, handled, and used in a way that does not pose a risk to people.[323] Persons liable to be exposed to hazardous substances must be warned of the relevant hazards and precautions, and adequate warning notices must be present.[324] A safety data sheet (SDS) of a hazardous substance must be provided by its seller; the occupier must assess the SDS and take adequate precautionary measures, and make the SDS available to all persons liable to be exposed to the substance.[325]

§3. Transport of Hazardous Substances

148. The EPM (Hazardous Substances) Regulations govern the transport, import, storage and supply of hazardous substances, as well as requirements for emergency action plans. The Schedule to the Regulations contains a list of hazardous substances and the quantity allowed for transport per trip. The limits vary from 0 kg for highly toxic chemicals such as ricin to 1,000 kg for corrosives such as sulphuric acid. Any person who wishes to transport any hazardous substance in excess of these limits must obtain a Transport Approval. He must possess a valid Hazardous Substances Licence before applying for transport approval. The transport approval will expire together with the Hazardous Substances Licence. There are detailed provisions on documentation, warning labels, supervision of vehicles, precautions against fire or explosions, overfill, carriage of multi-loads, and instructions for drivers (who must be properly trained). There are guidelines on storage, transport, and emergency response plans.[326]

The containers and tankers used for bulk chemical transportation must be designed, manufactured and tested according to internationally acceptable standards. All tankers must be certified as meeting the stipulated standards. All containers, tankers and vehicles must be properly labelled and carry appropriate hazard

319. https://www.nea.gov.sg/our-services/pollution-control/chemical-safety/hazardous-substances/management-of-hazardous-substances. *See also* Part IV EPM (Hazardous Substances) Regulations.
320. Section 25 EPMA.
321. Section 26 EPMA.
322. Section 16 WSHA. This applies to the categories of hazardous substances specified in Part 2 of the Fifth Schedule of the WSHA.
323. Reg. 41 WSH (General Provisions) Regulations.
324. *Ibid.*
325. Reg. 43 WSH (General Provisions) Regulations.
326. *See* NEA 'Management of Hazardous Substances' – https://www.nea.gov.sg/our-services/pollution-control/chemical-safety/hazardous-substances/management-of-hazardous-substances.

warning panels. The transport routes and times must be approved. All drivers must have received special training. There are duties on the consignor as well as the carrier.[327]

149. All imports of controlled hazardous substances must be approved by NEA's Chemical Control and Management Department (CCMD). The CCMD will approve the import only if the Hazardous Substances are stated in the importer's licence and there is a valid transport approval for the Hazardous Substances.[328]

§4. Enforcement and Offences

150. The laws empower PCD officers to carry out regular inspections to check on matters relating to the import, purchase and sale of hazardous substances, storage, transportation, labelling, maintaining and updating of records and sales documents, ensuring the safe disposal of all hazardous substances. PCD officers may check and search premises, extract records and documents for investigations, and conduct surprise checks on road tankers used for transportation on the road.

Contraventions of laws regarding hazardous substances constitute offences, and generally entail a fine of up to SGD 50,000 and/or imprisonment of up to two years, and a daily fine of up to SGD 2,000 for continuing offences.[329] Other penalties apply for certain offences: failing to remove hazardous substances from premises when required to do so entails a fine of up to SGD 50,000 (section 25 EPMA). Failure to carry out an impact analysis study as required entails a penalty of SGD 20,000 (section 26).

§5. Regional Collaboration

151. The NEA works closely with the Department of Environment (DOE) of Malaysia to organise regular emergency response exercises to manage chemical spill incidents on the Tuas Second Link. This is part of the bilateral cooperation programme under the Malaysia-Singapore Joint Committee on the Environment (MSJCE). As of 2025, NEA and the DOE of Malaysia have organised thirteen exercises, with the most recent conducted in 2023.[330]

---

327. Part II EPM(HS)R.
328. https://www.nea.gov.sg/our-services/pollution-control/chemical-safety/hazardous-substances/management-of-hazardous-substances.
329. Section 27 EPMA.
330. *See* https://www.nea.gov.sg/media/news/news/index/singapore-and-malaysia-conduct-joint-emergency-exercise-to-respond-to-a-simulated-chemical-spill-on-the-tuas-second-link-2023.

§6. Petroleum and Flammable Materials

152. Part VI (sections 77–90) of the Fire Safety Act applies to petroleum and flammable materials. It prohibits the storage of petroleum or any flammable materials without a licence (section 78), as well as their import without a licence (section 79). It also regulates their transport and their dispensing (sections 80 and 81) – all these require a licence from the Commissioner of Civil Defence.[331]

331. Act 39 of 1993, 2020 Rev. Ed. *See also* The Fire Safety (Petroleum and Flammable Materials) 2005 Regulations, GN S 81/2005.

Chapter 5. Waste Management

§1. Background

153. The amount of solid waste disposed of in Singapore has increased sevenfold from 1,260 tonnes a day in 1970 to 9,058 tonnes a day in 2023; this can be attributed to population and economic growth.[332] In light of this continuing growth and existing land scarcity, the main challenge facing Singapore is the allocation of land for waste disposal. Singapore has a comprehensive, highly automated and efficient refuse collection system. All solid wastes are collected and disposed of daily. For domestic and trade premises, private companies are appointed by NEA through open tender to serve as public waste collectors (PWCs).[333] For commercial and industrial premises, general waste collectors (GWCs) are licensed by NEA to collect one or more classes of general waste.[334] General waste disposal facilities (GWDFs) must also be licensed to receive, store, process, or treat general waste (including recyclables).[335] To maintain workplace safety, NEA mandates inspections for vehicles and equipment, and there is a set of Workplace Safety and Health Guidelines for General Waste Management that provides information and best practices.[336]

154. In the case of domestic refuse, almost all apartments are provided with individual chutes for garbage disposal. The garbage falls into huge bins on the ground level, which are then collected daily.[337] Over 90% of the public live in high-rise apartments, of which 82% live in apartments built by the HDB, the country's public housing authority. This efficient system of garbage disposal from high-rise buildings has made it more difficult to encourage recycling. For private apartments, under the Building Maintenance and Strata Management Act, 2004 and its Regulations, it is mandatory for the management corporations of strata title buildings and condominiums constituted on or after 1 April 2005 to separate and prepare recyclable materials or waste intended for recycling. From 1 November 2008, when required by the DG of Public Health in writing, it is mandatory for all condominiums and private apartments to have receptacles within the estate for the collection of recyclables like paper, plastic, metal and glass products for recycling (section 10 (1)(c) EPHA, 1987). The EPHA (General Waste Collection) Regulations require all recyclables that have been deposited in any receptacle, which is referred to in section 10(1)(c) of the EPHA or provided in any residential property for the purpose of recycling, to be sent to a recycling facility for recycling.

---

332. *See* https://www.nea.gov.sg/our-services/waste-management/waste-statistics-and-overall-recycling.
333. https://www.nea.gov.sg/our-services/waste-management/waste-collection-systems.
334. https://www.nea.gov.sg/our-services/waste-management/waste-collection-system.
335. https://www.nea.gov.sg/our-services/waste-management/waste-management-infrastructure/refuse-disposal-facility/waste-disposal/general-waste-disposal-facility.
336. https://www.nea.gov.sg/our-services/waste-management/waste-collection-systems.
337. *See* Guidebook on Setting Up Structured Waste Recycling Programme in Condominiums and Private Apartments, https://www.nea.gov.sg/docs/default-source/our-services/waste-management/20211115_guidebook-on-setting-up-a-structured-waste-recycling-programme-in-condos_2021.pdf.

155. After collection, solid waste is sent to one of four waste-to-energy (WTE) incineration plants to be incinerated, namely Tuas, Tuas South, Senoko and Keppel Seghers Tuas Plant (KSTP). Solid waste used to be sent directly to landfills until WTE incineration was adopted, with the first WTE plant completed in 1979. Incineration reduces waste volume by about 90%, significantly reducing the landfill space required. Around 37% of refuse is incinerated, while 60% is recycled and 3% is non-incinerable waste that is landfilled directly.[338] WTE plants are fitted with flue gas cleaning systems to remove dust and pollutants before the flue gas is released into the atmosphere. Heat from the combustion is used to heat steam to produce electricity, and ferrous scrap metal contained in the ash is recovered and recycled.[339] Incineration ash and non-incinerable waste are sent (via the Tuas Marine Transfer Station, TMTS) to Semakau Landfill, Singapore's only operating landfill.[340] Semakau Landfill was constructed offshore south of mainland Singapore and commenced operations in 1999. The inhabitants of two islands, Pulau Semakau and Pulau Seking, were relocated to mainland Singapore from the 1970s to the 1990s, and the two islands were merged through reclamation for the landfill complex to be built.[341] Efforts have been taken to protect the ecosystems and biodiversity on and around the landfill, and the area is of great biological interest; guided tours are available to promote public education.

156. Semakau Landfill is Singapore's only active landfill, and based on current waste disposal trends, it is slated to reach full capacity in 2035.[342] The authorities are seeking to extend its lifespan, through reducing waste and repurposing ash. Researchers are exploring reusing incineration ash as material for construction and reclamation. However, considering contamination risks and the costs of reprocessing ash, reducing waste and encouraging recycling remains a key strategy.[ibid.] Domestic waste generated per day per capita has decreased from 1.08 kg in 2013 to 0.88 kg in 2023.[343] While 52% of all waste was recycled in 2023, most of this is attributable to non-domestic (industrial and commercial) waste; only 12% of domestic waste was recycled.[344]

157. Under the Green Plan 2030, the government aims to reduce the amount of waste to landfill per capita per day by 30%.[345] To this end, there has been an increasing push in laws and campaigns relating to waste and recycling. There are also plans for an Integrated Waste Management Facility (IWMF) to be constructed, with

338. These figures are from 2017: https://www.nea.gov.sg/docs/default-source/resource/iwmf.pdf.
339. https://www.nea.gov.sg/our-services/waste-management/waste-management-infrastructure/semakau-landfill/waste-to-energy-and-incineration-plants.
340. https://www.nea.gov.sg/our-services/waste-management/waste-management-infrastructure.
341. *See* https://www.nlb.gov.sg/main/article-detail?cmsuuid=adb326ee-05ef-4c6e-a53c-8e1fceb7daa2 (Pulau Semakau) ; https://www.nlb.gov.sg/main/article-detail?cmsuuid=21302018-f13a-4d20-9889-d3edb1f3b1b7 (Pulau Seking).
342. https://www.straitstimes.com/singapore/can-semakau-landfill-s-lifespan-be-extended-with-full-capacity-looming; https://www.channelnewsasia.com/singapore/semakau-landfill-filling-waste-management-incineration-reduce-reuse-recycle-3909436.
343. https://www.nea.gov.sg/our-services/waste-management/waste-statistics-and-overall-recycling.
344. *Ibid.*
345. https://www.greenplan.gov.sg/targets/.

greater efficiency in terms of energy use, resource recovery, and land use.[346] Additional plans include developing a zero-waste food district in Jurong Lake District, with food waste segregation and treatment for new developments. This ties in with plans to develop Jurong Lake District as a model for sustainable mixed-use (residential, commercial, industrial) district with district cooling, solar power deployment and super-low-energy buildings.

§2. General Waste

158. Different types of wastes are subject to different measures. The general law on waste is discussed here. The management of solid waste is governed by the Environmental Public Health Act (EPHA)[347] and its subsidiary legislation, including the Environmental Public Health (EPH) (General Waste Collection) Regulations, the EPH (General Waste Disposal Facility) Regulations 2017, and the EPH (General Waste Disposal Facility — Exemption) Regulations 2023. Part III of the EPHA contains provisions on the cleansing of streets, the removal of refuse, the provision of public disposal facilities and the disposal and treatment of industrial waste. It also contains provisions on public nuisances.

I. Definition of Waste

159. Section 2, EPHA defines waste to include:

a. any substance which constitutes a scrap material or an effluent or other unwanted surplus substance arising from the application of any process; and
b. any substance or article which requires to be disposed of as being broken, worn out, contaminated or otherwise spoiled,

and anything which is discarded or otherwise dealt with as if it were waste shall be deemed to be waste unless the contrary is proved.

It defines 'industrial waste' to mean 'any waste whether solid, liquid or gaseous produced in the course of or is the waste product of any trade, business, manufacture or building construction, and includes toxic industrial waste and any dangerous substance'.

It defines 'toxic industrial waste' to mean 'any industrial waste which owing to its nature, composition or quantity constitutes a danger to human health or the environment or which contains or may produce pathogens or transmissible diseases'.

---

346. https://www.nea.gov.sg/our-services/waste-management/waste-management-infrastructure/integrated-waste-management-facility.
347. Act 14 of 1987, 2020 Rev. Ed. *See also* the Codes of Practice on Environmental Health; for Environmental Control Officers; and for Licensed General Waste Collectors – https://www.nea.gov.sg/corporate-functions/resources/practices-and-guidelines/practices.

II. Waste Collection

160. All parties involved in waste management must be licensed and adhere to the relevant legislation and guidelines. For domestic and trade premises, private companies are appointed by NEA through open tender to serve as public waste collectors (PWCs). PWCs are awarded licences for seven to eight years to provide refuse and recyclables collection services for specified geographic sectors.[348] Refuse collection fees are charged depending on the type of premises and the amount of refuse output. NEA also provides guidelines for the disposal of bulky items, garden waste, and dead pets.[349] PWCs are also required to provide recycling bins and recycling collection services to all HDB estates and private landed properties.[350] For private developments (e.g., condominiums, private apartments), the management (the Management Corporation Strata Title, MCST) can choose to opt in or out of the public waste collection scheme.[351] Those that opt out must provide their own waste and recycling receptacles and convey the waste and recyclables to disposal facilities as frequently as necessary.[352]

161. For commercial and industrial premises, general waste collectors (GWCs) are licensed by NEA. General waste is categorised into four classes, and each GWC is licensed to collect one or more classes of waste. Broadly, the classes are: (Class A) inorganic, bulky, non-putrefiable, and recyclable wastes; (Class B) organic and putrefiable wastes; (Class B1) cooking oil; (Class C) sludge, sewage, and other sanitary wastes. GWCs must adhere to the relevant legislation (the EPHA and EPH (General Waste Collection) Regulations) and the guidelines and best practices set out in the Code of Practice for Licensed GWCs.[353]

GWCs must apply for and maintain a licence.[354] Specified vehicles must be used for different classes of wastes and vehicles and equipment must be adequately labelled.[355] Recyclable waste may be collected by GWCs if they obtain a permit to do so;[356] recyclables must be kept segregated from non-recyclables.[357] Waste must be disposed of at disposal facilities: incinerable waste at incineration plants, non-incinerable waste at TMTS, and recyclable waste at recycling facilities.[358] GWCs must clean and maintain their vehicles, equipment, and waste collection points,[359]

348. There are currently six sectors, served by three PWCs: https://www.nea.gov.sg/our-services/waste-management/waste-collection-systems.
349. https://www.nea.gov.sg/our-services/waste-management/waste-management-infrastructure/refuse-disposal-facility/waste-disposal/bulk-item-disposal-disposal-of-garden-wastes-and-dead-pets.
350. https://www.nea.gov.sg/our-services/waste-management/3r-programmes-and-resources/national-recycling-programme.
351. https://www.nea.gov.sg/our-services/waste-management/waste-collection-systems.
352. EPHA s. 10; https://www.nea.gov.sg/docs/default-source/our-services/waste-management/20211115_guidebook-on-setting-up-a-structured-waste-recycling-programme-in-condos_2021.pdf.
353. *See* https://www.nea.gov.sg/our-services/waste-management/waste-collection-systems.
354. Reg. 3 EPH (General Waste Collection) Regulations.
355. Regs 8–13 EPH (General Waste Collection) Regulations.
356. Reg. 7A, EPH (General Waste Collection) Regulations.
357. Section 7, Code of Practice for Licensed General Waste Collectors.
358. Regs 16–17A, EPH (General Waste Collection) Regulations.
359. Regs 14–15, EPH (General Waste Collection) Regulations.

and must maintain proper records on the collection service they render.[360] A contravention of any of these regulations attracts a fine of up to SGD 10,000, and a daily fine of up to SGD 500 for continuing offences.[361]

162. General waste disposal facilities (GWDFs) must be licensed to receive, store, process, or treat general waste (including recyclables).[362] There are some exceptions for which licensing is not required, including refuse bin centres, residential waste storage premises, and small-scale facilities built for the purposes of research and development.[363] Licensed GWDFs must comply with the relevant legislation (the EPHA and EPH (General Waste Disposal Facility) Regulations). They must adhere to the types and quantities of waste approved in their licence,[364] and must maintain a daily register of the waste dealt with.[365]

163. To maintain workplace safety, NEA mandates inspections for vehicles and equipment, and there is a set of Workplace Safety and Health Guidelines for General Waste Management that provides information and best practices.[366] Waste management workers are also covered by the wage and training requirements in the Progressive Wage Model (PWM), and employers must meet these requirements.[367]

III. Offences

164. Businesses involved in waste management must be licensed, and are otherwise guilty of the following offences:

- Collecting, removing, transporting, storing, or importing any kind of refuse or waste without a waste collector licence (fine of up to SGD 10,000 and/or imprisonment for up to twelve months).[368]
- Constructing, establishing, maintaining, or operating any disposal facility without a waste disposal licence (first offence: fine of up to SGD 50,000 and/or imprisonment for up to twelve months; subsequent offences: fine of up to SGD 100,000 and/or imprisonment for up to twelve months.[369]

165. Apart from licensing issues, the following are the main offences in relation to general waste:

360. Reg. 18, EPH (General Waste Collection) Regulations.
361. Reg. 22, EPH (General Waste Collection) Regulations.
362. https://www.nea.gov.sg/our-services/waste-management/waste-management-infrastructure/refuse-disposal-facility/waste-disposal/general-waste-disposal-facility.
363. *Ibid. See also* the EPH (General Waste Disposal Facility — Exemption) Regulations 2023.
364. Regs 7–8, EPH (General Waste Disposal Facility — Exemption) Regulations 2023.
365. Reg. 10, EPH (General Waste Disposal Facility — Exemption) Regulations 2023.
366. https://www.nea.gov.sg/our-services/waste-management/waste-collection-systems.
367. https://www.mom.gov.sg/employment-practices/progressive-wage-model/waste-management-sector. This only applies to workers who are citizens or permanent residents.
368. Section 31 EPHA.
369. Section 23(1) EPHA.

- Littering – i.e., throwing or leaving behind any refuse in a public place (fine of up to SGD 2,000 for a first conviction, SGD 4,000 for a second conviction, and SGD 10,000 for subsequent convictions).[370]
- Abandoning any vehicle, furniture, or any other bulky article (fine of up to SGD 5,000 for a first conviction, a fine of SGD 10,000 and/or imprisonment for up to three months for subsequent convictions).[371]
- Non-compliance with the Regulations regarding collection and disposal of general wastes (fine SGD 2,000 plus daily fine of SGD 100).[372]
- Illegal dumping, i.e., dumping or disposal of any refuse, waste or any other article from a vehicle in a public place.[373] This is a serious offence and persons may be arrested without warrant by any police officer or public health officer.[374] For first offences, the penalty is a fine up to SGD 50,000 and/or imprisonment for up to twelve months; for subsequent offences, it is a fine up to SGD 100,00 and mandatory imprisonment of one to twelve months.[375] Any vehicle used in the illegal dumping may also be forfeited.[376]
- Spillage of any noxious liquid, dirt, sand, earth, stone waste, etc. in any public place – this offence carries the same penalties as littering.[377]

---

370. Sections 17(1)(a)–(g); 21(1)(c) EPHA. In *Public Prosecutor v. Yong Heng Yew* [1996] 3 SLR(R) 22; [1996] SGHC 199, the accused threw a cigarette butt on the floor. The question was whether the prosecution is required to show intention on accused's part to walk away without properly disposing of the butt. Held that an offence under s. 18(1) of the Act was a 'strict liability' offence. The phrase did not refer to an offence where no mental element existed at all; rather it referred to an offence where no blameworthy mental element need be shown. Once the act of throwing down the cigarette butt was shown to be a deliberate one, the Prosecution did not need to go on to show the presence of some blameworthy state of mind (Yong CJ). *See also Public Prosecutor v. Viknesh s/o Karishnan* [2010] SGDC 88; *Public Prosecutor v. Teo Yong Guang Robin* [2010] SGDC 32; *Public Prosecutor v. Liew Yong Liang* [2019] SGDC 171; [2020] SGHC 30; [2020] 4 SLR 1106.
371. Sections 17(1)(h), 21(1)(b), EPHA.
372. EPHA s. 21(1)(c).
373. Section 20(1) EPHA.
374. *Toh Teong Seng v. Public Prosecutor* [1995] 2 SLR 273; *Public Prosecutor v. Lim Ah Heng and Another* [1999] 1 SLR 827 – held by Yong CJ that dumping at a military site was still a 'public place', as a 'public place' was any place to which the public had access whether in fact or by right. A place could qualify as a 'public place' under s. 20(1) EPHA even if the public did not have a right of access, if it was established that they did in fact go there.
375. Section 21(1)(a) EPHA. These penalties were raised from an SGD 1,000 fine to a maximum fine of SGD 20,000 in 1996 (Act 2 of 1996), and further increased in 1999 (Act 22 of 1999), 2002 (Act 4 of 2002), and 2014 (Act 15 of 2014).
376. *Chandra Kumar v. Public Prosecutor* [1995] 2 SLR(R) 703; [1995] SGHC 164 – Held (Yong CJ) that a number of factors were relevant in determining whether the discretion to forfeit the vehicle should be exercised. These included: (a) the participation of the vehicle owner in the commission of the offence; (b) the benefit derived by the owner from the offence; and (c) peripherally, the value of the vehicle in question. However, where the owner himself was not guilty of an offence, the element of deterrence became irrelevant. Similarly, the extent to which the vehicle had been used in the commission of the offence, as well as the steps taken by the owner to prevent the use of the vehicle in the commission of the offence were irrelevant factors. *See also Ang Poh Chuan v. Public Prosecutor* [1995] 3 SLR(R) 929; [1995] SGHC 290 and *Toh Teong Seng v. Public Prosecutor* [1995] 1 SLR(R) 757; [1995] SGHC 100. *See* Lye Lin Heng 'The Judiciary and Environmental Governance in Singapore', *Journal of Court Innovation*: *The Role of the Environmental Judiciary (NY)*, Vol. 3 No. 1, Winter 2010, pp. 133–155.
377. Sections 19, 21(1)(c) EPHA.

- Littering – It is an offence to litter any public place or public street (section 18 EPHA). The maximum fine is SGD 1,000 for a first offence and SGD 2,000 for a subsequent offence (section 21 EPHA). The offence may be compounded for SGD 150 if it is a first offence – the offender must attend a fifteen-minute briefing on how littering can harm the environment.[378]

In 1992, the EPH (Corrective Work Order) Regulations ('CWO') were passed, under which persons found guilty of littering may be required to clean up a public place.[379] The Court can impose a CWO if it considers it 'expedient with a view to [the convicted person's] reformation and the protection of the environment and environmental public health'.[380] The number of hours the person is required to work must not exceed twelve hours in total, and must not exceed three hours per day.[381]

Prosecutions are instituted by the DG of Public Health and his officers. Appeals are heard by the High Court. It has been held that whether a CWO should be imposed is a matter for the court to determine in the exercise of its discretion. The Prosecution need not prove beyond reasonable doubt that a CWO would be expedient. Evidence of previous convictions was not a precondition for the imposition of a CWO. The implementation of section 21A(1) of the Act depended either on evidence of commission of previous similar offences or on evidence that a serious littering offence had been committed. The former type of evidence would demonstrate whether a person was a recalcitrant offender. To show that an offender was 'recalcitrant' for the purpose of imposing a CWO, it would be sufficient to show that he had previously committed the same offence on at least one occasion. He need not have been convicted of the offence. As such, evidence of a compounded offence could be relied upon for the specific purpose of imposing a CWO.[382]

§3. Resource Sustainability Act

166. A major development in recent years is the passing of the Resource Sustainability Act 2019 (RSA) and its subsidiary legislation. Implemented in stages starting from 2020 and amended in 2023, the RSA forms a significant part of Singapore's push towards a circular economy with a high recycling rate.[383] The RSA

378. Environmental Public Health (Notice to Attend Court) Regulations 1995 (S 449/95).
379. Section 447/92. *See Public Prosecutor v. Lim Niah Liang* [1996] 3 SLR(R) 702; [1996] SGHC 265.
380. Section 21A(1) EPHA.
381. Sections 21A(2), 21B(3), EPHA.
382. *Public Prosecutor v. Lim Niah Liang* [1996] 3 SLR(R) 702; [1996] SGHC 265, per Yong CJ. Principles on imposition of Corrective Work Order cited with approval in *Public Prosecutor v. Koh Thiam Huat* [2017] 4 SLR 1099 and *Public Prosecutor v. Azahar Bin Mohamed Nor* [2020] SGDC 185 albeit in the context of road traffic offences.
383. https://www.mse.gov.sg/latest-news/opening-speech-for-the-second-reading-of-the-rsa ; https://www.greenplan.gov.sg/key-focus-areas/sustainable-living/.

focuses on three priority waste streams: e-waste, packaging waste, and food waste. These waste streams have relatively high generation and low recycling rates, and thus are of particular concern.[384]

I. E-waste

167. Electrical and electronic waste is a source of concern. It is highly variable in composition and requires special treatment to manage hazardous and environmentally harmful substances. E-waste also contains valuable materials that can be recovered through recycling and reused in new products, reducing the need for resource extraction. The rate of e-waste generation is expected to continue increasing, together with economic growth and adoption of technology.[385]

The RSA introduced a regulated e-waste management system, underpinned by the principle of extended producer responsibility (EPR). Under the EPR framework, producers of regulated products are responsible for the collection and treatment of their products when they reach end-of-life. This includes companies that manufacture or import products to supply the local market.[386]

168. Producers of regulated products which come under the EPR scheme of the RSA must be registered with NEA[387] and keep and submit records on the weight and number of regulated products they supply.[388] NEA has published a set of Producer Guidelines outlining the EPR scheme and its obligations for producers.[389] Regulated products are categorised into consumer and non-consumer products.[390] Consumer products refer to equipment largely used by the general public (e.g., phones, laptops, refrigerators), while non-consumer products refer to commercial and industrial equipment largely used by businesses (e.g., servers, solar photovoltaic panels).[391] Non-regulated products (e.g., microwave ovens, vacuum cleaners, medical equipment) do not currently come under the EPR scheme, and can be disposed of through other bins and collection avenues.[392]

For regulated consumer products, e-waste is collected through the Producer Responsibility Scheme (PRS), in-store collection, and take-back services. NEA has

384. https://www.mse.gov.sg/latest-news/resource-sustainability-act.
385. *See* https://www.nea.gov.sg/our-services/waste-management/3r-programmes-and-resources/e-waste-management/extended-producer-responsibility-(epr)-system-for-e-waste-management-system.
386. Section 7(2) RSA; https://www.mse.gov.sg/latest-news/resource-sustainability-act.
387. Sections 8–11 RSA.
388. Section 18 RSA.
389. https://www.nea.gov.sg/our-services/waste-management/3r-programmes-and-resources/e-waste-management/extended-producer-responsibility-(epr)-system-for-e-waste-management-system.
390. Section 7(1) RSA; Resource Sustainability (Prescribed Regulated Products) Regulations 2019 (RSPRPR), First and Second Schedules.
391. *Ibid*; https://www.mse.gov.sg/latest-news/resource-sustainability-act.
392. https://www.nea.gov.sg/our-services/waste-management/3r-programmes-and-resources/e-waste-management/where-to-recycle-e-waste.

appointed a PRS Operator[393] to organise the collection of e-waste and its transportation to recyclers. Large producers of consumer products must join the PRS and finance the collection and recycling of the e-waste in proportion to their market share.[394] Large retailers must provide in-store collection of e-waste from consumers and convey the e-waste to the PRS Operator.[395] There are exemptions for small producers and retailers: small producers that supply less than a threshold amount of products are exempt from the PRS,[396] and retailers with a floor area of less than 300 m^2 are not required to provide in-store collection.[397] During delivery of a product, all retailers are required to offer a free take-back service of a product of the same class or type.[398]

For regulated non-consumer products, producers are required to offer a take-back collection service for all their products.[399] Collected products must be disposed of through licensed wasted collectors or e-waste recyclers, and producers must maintain and submit records of the products collected and disposed of.[400]

169. E-waste recyclers must be licensed[401] and are subject to obligations under the Resource Sustainability (E-waste Recyclers) Regulations 2021. These obligations include meeting material recovery targets, removing and processing specified pollutants, ensuring data security, and maintaining and providing records of e-waste processed. Recyclers must not prepare products for re-use if the person who provided the product gives notice that the product is not to be re-used, and must also not transfer products to another recycler outside Singapore unless the foreign recycler can ensure the material recovery target will be met. Some progress has been made since the commencement of these initiatives. The total amount of e-waste collected for recycling has increased from 3,500 tonnes in February 2022 to more than 22,300 tonnes as of September 2024, and the rate of e-waste recycling has increased over the years. The number of e-waste collection points has also increased from 300 in 2021 to 870 in 2024.[402]

---

393. The current PRS Operator is ALBA E-Waste Smart Recycling Pte Ltd (ALBA), and the appointment is for a period of five years until 30 Jun. 2026: https://alba-ewaste.sg/about-us/. *See also* RSA Part 6 and the Resource Sustainability (Producer Responsibility Schemes) Regulations 2021.
394. Section 12 RSA; https://www.mse.gov.sg/latest-news/resource-sustainability-act.
395. Section 15 RSA; https://www.nea.gov.sg/our-services/waste-management/3r-programmes-and-resources/e-waste-management/extended-producer-responsibility-(epr)-system-for-e-waste-mana gement-system. *See also* the Resource Sustainability (In-store Collection of E-waste) Regulations 2021.
396. Section 12 RSA; RSPRPR First Schedule. Some of these thresholds were lowered in 2023, narrowing the exemption and necessitating producers to either produce less of the products or join the PRS: RSPRP (Amendment) Regulations 2023.
397. Section 15 RSA.
398. Section 14 RSA.
399. Section 13 RSA.
400. Section 18 RSA.
401. Section 23 EPHA.
402. https://www.straitstimes.com/singapore/free-collection-of-bulky-e-waste-from-doorstep-of-all-households-in-singapore-from-2025.

II. Packaging Waste

170. Packaging waste (including plastics) makes up about one-third of domestic waste in Singapore.[403] Given Singapore's low littering rate and prevailing practice of incinerating waste, the focus here is on reducing the use of materials (including plastics) and increasing the recycling rate by improving systems and practices.[404] To this end, the RSA implements three main schemes: (i) mandatory packaging reporting, (ii) beverage container returns, and (iii) charging for disposable carrier bags.

A. Mandatory Packaging Reporting Scheme

171. Under the Mandatory Packaging Reporting (MPR) scheme, producers of packaged products must submit packaging data and 3R plans to the NEA.[405] This includes brand owners, manufacturers, importers, and retailers.[406] Producers must report the amount of packaging they import or use yearly in terms of weight, broken down according to form (e.g., bags, bottles) and material (e.g., plastic, metal, glass).[407] Producers must submit a plan to reduce, reuse, or recycle packaging (3R plan) yearly, including details of key initiatives, key performance indicators (KPIs), and targets. Producers must also report on the progress of these plans in subsequent years.[408] Producers with an annual turnover of less than SGD 10 million are exempted,[409] and there are exclusions for certain types of packaging and goods.[410] The NEA has published a guidebook on the MPR scheme.[411]

172. In 2021, the Packaging Partnership Programme (PPP) was launched, supporting companies in adopting sustainable packaging waste management practices and fulfilling their regulatory requirements under the MPR scheme.[412] The PPP has published guidelines on sustainable e-commerce packaging[413] and a 3R guidebook

403. https://www.nea.gov.sg/our-services/waste-management/mandatory-packaging-reporting.
404. https://www.mse.gov.sg/latest-news/opening-speech-for-the-second-reading-of-the-rsa.
405. https://www.nea.gov.sg/our-services/waste-management/mandatory-packaging-reporting.
406. *Ibid*; Section 19(2) RSA.
407. Section 20 RSA; Resource Sustainability (Packaging Reporting) Regulations (RSPRR) 2020 reg. 7.
408. Sections 21–23 RSA; RSPRR reg. 8; https://www.nea.gov.sg/our-services/waste-management/mandatory-packaging-reporting.
409. Section 20 RSA; RSPRR reg. 5.
410. RSPRR regs 3–4, Schedule.
411. https://www.nea.gov.sg/docs/default-source/mandatory-packaging-reporting/nea-mandatory-packaging-reporting-guidebook.pdf.
412. https://www.nea.gov.sg/programmes-grants/schemes/packaging-partnership-programme.
413. https://www.packaging-partnership.org.sg/resources/sustainable-e-commerce-packaging-guidelines.

for packaging,[414] playing a key role in developing technical standards for sustainable packaging.[415] The MPR scheme aims to raise companies' awareness of the benefits of packing reduction and encourage companies to reduce the amount of packaging used.[416] It also lays the foundation for EPR schemes for packaging waste management, to be implemented first by way of the beverage container return scheme.

B. Beverage Container Return Scheme

173. The beverage container return scheme (BCRS) adopts an EPR approach, placing more responsibility on producers for the collection and end-of-life treatment of their products. The scheme was introduced in 2023 by an amendment to the RSA[417] and is expected to be implemented starting from 2026.[418]

174. Under the BCSRS, a 10-cent (SGD) refundable deposit will be applied to all pre-packaged beverages in plastic and metal containers between 150mL–3L in volume (both inclusive).[419] The deposit will be fully refunded when consumers return beverage containers at designated return points.[420] Supermarket outlets larger than $200m^2$ will be required to set up return points, and the setting up of additional return points in community spaces will be explored to ensure convenience for the public.[421] All beverage producers that import or manufacture covered beverages must participate in the scheme,[422] and they will pay fees (per container placed on the market) to the Scheme Operator. The Scheme Operator is licensed by NEA and will be responsible for collecting and recycling empty beverage containers on behalf of all beverage producers in Singapore.[423] The target set by NEA is a return rate of 80% by the third year of the scheme.[424]

---

414. https://www.packaging-partnership.org.sg/resources/3r-guidebook-packaging.
415. *See* https://www.singaporestandardseshop.sg/Product/SSPdtDetail/17bbdf4c-5954-4197-ac58-2a3f347b1522.
416. https://www.nea.gov.sg/our-services/waste-management/mandatory-packaging-reporting.
417. Resource Sustainability (Amendment) Act 2023.
418. https://www.channelnewsasia.com/singapore/beverage-container-return-scheme-pushed-back-recycling-producers-request-4516481.
419. Sections 23P-Q RSA; Resource Sustainability (Beverage Container Return Scheme) Regulations 2024 (RSBCRSR) regs 2–3.
420. Section 23U RSA.
421. https://www.nea.gov.sg/our-services/waste-management/beverage-container-return-scheme.
422. Section 23O RSA.
423. The licenced Scheme Operator is Beverage Container Return Scheme Ltd. (BCRS Ltd.), a not-for-profit company incorporated by a consortium of beverage producers. Their licence will run for a period of seven years, from 1 Apr. 2026 to 31 Mar. 2033. (https://www.nea.gov.sg/our-services/waste-management/beverage-container-return-scheme). *See also* RSA Part 6 and the Resource Sustainability (Producer Responsibility Schemes) Regulations 2021.
424. *See* https://www.channelnewsasia.com/singapore/beverage-container-return-scheme-pushed-back-recycling-producers-request-4516481.

C. Disposable Carrier Bag Charge

175. The disposable carrier bag charge was introduced in 2023 by an amendment to the RSA[425] and came into effect from 3 July 2023.[426] Larger supermarket operators with an annual turnover of more than SGD 100 million[427] must charge at least 5 cents (SGD) per disposable carrier bag provided.[428] These operators account for around two-thirds of supermarket outlets in Singapore.[429]

Supermarket operators must record and report to NEA the number of bags provided.[430] Operators are allowed to decide how to use their proceeds from the bag charge and are encouraged by the government to apply them to environmental or social causes.[431] To ensure transparency and accountability, operators are required to publish information annually on the number of bags supplied, the proceeds collected, and how the proceeds are used.[432] For illustration, the supermarket operator Sheng Siong Group Ltd collected a total of SGD 703,802.27 (SGD 760,106.45 before tax) from the provision of 15,202,129 disposable bags in 2023, and donated the entire amount to the President's Challenge, a government campaign that supports various charitable causes.[433]

The bag charge has had visible impacts. In the first year of implementation, participating supermarket operators reported a 70%–80% reduction in the number of bags issued.[434] An NEA survey also found over 90% of customers brought their own bags after the charge was implemented, compared to 61% before.[435]

III. Food Waste

176. Food waste is a major waste stream. In 2023, 755,000 tonnes of food waste were generated, accounting for about 11% of total waste, but only 18% of it was recycled.[436] The RSA (as amended in 2023) therefore introduced measures to improve food waste outcomes.

---

425. Resource Sustainability (Amendment) Act 2023.
426. *See* https://www.nea.gov.sg/our-services/waste-management/disposable-carrier-bag-charge.
427. Section 23B RSA; Resource Sustainability (Disposable Carrier Bag Charge) Regulations 2023 (RSDCBCR) reg. 4.
428. Section 23F RSA.
429. *See* https://www.channelnewsasia.com/singapore/supermarket-plastic-bag-charge-disposable-carrier-drop-use-grace-fu-4035166.
430. Secrion 23I RSA.
431. *See* https://www.mse.gov.sg/latest-news/closing-speech-for-resource-sustainability-amendment-bill.
432. Sections 23J- 23K RSA.
433. https://corporate.shengsiong.com.sg/disposable-carrier-bag-charge-report-2023/.
434. *See* https://www.mse.gov.sg/latest-news/written-reply-to-parliamentary-question-on-disposable-carrier-bag-charge-mar-2025.
435. https://www.straitstimes.com/singapore/over-90-of-customers-bring-own-bags-since-mandatory-5-cent-charge-for-plastic-bags-nea-survey.
436. https://www.nea.gov.sg/our-services/waste-management/3r-programmes-and-resources/food-waste-management.

177. The measures in the RSA aim to promote food waste treatment as well as food waste valorisation, which refers to the conversion of waste into higher-value products that contribute back to the food supply chain.[437] Compared to incineration, food waste valorisation is preferable as it extracts more resources and reduces landfill space requirements. For instance, food waste can be processed into animal feed, fertilisers, or fermentation substrate (e.g., for beer production), closing the resource loop and contributing to the circular economy.[438]

178. To this end, the RSA creates obligations for owners and operators of commercial and industrial premises where large amounts of food waste are generated, such as hotels, malls, industrial development housing caterers and food manufacturers.[439] The requirements are in force for new buildings, and will commence progressively for existing buildings.[440] Building managers of affected buildings ('prescribed buildings') must provide a designated facility within the building or its premises to allow occupiers (tenants) to segregate and dispose of food waste separately from other waste.[441] Occupiers must segregate and dispose of food waste at the provided facility or obtain approval from NEA to manage their food waste separately.[442] As to food waste treatment, building managers of existing buildings must either treat the food waste on-site (in the building or its premises) or have the food waste treated at a licensed off-site facility. For new buildings, developers have been required since 2021 to allocate space in their design plans for on-site food waste treatment systems, and building managers must treat food waste on-site unless they obtain prior permission from NEA to have it treated off-site.[443] Building managers must report annually the amount of food waste treated on-site and off-site, and keep records relating to the reports and the monitoring and evaluation undertaken to comply with the RSA.[444] NEA has published guidelines for owners and operators seeking to implement on-site food waste treatment, as well as a Food Waste Segregation and Treatment Guidebook.[445]

---

437. *See* https://www.nea.gov.sg/our-services/waste-management/3r-programmes-and-resources/food-waste-management/food-waste-valorisation.
438. *Ibid.*
439. The requirements can be found in Resource Sustainability (Food Waste Segregation, Treatment and Reporting) Regulations 2024 (RSFWSTRR) reg. 4; they are defined in terms of building type and floor area used for food processing activities.
440. https://www.nea.gov.sg/our-services/waste-management/3r-programmes-and-resources/food-waste-management.
441. Section 27A RSA.
442. Sections 26–27 RSA. An occupier given an approval under s. 27(1) must report to the building manager the amount of food waste treated on-site and off-site: s. 27C(2) RSA.
443. Section 27B RSA.
444. Sections 27C–27E RSA.
445. https://www.nea.gov.sg/our-services/waste-management/3r-programmes-and-resources/food-waste-management/food-waste-management-strategies.

§4. Toxic Waste Control

I. Industrial Waste and Toxic Industrial Waste

179. Several other types of waste are of special concern to the environment. They generally come under the definition of 'toxic industrial waste' (TIW), to which certain laws apply.[446]

180. The EPHA contains specific provisions relating to industrial waste and its disposal (sections 24–30). Industrial waste must be disposed of at a public disposal facility or licensed waste disposal facility.[447] Before disposal, industrial waste must be stored properly to avoid causing any nuisance, injury, or pollution.[448] The DG of Public Health may require the occupier of any workplace to periodically remove industrial waste to a disposal facility.[449] The DG of Public Health may require the owner or occupier of any workplace to furnish information on the amount, type and nature of any industrial waste found on his premises. The owner/occupier may also be required to treat the industrial waste at his own expense before disposal.[450]

181. The generation, import, collection, sale, supply, transport, storage, treatment and disposal of toxic industrial wastes is regulated by the EPHA and the EPH (Toxic Industrial Waste) Regulations (TIWR). The Schedule to the TIWR contains the list of controlled toxic industrial wastes and prescribed amounts for generation and transportation. Duties are imposed on generators and collectors by the Pollution Control Division, NEA.[451]

182. At the planning stage, NEA checks the generation and disposal of wastes from proposed industrial developments, and approves the development only if the wastes generated can be safely treated and disposed of in Singapore. NEA also requires industries to use processes that minimise waste generation and facilitate their proper treatment.[452]

183. Generators of TIW must keep records of all the waste generated and may be required to submit samples of TIW to be analysed by an approved laboratory. If

446. 'Industrial waste' is defined as 'any waste whether solid, liquid or gaseous produced, or removed or recovered, in the course of or is the waste product of any trade, business, manufacture or building construction, and includes toxic industrial waste and any dangerous substance'. 'Toxic industrial waste' is defined as 'any industrial waste which owing to its nature, composition or quantity constitutes a danger to human health or the environment or which contains or may produce pathogens of transmissible diseases' (s. 2 EPHA).
447. Section 24 EPHA.
448. Section 25 EPHA.
449. Section 26 EPHA.
450. Section 28 EPHA.
451. *See* https://www.nea.gov.sg/our-services/pollution-control/toxic-industrial-waste/toxic-waste-control.
452. Management of Toxic Industrial Waste information paper (https://www.nea.gov.sg/docs/default-source/tiw/enhancement-mar-2025/management-of-toxic-industrial-waste-(jan-2025).pdf).

the DG thinks the quantity produced is excessive or unduly toxic, he has wide powers to require remediation by the occupier of the workplace, e.g., by altering the method of production, equipment or materials used.[453] The generator must inform the DG of any change in the type or nature of TIW generated, and the quantity or concentration of any TIW generated in excess of that prescribed in the Schedule to the TIWR (and the corresponding remedial action).[454] The generator must keep a register specifying the type and quantity of waste generated, the manner of disposal, the date and quantity supplied or sold to the collector, the name and address of the collector and the quantity held in stock.[455] He must also give all necessary information to the toxic industrial waste collector to ensure that he can properly carry out his work.[456]

184. TIW collectors (TIWC) must be licensed.[457] TIWCs must comply with their licence conditions and the relevant laws and requirements. TIWCs must, *inter alia*, carry out their work in a suitable industrial area with sufficient facilities and processes, provide adequate pollution control measures and emergency response plans, and keep and submit records of TIW dealt with. NEA publishes a list of requirements for TIWCs and a set of guidelines for special waste incinerators meant for incinerating TIW.[458] Written permission is required to import TIW into Singapore, and it may only be collected at specified locations.[459]

185. For the transportation of TIW, written permission is required to transport TIW in amounts exceeding the quantities prescribed in the Schedule of the TIWR.[460] Containers conveying the TIW must be designed and tested in accordance with an acceptable code of practice.[461] There are responsibilities placed on the consignor, consignee, and carrier, including a consignment note, warning panels and labels, approved transport routes and times, supplementary operational requirements, and safety precautions.[462] Drivers conveying TIW must possess a Hazardous Materials Transportation Driver Permit (HTDP) issued by the Singapore Civil Defence Force (SCDF).[463] When transporting or consigning TIW in amounts exceeding the quantities prescribed in the Schedule of the TIWR, consignees (i.e., generators) must prepare and submit electronic consignment notes on the Waste &

---

453. Section 30 EPHA.
454. Reg. 4 TIWR.
455. Reg. 6 TIWR.
456. Reg. 5 TIWR.
457. Reg. 9 TIWR; Section 23 EPHA. NEA publishes a list of licensed TIWCs: https://www.nea.gov.sg/docs/default-source/tiw/enhancement-mar-2025/list-of-tiw-collectors-(jan-2025).pdf.
458. https://www.nea.gov.sg/our-services/pollution-control/toxic-industrial-waste/toxic-waste-control/instructions-to-register-as-a-user.
459. Regs 14–15 TIWR.
460. Reg. 16 TIWR.
461. https://www.nea.gov.sg/our-services/pollution-control/toxic-industrial-waste/toxic-waste-control/instructions-to-register-as-a-user.
462. Part 6 TIWR.
463. https://www.nea.gov.sg/our-services/pollution-control/toxic-industrial-waste/toxic-waste-control/instructions-to-register-as-a-user.

Resource Management System (WRMS). A trip-ticket system monitors the movement of TIW between generators and licensed TIWCs.[464]

186. NEA encourages companies to incorporate circular economy principles in their TIW management operations. These principles maximise resource recovery and utilisation and minimise waste generation, which reduces the volume of waste sent to landfill and channels valuable resources back into the industry. Some exemplary circular economy practices adopted by TIWCs are featured on the NEA website.[465]

II. Treatment of TIW Before Disposal at Landfill

187. TIW must be treated before disposal at a landfill. Solid residues such as sludge from wastewater treatment facilities and fly ash from waste incinerators may contain toxic contaminants such as heavy metals.[466] Such waste must be treated to comply with leachate test standards[467] before disposal at Semakau Landfill. Applications for written permission to dispose of such wastes must be accompanied by a recent report of analytical results from leachate tests carried out on the wastes. The report must be from an accredited laboratory.

III. Biohazardous Wastes and Other Healthcare and Research TIW

188. Healthcare facilities (e.g., hospitals) and research facilities (e.g., laboratories) produce various types of waste. Biohazardous wastes are a specific type of TIW, and include infectious waste, pathological waste, contaminated sharps, routine clinical waste, cytotoxic waste, and pharmaceutical waste.[468] Other types of waste include chemical waste, mercury-containing waste, radioactive waste, and general waste.[469] Biohazardous wastes must be disposed of by licensed TIWCs authorised to handle the specific waste in question.[470] Some types of waste must be segregated.[471]

---

464. Reg. 17 TIWR; https://www.nea.gov.sg/our-services/pollution-control/toxic-industrial-waste/toxic-waste-control/e-tracking. The WRMS replaced the previous electronic consignment note system, e-Tracking, in 2019.
465. *See* https://www.nea.gov.sg/our-services/pollution-control/toxic-industrial-waste/toxic-waste-control/moving-towards-circular-economy-of-tiw.
466. *See* https://www.nea.gov.sg/our-services/pollution-control/toxic-industrial-waste/toxic-waste-control/disposal-of-treated-tiw-at-semakau-landfill.
467. *See* https://www.nea.gov.sg/docs/default-source/our-services/hazardous-waste/leaching-test.pdf.
468. *See* classification of biohazardous wastes in https://www.nea.gov.sg/docs/default-source/our-services/20090316432165744138.pdf.
469. https://www.nea.gov.sg/our-services/pollution-control/toxic-industrial-waste/toxic-waste-control/control-of-biohazardous-wastes-and-other-tiw-from-healthcare-and-research-facilties.
470. *Ibid.*
471. *Ibid.*

- Non-biohazardous mercury-containing waste (e.g., non-contact amalgam, unused pre-capsulated amalgam (scrap), empty amalgam capsules) is considered TIW, but should be separated from other chemical waste.
- Radioactive wastes should also be separated from biohazardous wastes, TIW, and other wastes.
- Biohazardous mercury-containing wastes such as contact amalgam (i.e., amalgam that has been in contact with the patient's blood) are classified as biohazardous wastes and must be properly segregated from other types of biohazardous waste and non-mercury-containing TIW. (Before disposing of contact amalgam, generators should inform the TIWC of the presence of mercury in the biohazardous waste so that appropriate measures can be taken to ensure their safe collection, treatment and disposal.)

Colour-coded disposal bags are used in hospitals to ensure proper segregation and handling of different types of waste.[472] Yellow bags are used for biohazardous wastes. Purple and red bags are used for cytotoxic and radioactive wastes, respectively. For general waste, black disposal bags are used. Used sharps (e.g., syringes, insulin pen needles) should be placed in a yellow sharps bin or any hard puncture-resistant, sealable container. The container should be labelled and sealed before disposal.[473]

IV. Asbestos

189. The use of asbestos in building materials and the import of raw asbestos have been prohibited in Singapore since the late 1980s. However, some older buildings may have asbestos-containing materials, and removal or demolition of such materials can generate asbestos fibres, posing a health hazard.[474]

190. To carry out asbestos removal works, a contractor must be approved to remove asbestos and must notify the Ministry of Manpower (MOM) at least one week before commencing work.[475] The contractor must also obtain written permission from NEA to dispose of asbestos wastes at Semakau Landfill. The contractor must engage a licensed TIWC capable of handling asbestos wastes to clean up and transport the asbestos wastes directly to Semakau Landfill. The NEA prescribes further instructions for contractors and TIWCs handling asbestos, including the use of

472. MOH, National Infection Prevention and Control Guidelines for Acute Healthcare Facilities 2017, s. 3.3 (https://isomer-user-content.by.gov.sg/95/52a4b3c3-d3e5-4649-ab92-30ddf097406f/the-national-infection-prevention-and-control-guidelines-for-acute-healthcare-facilities---2017.pdf); https://www.nea.gov.sg/our-services/pollution-control/toxic-industrial-waste/toxic-waste-control/frequently-asked-questions-(faqs).
473. *See* https://www.nea.gov.sg/our-services/pollution-control/toxic-industrial-waste/toxic-waste-control/frequently-asked-questions-(faqs).
474. https://www.nea.gov.sg/our-services/pollution-control/toxic-industrial-waste/toxic-waste-control/asbestos-waste. Non-friable asbestos materials (which are solid, rigid, and cannot be crumbled, pulverised, or reduced to powder by hand pressure) should not pose a health hazard if in good condition, and their removal is not necessary.
475. Workplace Safety and Health (Asbestos) Regulations 2014.

sealed and labelled containers for containing asbestos wastes and materials used in removal works, and care to be taken when transporting asbestos wastes.[476]

V. Offences

191. The following are the main offences in relation to industrial waste:

- Collecting, removing, transporting, storing or importing any kind of refuse or waste without a waste collector licence (fine of up to SGD 10,000 and/or imprisonment for up to twelve months).[477]
- Bringing any dangerous substance, toxic industrial waste or the residue from its treatment to any disposal facility for disposal without written permission from the DG of Public Health (fine of up to SGD 10,000 and/or imprisonment for up to twelve months).[478]
- Breach of any other provisions in the EPH (Toxic Industrial Waste) Regulations (fine of up to SGD 10,000, and a daily fine of up to SGD 100 for continuing offences).[479]

§5. Multilateral Environmental Agreements

I. The Basel Convention: Transboundary Movement of Hazardous Wastes and Their Disposal

192. Singapore acceded to the Basel Convention on the Control of Transboundary Movements of Hazardous Waste and their Disposal on 2 January 1996.[480] In accordance with the Basel Convention, the Hazardous Waste (Control of Export, Import and Transit) Act, 1997[481] came into effect on 16 March 1998. It was modelled on the Commonwealth of Australia Hazardous Waste (Regulation of Exports and Imports) Act 1989. Under the Act and its Regulations, any person who wishes to export, import or transit hazardous wastes shall obtain a permit from NEA's Chemical Control and Management Department (CCMD). CCMD adopts the Prior Informed Consent (PIC) procedure of the Basel Convention in granting any permit for the export, import or transit of hazardous wastes. The NEA website contains

476. *See* https://www.nea.gov.sg/our-services/pollution-control/toxic-industrial-waste/toxic-waste-control/asbestos-waste.
477. Section 31 EPHA.
478. Section 29 EPHA.
479. Reg. 41 TIWR.
480. For more information, *see* the Basel Convention website: https://www.basel.int/.
481. Act 13 of 1997, Cap. 122A, 2020 Rev. Ed, amended by Act 6 of 2020 and S 871/2024, supplemented by the Hazardous Waste (Control of Export, Import and Transit) Rules, No. 71/98, Rg 1, 2020 Rev. Ed., amended by GN S 862/2020. *See also* Hazardous Waste (Extended Meaning of Wastes) Indonesia Notification GN S 838/2005; Malaysia Notification GNS 839/2005; Philippines Notification GN S 840/2005; Thailand Notification GN S 841/2005.

guidelines on implementing the Convention.[482] Severe penalties apply for importing, exporting, or carrying out the transit of hazardous waste: for individuals, a fine of up to SGD 100,000 and/or imprisonment not exceeding two years; for corporations, a fine of up to SGD 300,000. In the case of offences by a body corporate, liability is extended to its officers, who are presumed to be guilty of the offence unless they prove otherwise (section 42).

II. The Stockholm Convention on Persistent Organic Pollutants (POPs)

193. Singapore signed the Stockholm Convention on Persistent Organic Pollutants on 23 May 2001, and ratified it on 24 May 2005. The Convention calls for measures and international cooperation to control the production, use, trade and disposal of substances termed as Persistent Organic Pollutants (POPs). POPs are chemicals that resist degradation, enabling them to be transported over long distances. They bioaccumulate easily in living tissues and are toxic and harmful to human and environmental health. Exposure to low amounts of certain POPs can cause cancer, nervous system damage, immune system diseases, reproductive disorders, and interference with normal infant and child development. The initial list of twelve POPs (commonly referred to as the 'dirty dozen') covered under the Stockholm Convention comprises: aldrin, chlordane, DDT, dieldrin, endrin, heptachlor, mirex, toxaphene, PCBs, hexachlorobenzene, dioxins and furans. Over the years, the Stockholm Convention has expanded the list to include new POPs such as lindane, dicofol, and more.[483] Many of these substances, which are commonly used as pesticides, have been banned in Singapore.[484] POPs such as dioxins and furans are the unintentional by-products of combustion, such as waste incineration. Processes and procedures are in place to minimise their production in Singapore's waste incineration processes. Emission levels are low and comparable to those in other developed countries.[485]

III. The Rotterdam Convention on Prior Informed Consent (PIC)

194. The Prior Informed Consent (PIC) procedure started as a voluntary process in the 1980s, requiring exporters trading in a list of hazardous substances to obtain

---

482. *See* NEA's notifications on the Basle Convention at https://www.nea.gov.sg/corporate-functions/resources/legislation-international-law/multilateral-environmental-agreements/chemical-safety/basel-convention.
483. *See* http://chm.pops.int/TheConvention/ThePOPs/ListingofPOPs/tabid/2509/Default.aspx.
484. *See* Lye Lin Heng, 'The Regulation, Control and Management of Pesticides in Singapore', *Environmental and Planning Law Journal* Vol. 35 (Special Issue: Regulation of Pesticides – The Need for a Paradigm Shift), 2018, pp. 430–442.
485. *See* NEA's site on the Stockholm Convention at https://www.nea.gov.sg/corporate-functions/resources/legislation-international-law/multilateral-environmental-agreements/chemical-safety/stockholm-convention.

the prior informed consent of importers before proceeding with the trade.[486] Since June 2001, Singapore has been participating in the Interim PIC Procedure (IPP). Singapore participated in the Interim PIP Procedure (IPP) from June 2001 onwards.[487]

195. Building on the voluntary PIC procedure, the Rotterdam Convention creates legally binding obligations for the implementation of the PIC procedure. Under the PIC procedure, countries exporting hazardous chemicals identified in the Convention are only allowed to export to parties that consent to the import of these said chemicals.[488] The import decisions of each country can be found in the PIC Circular, updated every six months.[489] The Convention entered into force on 24 February 2004. Singapore acceded to the Convention on 24 May 2005, and it came into force for Singapore on 21 August 2005. The NEA's PCD is Singapore's Designated National Authority (DNA) under the PIC procedure, and hazardous chemicals in Singapore are already subject to stringent controls under the NEA's EPMA and its Regulations. Through the control of export licences, NEA can ban or restrict the import or export of hazardous chemicals.[490]

IV. The Minamata Convention on Mercury[491]

196. Singapore signed the Minamata Convention on Mercury in October 2013 and ratified it on 22 September 2017.[492] Mercury is of significant concern as it is toxic to humans and the environment, can be transported over long distances, and bioaccumulates easily in living tissue. It is used widely across various applications. The Minamata Convention aims to protect human health and the environment from the adverse effects of mercury and mercury compounds by addressing, *inter alia*, the mining, use, release, import and export, storage, and disposal of mercury, and improving management of mercury-related health issues.[493]

As a Party to the Convention, Singapore's key obligations are to:[494]

486. https://www.nea.gov.sg/corporate-functions/resources/legislation-international-law/multilateral-environmental-agreements/chemical-safety/rotterdam-convention.
487. https://www.nea.gov.sg/docs/default-source/resource/publications/environmental-protection-division-annual-report/epd-2003.pdf (p. 60).
488. The list of chemicals are found in Annex III of the Convention: https://www.pic.int/Default.aspx?tabid=1132.
489. https://www.pic.int/Implementation/PICCircular/tabid/1168/language/en-US/Default.aspx.
490. The list of chemicals subjected to the IPP procedure (PIC chemicals) can be found at Annex A of NEA's website – https://www.nea.gov.sg/docs/default-source/our-services/pcd-pic-prod-code2-cas-(300614).pdf.
491. https://www.mercuryconvention.org/en.
492. https://www.nea.gov.sg/corporate-functions/resources/legislation-international-law/multilateral-environmental-agreements/chemical-safety/minamata-convention-on-mercury.
493. https://minamataconvention.org/en.
494. https://www.nea.gov.sg/corporate-functions/resources/legislation-international-law/multilateral-environmental-agreements/chemical-safety/minamata-convention-on-mercury.

- Ensure that the export of mercury is only to countries that have provided written consent to the export and for a use/purpose allowed under the Convention.
- Ensure that mercury imported is not from sources that are not allowed under the Convention.
- Reduce or phase out specific manufacturing processes listed under Annex B of the Convention in which mercury or mercury compounds are used.
- Phase out the manufacture, import and export of specific mercury-added products that are listed under Annex A of the Convention.
- Control emissions of mercury or mercury compounds to the atmosphere.
- Control releases of mercury or mercury compounds to land and water.

To this end, mercury is subject to strict regulatory control in Singapore. Singapore has developed an inventory of mercury emissions as per the UN Environment Programme (UNEP) guidelines. Imports of certain mercury-containing products are banned, and there are no domestic production and processing activities that use mercury. Pollution control equipment is required at incineration plants and industries to ensure compliance with the mercury emissions limits in the EPM (Air Impurities) Regulations. Wastewater discharged into watercourses must be treated to comply with the mercury limits prescribed in the EPM (Trade Effluent) Regulations.[495]

495. *Ibid.*

Chapter 6. Land Contamination

197. Section 20 EPMA provides that the Minister may make regulations to control the pollution of land 'whereby the condition of the land is so changed as to make or be likely to make the land or the produce of the land obnoxious, noxious or poisonous'. No regulations have been passed as yet.

198. However, NEA's Code of Practice on Pollution Control[496] contains substantive provisions on the remediation of polluted sites, if the site is to be re-developed, re-zoned or re-used for a non-pollutive activity. A study shall first be conducted on the site to assess the extent of land contamination. The Code provides guidance on who can conduct these studies, the standards and technical guidelines to be followed, the consultants that may be engaged, and what their report should contain. If the site is found to be contaminated, 'it shall be cleaned up to standards acceptable for the intended use'.[497] Appendix 21 lists the 'pollutive activities' that require remediation. Remediated sites must be certified by experts or specialist consultants. The Guidelines allow the adoption of various clean-up standards, including the Dutch Guidelines for Soil Protection, ASTM (American Society for Testing and Materials) standards, and New Zealand Standards for Assessing and Managing Petroleum Hydrocarbon Contaminated Sites.

496. Singapore Standards 593/2013 at p. 21.
497. The 2024 JTC ESA guidelines provides further guidance for conducting the Environmental Site Assessment for assessing contamination of a site (https://www.jtc.gov.sg/-/media/project/jtc-cx/corpweb/assets/get-help/jtc-environmental-site-assessment-requirements-and-technical-guidelines-2024-edition.pdf).

Chapter 7. Noise

199. The main sources of noise pollution in Singapore are: vehicular traffic, mass rail transit (MRT) systems, construction sites, industries, aircraft, public entertainment activities and community activities. Noise-induced deafness is a major occupational hazard in Singapore factories. The Singapore Green Plan (SGP) 1992 identified noise as a major concern.

200. An Environmental Noise Management Unit (ENMU) was set up by the Ministry of Environment in May 1994 to look into the integrated control and management of noise, particularly from construction activities and from transport, and to develop an action plan for noise emanating from trade and industrial activities. In November 1994, an Environmental Noise Advisory Committee was formed to facilitate discussion and feedback. The ENMU has since identified nineteen action programmes, viz. the development of an environmental noise monitoring system; control of road traffic noise and MRT train noise; acceptable indoor noise for future residential buildings; control of noise from indoor places of public entertainment and outdoor public entertainment sites; boundary noise limits for factory premises; promotion of good management practices and use of quieter plant and equipment at construction sites; and planning guidelines for noise control.

These programmes have resulted in more stringent laws being passed to control noise pollution from these sources:

§1. Noise from Vehicular Traffic and Mass Railway Transit (MRT)

201. Noise from vehicular sources used to be regulated under the Road Traffic (Construction and Use) Rules. These have now been replaced by the Environmental Protection and Management (Vehicular Emission) Regulations 1999,[498] which prescribe vehicular emission standards as well as noise levels for various categories of vehicles.[499] The registration standards of exhaust noise for new vehicles and those registered on or after 1 July 1999 have been tightened, taking effect as from 1 October 2010. The noise emission standards vary depending on type of vehicle and whether the engine is at the rear end of the vehicle. Failure to comply constitutes an offence carrying a maximum fine of SGD 2,000 for the first offence and SGD 5,000 for a second or subsequent offence. While the NEA sets the noise emission standards for new and in-use vehicles, the Land Transport Authority (LTA) requires vehicles to undergo mandatory, periodic inspections to ensure they meet NEA's noise emission standards for in-use vehicles and have not been illegally modified.

498. Rg 6, GN S 291/1999, amended S 625/2008, S 564/2010, S 301/2012, S 199/2014, S 372/2016, S 26/2017 S 781/2017, S 877/2018, S 57/2019.

499. *See* the noise emission standards for vehicles at https://www.nea.gov.sg/our-services/pollution-control/noise-pollution/vehicular-noise-control.

Enforcement efforts are conducted with the Traffic Police (TP).[500] Vehicles that do not meet the prescribed noise standards during the mandatory periodic inspections at authorised inspection centres will not have their road tax renewed and cannot be used on the road. LTA, TP and NEA conduct regular joint enforcement operations against modified vehicles/overloaded/speeding/noisy local and foreign vehicles. The modified and noisy foreign vehicles are also reported to the Malaysian authorities for their follow-up action.

202. The noise emission standards were tightened from 1 April 2022, when the Fourth Schedule to the EPM (Vehicular Emissions) Regulations was amended.[501] This was further tightened to follow internationally recognise UN standards with effect from 1 April 2023.[502]

203. The Mass Railway Transit Corporation (MRTC) initially adopted a noise emission standard of 86 dBA for MRT trains, as a self-regulatory initiative, measured at a distance of 15 m and at a speed of 80 km/hour. All underground MRTs are generally kept to an interior noise threshold of 85 decibels Laeq (a measurement of sound pressure over a period of time). In 2011, the LTA embarked on a study of noise levels emitted by the MRT trains.[503] It has since built noise barriers in various parts of Singapore, and by 2019, it was into its third phase to reduce the impact of railway locations near residential areas.[504] Noise is also reduced by planning guidelines, which require setback distances for residential premises adjacent to MRT tracks.[505] LTA also has plans to reduce noise levels on future new MRT lines by slowing down the trains in these areas and grinding the surface of the tracks to smooth the contact between the tracks and wheels.

§2. Noise from Construction

204. Part VIII of the EPMA, 1999 (sections 28–30) relates to noise control. Section 28 applies to construction activities and allows the Director-General (DG) to give written notice imposing conditions for carrying out such works, relating, *inter alia*, to the type of plant/machinery to be used, hours of work, and the noise and vibration levels. A stop-work order may be issued if there is non-compliance. The penalties for breach are a daily fine of SGD 10,000 per day, imprisonment up to

---

500. *See* https://www.mot.gov.sg/news-centre/news/Detail/written-reply-by-minister-for-transport-ong-ye-kung-to-parliamentary-question-on-proposal-to-install-acoustic-cameras-to-identify-noisy-vehicles-for-enforcement-action/ (5 Oct. 2020).
501. EPM (Vehicular Emissions) (Amendment) Regulations, 2022 – No. S 249/2022 with effect from 1 Apr. 2022.
502. https://www.nea.gov.sg/media/news/news/index/in-use-emission-standards-for-older-motorcycles-and-noise-standards-for-all-vehicles-will-be-tightened-in-april-2023.
503. https://www.eco-business.com/news/lta-to-study-noise-levels-from-mrt-trains/ (15 Jun. 2011).
504. https://www.lta.gov.sg/content/ltagov/en/newsroom/2019/10/1/contract_for_phase3_railway_noise_barrier.html.
505. *See Lim Sor Choo v. Sato Kogyo Pte Ltd* [2006] SGDC 212 – owner of apartment failed in an action in nuisance and for breach of the EPC (Noise at Construction Site) Regulations against contractor building the MRT system, and had to pay legal costs amounting to SGD 45,000.

three months or both fine and imprisonment. Section 29 relates to the control of noise from workplaces. The DG may prohibit certain activities or use of a specified plant if the noise emitted is in excess of permitted levels. If the noise exceeds permitted levels, the DG may impose certain requirements such as the installation of noise control equipment, noise barrier, or adjustments to machinery. If any of the regulations relating to when construction works can be carried out are contravened, the DG may require an electronic video surveillance system to be set up on the premises to monitor whether and when construction works are being carried out.

205. The EPM (Control of Noise from Construction Sites) Regulations 1999[506] regulate the noise level from construction sites by imposing two different maximum permissible noise levels for two different twelve-hour periods (one in the day, and one at night). The levels allowed vary, with lower levels required for hospitals, schools, institutions of higher learning, homes for the aged, etc. The EPMA empowers the DG to give written notice imposing requirements on the carrying out of building, demolition and construction works. As there were many complaints about construction noise, the NEA tightened permissible noise limits for construction sites within 150 m of residential premises and noise-sensitive premises such as hospitals and nursing homes. There are now three different periods with permitted noise levels. The first period is for construction work commenced on or before 1 October 2007; the second is for construction work commenced after 1 November 2007; the third is for work that commenced on or after 1 September 2011. For construction work that commenced after 1 September 2011, no work is allowed from 10 pm on Saturday to 7 am on the following Monday; and no work is allowed from 10 pm on the eve of public holidays to 7 am on the day after the public holiday. Work is prohibited on Sundays and public holidays.[507] However, since 1 January 2017, construction sites at the architectural/project completion stage are allowed to carry out quieter forms of work (list of permitted works on the NEA ePortal) on specific Sundays and public holidays. Contractors must submit an application via the NEA ePortal for a permit to carry out quieter works on specific Sundays and public holidays, subject to compliance with stringent conditions in the application form and comply with any other conditions imposed by NEA.[508]

From 1 April 2025, noise barriers are required to be installed along the perimeter of a construction worksite if they have a project value of SGD 50 million and above, and it is located within 75 metres of sensitive premises.

---

506. Cap. 94A Rg 2, GN S 157/1999 (2008 Rev Ed), amended S 276/2001, S 145/2007, S 484/2011. *See Public Prosecutor v. China Construction (South Pacific) Dev Co Pte Ltd* [2006] SGDC 100; *Public Prosecutor v. Tat Hin Builders Pte Ltd* [2007] SGDC 206; *Public Prosecutor v. M/s Universe Builders Pte Ltd* [2013] SGDC 87.

507. *See* the new standards for noise from construction sites at https://sso.agc.gov.sg/SL/EPMA1999-RG2. *See also* https://www.nea.gov.sg/our-services/pollution-control/noise-pollution/construction-noise-control.

508. *See* https://www.nea.gov.sg/our-services/pollution-control/noise-pollution/construction-noise-control;https://www.straitstimes.com/forum/letters-in-print/nea-acts-on-contractors-violating-noise-regulations-and-not-only-when-there (28 Mar. 2019).

206. The maximum fine for violating the permissible noise limits has been increased to SGD 40,000 (up from a maximum fine of up to SGD 10,000 and SGD 20,000 for the first and second prosecution, respectively). The penalty for a continuing offence after conviction is also increased from SGD 500 to SGD 1,000 for every day the offence is continued. The increase in penalties came into effect on 1 October 2007.[509]

207. A construction noise alert system was also implemented in 2008. NEA now requires all construction projects above SGD 10 million to install and operate real-time noise monitoring system to monitor construction noise. In September 2011, this requirement was extended to include all construction projects above SGD 3 million and all projects involving piling and demolition. With this real-time noise monitoring system in place, NEA can assess the noise monitoring website at any time to check the real-time noise levels measured on site. This improves operational responsiveness and efficiency as officers do not need to travel to the construction site to take noise measurements. Owners/occupiers of the construction site are also required to submit all records of the noise readings, including relevant facts which may influence the values of the noise level readings. In addition, project managers of construction sites are able to access the noise monitoring website to review the noise levels generated at the site. The system can also be programmed to send SMS alerts to these project managers if the noise level exceeds a certain limit. This enables the contractor to take immediate corrective measures to reduce their noise levels.

In October 2020, the MSE stated it was reviewing construction noise limits and penalties, taking into account that Singaporeans are working and studying from home during the COVID-19 pandemic.[510] The Republic of Singapore Air Force (RSAF) has also said that it will reduce the frequency of its flights island-wide and end night flying activities earlier during periods of major examinations for students.

§3. Noise Within Factories and Industrial Premises

208. The Workplace Safety and Health Act 2006 (WSHA)[511] requires employers of factories with excessive noise or vibration to take steps to reduce the noise. They must also provide hearing protectors to workers who are exposed to a daily equivalent noise level exceeding 85 dBA over an eight-hour exposure period. The WSHA extends liability to all who create and have control over safety and health risks at a workplace (section 10). These include the employer, principal, occupier, contractor, sub-contractor, platform operator, platform worker, designer, manufacturer or supplier of any machinery; erector, installer or modifier of machinery or

509. *See* NEA News Release no. 12/2007, issued 30 Mar. 2007. In *Public Prosecutor v. M/s Universe Builders Pte Ltd* [2013] SGDC 87, a first offender who pleaded ignorance of the new laws was fined SGD 5,000.

510. *See* https://www.todayonline.com/singapore/review-construction-noise-limits-penalties-singaporeans-work-study-home-desmond-tan (14 Oct. 2020).

511. Act 7 of 2006 2020 Rev. Ed.; amended by Act 18/2001, Act 9,/2008, Act 44/2017, Act 18/2011 and Act 40/2019.

equipment for use at work; an owner, hirer or lessee of machinery or a person who maintains such machinery for use at work; a worker, and a self-employed person. These terms are defined in sections 4 and 6 of the Act. A worker who fails to wear hearing protectors when required will therefore be committing an offence under the WSHA.

209. The Factories (Noise) Regulations[512] came into effect on 1 January 1997 and remained in effect despite the repeal of the Factories Act until 1 September 2011, when it was replaced by the WSH (Noise) Regulations, 2011.[513] The Regulations impose a duty on the occupier of a workplace 'to take, so far as is reasonably practicable, such measures to reduce or control the noise from any machinery or equipment used, from any process, operation or work carried on by him in a workplace, so that no person at work in the workplace is exposed or is likely to be exposed to excessive noise'. The Schedule sets out the permissible limits for exposure to noise. The Regulations require persons exposed to excessive noise to wear hearing protectors; noisy factories must appoint noise control advisors; noise monitoring must be carried out; suppliers of noisy machines must provide more information on noise emissions to assist buyers in picking quieter machines. Breach of these regulations entails a maximum fine of SGD 20,000 or imprisonment for a term not exceeding two years or both. A second or subsequent conviction may result in a maximum fine of SGD 50,000, or imprisonment for a term not exceeding two years or both. Additionally, a company with ten or more people likely to be exposed to excessive noise must submit noise monitoring reports to the Ministry of Manpower (MOM).[514]

The WSH (Medical Examinations) Regulations[515] require persons exposed to excessive noise to undergo hearing examinations every twelve months. Prosecutions are instituted by MOM.

§4. Noise Emanating from Factories

210. The Environmental Management and Protection (Boundary Noise Limits for Factory Premises) Regulations[516] specify the maximum noise levels that can be emitted from factory premises. Breaches carry a maximum fine of SGD 5,000 and a daily fine of SGD 200. Prosecutions are instituted by the NEA. The fine is doubled to SGD 10,000 for a second or subsequent conviction, and a daily fine of SGD 300.

512. GN S 372/1996.
513. GN S 424/2011.
514. *See* https://www.mom.gov.sg/faq/hygiene-monitoring/is-my-company-required-to-submit-noise-monitoring-report-to-mom.
515. GN S 516/2011.
516. GN S 156/1999, Rg. 1.

§5. Aircraft Noise

211. Singapore pursues a liberal aviation policy, which ensures the continued growth of air traffic. Singapore's Changi International Airport is one of the busiest and best in the world, and is the airport that has received the most 'Best Airport' awards, winning some 704 awards.[517] It was the fourth busiest international airport in 2024, and is a major air hub in Asia, serving more than 100 international airlines flying to over 160 destinations across close to fifty countries worldwide. It handled more than 67.7 million passengers in 2024 (more than ten times the size of Singapore's population). A flight takes off or lands at Changi almost once every eighty seconds.[518] All aircraft that take off and land must comply with the noise standards set out in Article 9, Annex 16, of the Chicago Convention on International Civil Aviation, 1944,[519] in accordance with the recommendations from the International Civil Aviation Organization (ICAO)'s guidelines on Balanced Approach to Noise. The Air Navigation Act, 1966,[520] provides that noise from aircraft overflight cannot be the subject of an action in trespass or nuisance if, having regard to the wind, weather and all the circumstances of the case, it is reasonable or ordinarily incidental to the flight.[521] Likewise, noise and vibration caused by aircraft in aerodromes are not actionable in nuisance.[522] In addition, Changi Airport has in place various operational and noise-abatement measures to protect the environment. These include:

i. Reducing the noise at source – Civil aircraft operating in Singapore are required to meet the noise standards stipulated by the International Civil Aviation Organisation (ICAO). To this end, a Noise Certificate issued by the Civil Aviation Authority of Singapore (CAAS) must be obtained to document that the aircraft in question complies with the ICAO requirements.[523]
ii. Land-use planning – here, noise abatement considerations are factored into Changi Airport's long-term airport master planning. Three out of four runways at Changi Airport lead almost directly into the sea. Only departures towards the south on Runway 1 fly over a small portion of land, which has been designated for non-residential use. The Urban Redevelopment Authority (URA) zones land surrounding Changi Airport for residential use in accordance with international norms on noise levels. Noise studies are conducted regularly to update the noise contours around Changi Airport. The results of these studies are shared with URA for future land-use planning.

---

517. https://www.changiairport.com/corporate/about-us/awards-and-accolades.html.
518. *See* https://www.changiairport.com/corporate/our-expertise/air-hub/traffic-statistics.html. These statistics were before the outbreak of the COVID-19 pandemic in 2020.
519. Compliance is evidenced by the manufacturer's certification in the flight manual that the noise standards in Annex 16 are complied with.
520. Act 11 of 1966, 2020 Rev. Ed. Amended by Act 28/2000, Act 12/f 2007, Act 10/2014, Act 16/2015, Act 10/2018, Act 18/2018, and Act 34 of 2019.
521. *See* Air Navigation Act, s. 42, . *See also* s. 3 (power to give effect to international obligations and regulate air navigation) and Air Navigation Order 2, 1985), paragraph 51 (control of aircraft noise).
522. *See* ss 8(4) and 9(1)(e).
523. *See* https://www.caas.gov.sg/operations-safety/aircraft/noise-certificate.

iii. Operational measures – The main priority of CAAS air traffic services when assigning runways to aircraft is to move air traffic (i.e., departures and landings) in the safest and most efficient manner possible. As departures are noisier than landings, where possible, Runway 1, which is located closer to residential areas, is used for arrivals and Runway 2, which is located further away from residential areas, is used for departures. All aircraft departing from Changi Airport follow defined routes designed to avoid flying directly overhead residential areas. Furthermore, the use of Runway 1 for aircraft departures towards the south is restricted in the early hours of the morning. Exceptions to this restriction are made only when Runway 2 is closed for maintenance and other works.

iv. Monitoring and Reporting – Regular inspections are conducted at Changi Airport to note any abnormal noise activity, particularly during the early hours of the morning. Changi Airport Group gathers feedback from local residents and has a process in place for reporting and responding to noise complaints. It also works closely with air agencies such as SASCO (ST Aviation Services Company) to ensure that the impact of noise from their compounds is minimised, especially between the hours of midnight to 6 am.

212. Noise from military aircraft is outside the purview of this Act. The Republic of Singapore Air Force (RSAF) has sought to explain its policies. It claims it has laid down strict rules to reduce noise levels around the airbases, including:

- lowering the speed of jets when operating over the main island;
- ceasing flying activities during school examinations for 'listening comprehension';
- dialling down frequency of flights island-wide and ending night flying activities earlier during the national examination season for schools more generally;[524]
- adjusting their flight schedule in response to feedback from residents;
- planning flight routes to reduce flying over populated areas where possible, to reduce impact of military aircraft noise on the public;
- conducting engine ground runs for fighter aircraft in the Hush House, an enclosure designed to absorb noise during the testing of jet engines.

213. Also, most of the training is done over the South China Sea and Pulau Pawai, and at training detachments overseas. Again, to reduce noise and minimise risk, RSAF aircraft avoid residential areas when taking off for training where possible, and adjust flying training tempo and hours during school examination periods; and also fly at higher altitudes on the departure routes. The relocation of the Flying Training School to Perth, Western Australia, and the introduction of Flight Simulators in the RSAF have significantly reduced aircraft noise. The RSAF has said that a portion of flying training is conducted using simulators and a significant

524. *See* https://www.todayonline.com/singapore/rsaf-reduce-frequency-flights-end-night-flying-activities-earlier-during-national-exam (1 Sep. 2020).

portion of flying training is also done overseas.[525] Similar noise abatement measures on foreign aircraft are imposed. MINDEF and RSAF are also working with government agencies such as HDB and NEA on noise mitigating measures for new infrastructure developments in the vicinity of air bases. This includes thicker window glass in public housing for better sound insulation, façade designs with overhangs or canopies to deflect and abate noise transmission, and orienting buildings away from the direct line of aircraft flight paths.

§6. Noise as a Public Nuisance

214. Section 44(m) EPHA 1987, recognises noise as a form of nuisance for which a Nuisance Order under section 45 may be issued by the DG of Public Health. Noise is defined to include vibrations (section 15(6) of the Miscellaneous Offences (Public Order and Nuisance) Act. The making of excessive noise so as to cause annoyance or inconvenience to an occupier of any premises in the vicinity or to any person lawfully using any public road or any public place is an offence under section 14 of that Act,[526] carrying a fine of up to SGD 1,000. Upon such complaint, a police officer may enter the premises and, after due warning, stop the noise, including removing the instrument that caused the noise. Section 15 allows a person to complain to a Magistrate who may order that the nuisance be abated. Failure to comply entails a fine of up to SGD 2,000. However, it is a defence for noise caused in the course of a trade or business if the defendant proves that the best practicable means was used for preventing that noise (section 15(5)).

525. *See* https://www.mindef.gov.sg/web/portal/mindef/news-and-events/latest-releases/article-detail/2020/January/10jan20_fr.
526. Ordinance 13 of 1906, 2020 Rev. Ed., amended by Act 21/1973, Act 10/1989, Act 12/1996, Act 2/2012, Act 5/2015.

Chapter 8. Radiation

§1. Introduction

215. The Radiation Protection Inspectorate (RPI) was formed as a unit of the Department of Scientific Services (DSS) in 1972. In 1976, with assistance from the International Atomic Energy Authority (IAEA), RPI started the use of Thermoluminescent Dosimeter (TLD) as a monitoring device, in addition to the film badge monitoring service being offered. RPI then set up an IAEA/WHO Secondary Standards Dosimetry Laboratory (SSDL), equipped with a constant potential X-ray machine. The SSDL continues to serve as a national calibration laboratory for radiation protection and environmental monitoring since 1988. In the following year in 1989, RPI was designated as the Singapore Contact Point for the following two IAEA Conventions: Convention on Early Notification of Nuclear Accident, and Convention on Assistance in the Case of Nuclear Accident. Singapore became a member of the International Atomic Energy Agency (IAEA) in 1967 and MSE/NEA has been Singapore's lead agency for IAEA matters since 1995. NEA serves as the national focal point for various IAEA conventions/agreements that Singapore is a party to. Singapore became a member of the IAEA's Regional Cooperative Agreement (RCA) for Research, Education and Training related to Nuclear Science and Technology for Asia and the Pacific in 1974.[527] NEA has served as the National RCA Representative since 2003 and is in charge of overseeing and facilitating local agencies' participation in RCA activities.

216. On 1 August 2013, the Radiation Protection and Nuclear Science Group (RPNSG), formerly known as the Centre for Radiation Protection and Nuclear Science (CRPNS), became the national authority for radiation protection in Singapore, administering and enforcing the Radiation Protection Act and Regulations through a system of licensing, notification, authorisation, inspection and enforcement.[528] The key functions of RPNSG include:

– administering and enforcing the Radiation Protection Act (RPA) and its Regulations;
– licensing the import, export, sale, possession, use and transport of radioactive materials and irradiating apparatus;
– ensuring the safe use of ionising and non-ionising radiation;
– monitoring radiation dose exposure for radiation workers;
– providing radiation-related and consultancy services (e.g., calibration of survey meters and radioactivity testing);
– controlling the disposal of radioactive waste;

527. The IAEA Regional Cooperative Agreement (RCA) was initiated in 1972, and has expanded from 10 to 22 Member States from East Asia and Oceania. The RCA is one of three cooperative agreements under the aegis of the IAEA, the other two being for Africa (AFRA) and Latin America (ARCAL). *See* http://www.rcaro.org/whatsrca.

528. *See* https://www.nea.gov.sg/our-services/radiation-safety/overview.

- implementing international conventions relating to nuclear safety, security and safeguards that Singapore is a party to; and
- jointly responding with the Singapore Civil Defence Force to radiological emergencies.

§2. Radiation Protection Act

217. The Radiation Protection Act was first passed in 1973 to control the import, export, sale, transport, possession and use of radioactive materials and irradiating apparatus, and was amended in 1991 to include the control of non-ionising radiation (NIR). In July 2007, the Act was repealed and re-enacted,[529] particularly to prepare for Singapore's ratification of the IAEA's Additional Protocol. In 2014, the Radiation Protection Act 2007 was amended to allow Singapore to implement its obligations under the IAEA Convention on Physical Protection of Nuclear Material (CPPNM).[530] Licences are required for the import, export, sale, manufacture, dealing in, possession and use of radioactive materials and irradiating apparatus. A licence is also required for the transport of radioactive materials. Licensees are required to keep careful records and offer them for inspection when required.

218. In relation to occupational health and safety, the Act requires every licensee to provide employees with a safe working environment so that they are protected from unnecessary exposure to radiation. They must be given training and supervision so they can perform their work safely. Employees must also be given prescribed radiation monitoring equipment, including personal monitoring devices, and prescribed medical examinations (section 10(2)(d), (e)). Part VI governs the disposal of radioactive waste. Disposals require the prior written consent of the DG of Environmental Protection (section 13).

219. The maximum penalty for infringement of the Act is SGD 100,000 or imprisonment for a term not exceeding five years or both. Section 43 empowers the court to order the forfeiture of all radioactive materials where a person is convicted.

§3. The Radiation Protection Regulations

220. There are four Regulations as follows:

1. Radiation Protection (Non-Ionising Radiation) Regulations, 1991.[531]
2. Radiation Protection (Ionising Radiation) Radiation Regulations 2023.[532]

529. Act 27 of 2007, 2008 Rev. Ed, amended by Act 20 of 2014.
530. *See* https://www.nea.gov.sg/our-services/radiation-safety/regulatory/summary-of-radiation-protection-(amendment)-act-2014.
531. Rg 1, GN S 479/1991, amended by S 517/2019 and S 34/2022.
532. Rg 2, GN S. 29/2000.

3. Radiation Protection (Transport of Radioactive Materials) Regulations 2000.[533]
4. Radiation Protection (Exemption for Transit, Transhipment and Carriage of Conveyance Equipment) Regulations 2014.[534]

I. Radiation Protection (Ionising Radiation) Regulations

221. The Ionising Regulations were first implemented in 1974. They were amended in 2000 to incorporate the 1990 Recommendations of the International Commission on Radiological Protection (ICRP) and the requirements of the International Basic Safety Standards (IBSS) published in 1996 by the International Atomic Energy Agency (IAEA). They regulate the use, handling, storage, labelling, and transportation of irradiating apparatus and radioactive materials. This was further amended in 2023 to incorporate the 2007 ICRP updates recommending a shift from a practice-based approach to an approach based on exposure situation for radiation protection and the 2014 IAEA's General Safety Requirements Part 3 Radiation Protection and Safety of Radiation Sources (GSR Part 3) recommending an approach based on exposure situation to radiation protection. The 2023 amendments also streamlined the licensing regime and reduced the administrative burden for both NEA as well as licensees.

222. The amended Radiation Protection (Ionising Radiation) Regulations 2023 provide the framework for the licensing regime, the responsibility of licensees, the exemptions and clearance. The Act also control the labelling of radiation sources and radiation areas, supply of irradiating apparatus and radioactive materials, accounting of radioactive materials, and checking of leakage of sealed sources. The Act also sets out the general responsibilities of licensees depending on if their employees are engaged in occupational exposure, medical exposure, or public exposure. Finally, the act covers radioactive waste management, management of disused sealed sources, emergency preparedness and response, security of radioactive materials, and radiation accidents.

223. The accumulation of radioactive waste is prohibited unless with the Director of Radiation Protection's written consent. Likewise, the transportation of radioactive waste requires the Director's prior written consent. Every approved person must ensure that the radioactive waste is properly stored and that they develop a suitable and comprehensive recording system for radioactive waste management activities under the person's responsibility, while ensuring that records related to radioactive waste inventory are kept up to date. The Director is also empowered to dispose of any radioactive waste on the premises if he is of the opinion that the waste is unlikely to be properly disposed of, and recover any expenses reasonably connected.

---

533. Rg 3, GN S 30/2000.
534. GN S 703/2014.

II. The Radiation Protection (Non-Ionising Radiation) Regulations

224. The Radiation Protection (Non-Ionising) Regulations[535] were passed in 1991 to regulate exposure to radiation. They apply to microwave ovens, ultraviolet sunlamps, medical and industrial ultrasound apparatus, and magnetic resonance imaging (MRI) apparatus, entertainment lasers, and high-power industrial and medical lasers. Licences are required for the manufacture, possession, use and sale of specified non-ionising radiation apparatus. A licence is required for importing or exporting each consignment of non-ionising radiation (NIR) apparatus. All NIR apparatus shall be manufactured and designed so that the requirements on shielding, interlocks and warning devices are met. All non-ionising irradiating apparatus shall be appropriately labelled to give adequate warning of radiation hazards.

III. The Radiation Protection (Transport of Radioactive Materials) Regulations

225. These Regulations were first implemented in 1974 and amended in 2000.[536] They are based on the IAEA Safety Standards Series No. ST-1, 1996 Edition – Regulations for the Safe Transport of Radioactive Material, and provide detailed requirements for the transport, handling and storage of radioactive materials.

226. 'Transport' has been defined to mean to move from any place, vehicle, vessel or aircraft to another place, vehicle, vessel or aircraft by road, rail, water or air and includes transport which is incidental to the use of the radioactive materials, such as carrying radiography devices to and from the operations site by the radiographer or carrying density measuring gauges to and from the construction site. The Regulations are not intended to be applied to movements of radioactive materials which form an integral part of a means of transport, such as depleted uranium counterweights or tritium exit signs used in aircraft.[537] Natural radioactive materials or ores which form part of the nuclear fuel cycle or which will be processed to use their radioactive properties need to comply with the Regulations. To minimise the possibility of radioactive material packages losing their containment integrity owing to the interaction of the package with other dangerous goods, they should be kept segregated from other dangerous cargo during transport or storage. The package design requirements for the various quantities and types of radionuclides are all stated in these Regulations.

535. GN S 479/1991.
536. GN S 30/2000.
537. *See* R 2(c), Regulations GN S 30/2000.

IV. Services of the Radiation Protection and Nuclear Science Division

227. The Radiation Protection and Nuclear Science Division (RPNSD), as the national regulatory authority for radiation protection in Singapore, offers the following radiation services.[538]

(1) Training and Education

228. To promote safe use of ionising and non-ionising radiation, Ngee Ann Polytechnic and Republic Polytechnic conduct courses for radiation workers on various aspects of radiation safety.

(2) Radiofrequency Radiation and Electromagnetic Field Measurement

229. The RPNSD provides radiofrequency radiation and electromagnetic field measurement services to industries, government agencies and the public. These services are done using broadband measurement meters.

(3) Analysis of Wipe Test Samples for Sealed Sources

230. Under the Radiation Protection (Ionising Radiation) Regulations, every person who possesses or has under his control any sealed source shall ensure that a wipe test for leakage of radioactive substance is made by a qualified individual at least once in every period of twelve months. This is to ensure that there is no leakage of radioactive substances. RPNSD provides analytical laboratory services to analyse the wipe sample for presence of radioactive contamination.

(4) Calibration of Survey Meters

231. Under the Radiation Protection (Ionising Radiation) Regulations, any radiation monitoring equipment used in connection with any radiation work (e.g., survey meters, direct reading personal dosimeters) must be calibrated once every twelve months by a person approved by the Director-General of Environmental Protection. For this purpose, RPNSD maintains a Secondary Standards Dosimetry Laboratory for radiation protection level dosimetry and is able to carry out calibration of such equipment and devices.

(5) Personal Dose Monitoring

232. Under the Radiation Protection (Ionising Radiation) Regulations, every individual who is working with ionising radiation shall wear a personal monitoring device. Under these Regulations, it is the responsibility of the licensee to provide radiation workers with approved personal monitoring devices and to ensure that these devices are processed at regular intervals. RPNSD provides the service of analysing the radiation dose recorded on the personal monitoring devices.

538. *See* https://www.nea.gov.sg/our-services/radiation-safety/radiation-protection-services.

Chapter 9. The Ozone

233. Ozone-depleting substances (ODS) are controlled as hazardous substances under the Environmental Protection and Management Act (EPMA). The import and export of controlled ODS are regulated under the EPM (ODS) Regulations.

234. Singapore acceded to the Vienna Convention on the Protection of the Ozone Layer (1985) and the Montreal Protocol on Substances that Deplete the Ozone Layer (1989) on 5 January 1989. The Control of Imports and Exports (Montreal Protocol) (Chloroflourocarbons) Order ('CFCs') was passed in 1989, amended in 1991 and consolidated in 1993.[539] A quota allocation system controls the amount of CFCs and halons for use. Since then, various measures have been undertaken to phase out ODS. Since 1 January 1996, the import of all CFCs has been prohibited.

235. Singapore has since acceded to the 1990 London Amendment (in 1993), the 1992 Copenhagen Amendment (in 2000), the 1997 Montreal Amendment (in 2000), and the Beijing Amendment on 10 January 2007. To implement these, the Environmental Protection and Management (EPM) (ODS) Regulations 2000 were passed to take effect as from 1 January 2000.[540] The 1992 Copenhagen Protocol stipulates control measures for three specific ODS, namely hydrochloroflourocarbons (HCFCs), hydrobromoflourocarbons (HBFCs) and methyl bromide (MBr). The 1997 Montreal Amendment prohibits Parties from trading in MBr with non-Parties to the Copenhagen Amendment. As a party to the Amendments, Singapore will phase out the consumption of HCFCs based on the schedule given in the Annex to the Amendment. Singapore has already banned the import of HBFCs since 1996. The phase-out schedule for (MBr) as given in the Annex will also be observed.[541] Local industries were informed of the implications of the Amendments before Singapore's accession. Reminders are sent to traders upon each accession, e.g., following Singapore's accession to the Beijing Amendment, a circular was sent by NEA to all HCFC licence holders that they will not be allowed to export HCFCs to countries that are not party to the Beijing Amendment, and that checks will be in place to ensure this is not violated.[542]

236. Under the Act and its Regulations, a licence is required for the import and export of ODS listed in the Schedules of the EPMA and its Regulations. Licences are valid for three months or one year and the corresponding fees are SGD 135 and SGD 525, respectively. ODS that are prohibited from use in Singapore are the CFCs, Halons and HBFCs. For these ODS, traders are only allowed to import the prohibited ODS if they are meant for re-export. This requirement is imposed as a

539. GN S 141/1993.

540. Rg 9, GN S 604/2000 (2008 Rev. Ed), with effect from 1 Jan. 2001, repealing the Regulation of Imports and Exports (Montreal Protocol) Order, via S 608/00.

541. *See* Press Release No. 175/2000 from ENV 'Singapore Reaffirms Its Commitment Towards Ozone Layer Protection', 20 Dec. 2000. https://www.nas.gov.sg/archivesonline/data/pdfdoc/MSE_200012 20002.pdf.

542. *See* https://www.nea.gov.sg/docs/default-source/our-services/circular-on-export-of-hydrochlorofl uorocarbons-(hcfcs).pdf.

licensing condition and licensees are required to comply with such requirements. Failure to do so may result in the revocation of the company's import and export licence. In addition, licensees are also required to submit electronic monthly returns to the NEA's PCD on the quantity of controlled ODS imported, sold and/or exported. Companies that wish to purchase prohibited ODS from local importers for export shall, prior to export, declare the intended transaction to the PCD using the relevant form.[543] Importers who wish to sell prohibited ODS to another company for export shall declare such transactions in the relevant form.[544]

237. As an Article 5 Party to the Montreal Protocol, Singapore is obliged to implement control measures to freeze the consumption of HCFCs on 1 January 2013, and to completely phase out HCFCs by 1 January 2030.[545] NEA has declared it will adopt a Cap and Allocation Framework for the freeze and phase out of HCFC consumption in Singapore.[546] Consumption of HCFCs is reported to the Montreal Protocol's Secretariat annually. In 2013, national HCFCs consumption was capped at 216 ODP Tonnes (ODPT). The reduction schedule is tagged to the national baseline of 2013. By 2015, the reduction should be 10% (ODPT Cap – 194); by 2020, the reduction should be 35% (140 ODPT), by 2025, 67.5% (70 ODPT); and from 2030 to 2040, 97.5% (5.4 ODPT).

543. Declaration by Licenced Exporter of Controlled Ozone Depleting Substances form., at https://www.nea.gov.sg/docs/default-source/our-services/declaration-by-licenced-exporter-of-controlled-ozone-depleting-substances-(ods)-form-.pdf.

544. Re-Export Debit Authorisation of Controlled Ozone Depleting Substances (ODS) form, found at https://www.nea.gov.sg/docs/default-source/our-services/re-export-debit-authorisation-of-controlled-ozone-depleting-substances-(ods)-form.pdf.

545. https://www.nea.gov.sg/docs/default-source/our-services/common-hcfcs-and-their-ozone-depleting-potential-(odp)-values.pdf.

546. *See* 'Latest circulars and news on ozone depleting substances' at https://www.nea.gov.sg/corporate-functions/resources/legislation-international-law/multilateral-environmental-agreements/chemical-safety/montreal-protocol/ozone-depleting-substances. *See also* 'HCFCs Phase-out Management Plan in Singapore', NEA Dialogue session, Kee Su Yin Scientific Officer, PCD at https://www.nea.gov.sg/docs/default-source/our-services/hydrochlorofluorocarbons-(hcfcs)-phase-out-management-plan-nbsp-in-singapore-nbsp-(presentation-slides).pdf. 8 Oct. 2012.

Chapter 10. Climate Change

§1. Introduction

238. Climate change has emerged as one of the most existential environmental problems of our time. The science that attributes anthropogenic emissions of greenhouse gases as causing adverse changes to our climate is now unequivocal and widely accepted.[547] In February 2021, the Singapore Parliament declared climate change a global emergency, sending a clear signal that the nation was committed to addressing 'one of the most long-term threats we face in the 21st century'.[548] Yet, actions by the Singapore government to address climate change have gone on for decades, and have only grown over the years as the climate crisis continues to intensify.

§2. International and Transnational Efforts

239. Singapore has been an active player in the international climate change negotiations. Singapore signed (1992) and ratified the UN Framework Convention on Climate Change (UNFCCC) (1997), and submitted its Initial Report to the Secretariat in August 2000.[549] On 12 April 2006, Singapore acceded to the Kyoto Protocol. Singapore further ratified the Doha Amendment to the Kyoto Protocol in 2014 and signed the Paris Agreement on 22 April 2016 and ratified it on 21 September 2016. A National Energy Efficiency Committee (NEEC) was set up in 2001 to spearhead programmes to encourage more efficient use of energy by industries, homes, commercial buildings and vehicles. With the announcement of Singapore's accession to the Kyoto Protocol, the NEEC was expanded in scope to cover climate change issues and has been renamed the *National Climate Change Committee (NCCC)* to better reflect its expanded function. NCCC was tasked with (i) promoting greater energy efficiency and less carbon-intensive energy in key sectors, (ii) raising awareness among the people, private and public sectors on the impacts and opportunities arising from climate change, and the actions they can take; (iii) building competency in Singapore to better respond to climate change such as through promoting research and development of low-carbon technologies; and (iv) understanding Singapore's vulnerability to climate change and facilitate the adaptation actions needed. An association was also formed to promote energy efficiency and awareness in construction, manufacturing and service sectors, the Sustainable Energy Association of Singapore (SEAS).[550] An Inter-Ministerial Committee on

547. *See* https://www.ipcc.ch/report/ar6/syr/downloads/report/IPCC_AR6_SYR_FullVolume.pdf.
548. *See* https://www.straitstimes.com/singapore/politics/singapore-parliament-declares-climate-change-a-global-emergency.
549. *Singapore's Initial National Communication Under the United Nations Framework Convention on Climate Change,* August 2000, Ministry of the Environment. *See also* https://www.nccs.gov.sg/media/publications/singapores-national-communications-and-biennial-update-reports (30 Dec. 2020).
550. Sustainable Energy Association of Singapore – *see* http://www.seas.org.sg/.

Climate Change (IMCCC) was established in 2007. The IMCCC enhances 'Whole-of-Government' coordination on climate change policies to ensure that Singapore is prepared for the impacts of climate change. It is presently chaired by Mr Teo Chee Hean, Senior Minister and Coordinating Minister for National Security.[551] NEA actively supports the strategic outcomes of the various IMCCC working groups.

240. In 2009, Singapore announced, just before the UNFCCC Climate Change Conference in Copenhagen, a pledge to reduce its GHG emissions by 16% below Business-as-Usual (BAU) levels in 2020. On the issue of whether emission reduction targets need to be legally binding, the government's position was espoused by Singapore's Chief Negotiator for Climate Change, Ambassador Kwok Foo Seng 'For Singapore, we see the emissions reduction target as a nationally determined commitment that each country communicates formally. Whether this target itself is bound legally or not is not so critical. The meaningful aspect of this agreement is that all parties under this agreement have a legal requirement to submit and maintain a continuing series of such emissions reduction targets over time. Furthermore, each country's achievement of such targets is subject to a measurement, reporting and verification system that is also legally binding. This is ultimately the mechanism that will lead to universal cooperation to lower global emissions.'[552]

241. On 1 July 2010, the National Climate Change Secretariat (NCCS) was set up as a dedicated agency under the Prime Minister's Office, to coordinate Singapore's domestic and international policies, plans and actions on climate change.[553] Singapore's Climate Action Plan was published in 2016 and comprises two complementary publications on Singapore's mitigation and adaptation plans. The first publication, *Take Action Today, for a Carbon-Efficient Singapore*, contains information on how Singapore intends to reduce GHG emissions and increase energy efficiency to meet its 2030 climate pledge. The second publication, *A Climate-Resilient Singapore, for a Sustainable Future*, explains how Singapore may be affected by climate change and its strategy to prepare for it. The plan covered four main areas: (1) improving energy and carbon efficiency, (2) reducing carbon emissions in power generation, (3) developing and deploying low-carbon technology, and (4) encouraging collective climate change.[554] Singapore also submitted its National Communication to the UNFCCC – first on 21 August 2000, then on 12 November 2010 and on 3 July 2015.[555] On 31 March 2020, Singapore submitted its enhanced Nationally Determined Contribution (NDC) and Long-Term Low-Emissions Development Strategy (LEDS) documents to the UNFCCC.[556] In

551. *See* https://www.nccs.gov.sg/who-we-are/inter-ministerial-committee-on-climate-change/.
552. *See* https://www.todayonline.com/commentary/climate-change-negotiations-tiny-spore-called-upon-be-honest-broker (27 Nov. 2015).
553. *See* https://www.nccs.gov.sg/.
554. Download at https://www.nccs.gov.sg/media/publications/climate-plan-take-action-today-for-a-sustainable-future.
555. *See* https://www.nccs.gov.sg/media/press-release/singapore-s-submission-to-the-united-nations-framework-convention-on-climate-change-(unfccc), 3 Jul. 2015.
556. *See* https://www4.unfccc.int/sites/ndcstaging/Pages/Party.aspx?party=SGP&prototype=1.

November 2022, Singapore submitted the second update to that NDC and an addendum to its LEDS. In February 2025, Singapore further submitted a revised 2035 NDC, which included a net-zero-by-2050 target.[557]

242. Singapore has sought to promote international cooperation on climate change.[558] Its efforts include participating in related multilateral efforts, including discussions hosted by the World Trade Organisation (WTO), the World Intellectual Property Organisation (WIPO), the International Maritime Organisation (IMO) and the International Civil Aviation Organisation (ICAO), in support of a comprehensive and holistic approach to deal with climate change. Singapore also actively engages in environmental cooperation through bilateral and regional platforms such as the Asia-Pacific Economic Cooperation (APEC) and the ASEAN. Singapore is also a partner in a number of key regional initiatives, such as the Sino-Singapore Tianjin Eco-city project[559] with China, and collaborates with Indonesia's Jambi Province to improve peatland management and promote sustainable land-use practices.[560] Singapore also provides technical assistance in human resource capacity building in climate-related areas through the Singapore Cooperation Programme (SCP).[561] Under the SCP, Singapore has a Small Island Developing States Technical Cooperation Programme that focuses on the specific needs of small island developing states, including climate-related issues and challenges.[562] As of December 2015, some 10,700 participants from about developing countries have attended SCP training courses on environment and climate change management in Singapore. The wide range of topics and issues relating to climate change and environment includes sustainable urban development, water management, energy efficiency and emissions reduction. Singapore joined the C40 Cities Climate Leadership Group (C40) as an observer city in March 2012. The C40 is a network of ninety-seven member cities (including Berlin, Hong Kong, Jakarta, Johannesburg, Los Angeles, London, New York, Sao Paulo, Seoul and Tokyo) committed to implementing meaningful and sustainable climate-related actions locally that will address global climate change. It collaborates with several international organisations such as the World Bank, the Organisation for Economic Cooperation and Development (OECD), the Clinton Climate Initiative and the World Resources Institute, on initiatives that advance urban action on climate change solutions. Singapore's participation in the C40 allowed it to learn from the best practices of other C40 cities in areas such as building energy efficiency, transportation, climate change resilience and adaptation.

557. *See* https://www.nccs.gov.sg/singapore-submits-2035-nationally-determined-contribution/.
558. *See* https://www.nccs.gov.sg/singapores-climate-action/singapore-and-international-efforts/.
559. http://www.tianjinecocity.gov.sg/–; this new city aims to be a thriving city which is 'socially harmonious, environmentally-friendly and resource-efficient', *see* https://www.mnd.gov.sg/tianjinecocity/progress#beyond.
560. This collaboration has since ended, and the haze continues to be an issue. *See* https://www.channelnewsasia.com/news/asia/fighting-haze-causing-forest-fires-in-indonesia-s-jambi-province-11976620 (7 Oct 2019).
561. *See* https://scp.gov.sg/startpublic/#!/home.
562. https://sustainabledevelopment.un.org/partnership/?p=11344.

Singapore has also contributed to C40 by sharing our experiences in urban development and transport infrastructure. Singapore's efforts in promoting urban sustainability and addressing climate change were also recognised by C40 in 2013 when it was presented with the C40 & Siemens City Climate Leadership Award.

243. Singapore has always emphasised that it is just a tiny island and that it accounts for less than 0.2% of global emissions. However, it acknowledges that it must still play its part in addressing climate change by reducing emissions. Thus, in 2009, Singapore pledged in the context of the UNFCCC negotiations to reduce its GHG by 16% below the BAU scenario in 2020 when a global agreement is achieved. The main contribution to Singapore's GHG emissions is carbon dioxide (CO_2) from the use of energy to meet development and human needs. In 2015, building on its earlier commitment, Singapore pledged to reduce its Emissions Intensity – the amount of GHGs emitted per dollar GDP – by 36% from 2005 levels by 2030, and to stabilise emissions with the aim of peaking around 2030. On 31 March 2020, Singapore's enhanced NDC document updated Singapore's climate pledge submitted in July 2015 under the Paris Agreement to state an absolute emissions target to peak emissions at $65MtCO_2e$ around 2030. Singapore is building on the enhanced NDC's target by aspiring to halve its emissions from their peak to $33MtCO_2e$ by 2050, with a view to achieving net zero emissions as soon as viable in the second half of the century.[563] In 2022, Singapore committed to reduce its 2030 target to around 60 MtCO2e and announced it would raise its national climate target to achieve net zero emissions by 2050. On 10 February 2025, Singapore committed to reduce emissions to between 45 and 50 $MtCO_2e$ in 2035 as part of its 2035 NDC. During the various COPs convened under the UNFCCC in recent years, Singapore has strengthened its commitment to tackle climate change through the following:

- During COP-26 in Glasgow in November 2021, Singapore joined the following initiatives to strengthen its collective global climate action: the Powering Past Coal Alliance and the Global Coal to Clean Power Transition Statement; the Global Methane Pledge; the Greening Government Initiative (GGI); the Agriculture Innovation Mission for Climate (AIM4C); and the Glasgow Leaders' Declaration on Forests and Land Use.
- At COP-27 in Sharm El-Sheikh in November 2022, Singapore joined several global initiatives, including the Forests and Climate Leaders' Partnership (FCLP), the UN Global Early Warnings Initiative (GEWI) and the Green Shipping Challenge. Singapore also signed the Joint Declaration from Energy Importers and Exporters on Reducing Greenhouse Gas Emissions from Fossil Fuels.[564]

563. *See* https://www.nccs.gov.sg/media/press-release/submission-of-singapores-enhanced-nationally-determined-contribution-and-long-term-low-emissions-development-strategy (1 Apr. 2020).
564. *See* https://2021-2025.state.gov/joint-declaration-from-energy-importers-and-exporters-on-reducing-greenhouse-gas-emissions-from-fossil-fuels/.

- During COP-28 in Dubai in November 2023, Singapore signed the Global Renewables and Energy Efficiency Pledge, the Emirates Declaration on Sustainable Agriculture, Resilient Food Systems, and Climate Action, the Global Cooling Pledge, and the Declaration of Intent on Mutual Recognition of Certification Schemes for Hydrogen and Derivatives.
- During COP-29 in Baku in November 2024, Singapore committed up to USD 500 million in concessional funding to support the Financing Asia's Transition Partnership (FAST-P). FAST-P is a blended finance initiative which brings together international public, private and philanthropic partners to support Asia's decarbonisation and climate resilience.

244. Singapore maintains that from the 1980s till 2020, its policies to actively green the nation have led to an increase of over 10% in green cover from 36% to 47% even though its population had increased from about 2.414 million to 5.850 million during this period. Despite being a small city-state, vegetation covers 56% of the total land area of the city-state, with 27% being actively managed, such as parks, gardens, and lawns.[565] This includes its nature reserves as well as an island-wide network of parks, park connectors, street-side and waterfront greenery. Its policies in the past have also contributed significantly to reducing its emissions. For example, in terms of transport, which is a key source of GHG emissions, Singapore has very stringent laws on the ownership and control of motor vehicles, significantly curbing the growth of its vehicle population, and hence reducing air pollution, traffic congestion, as well as GHG emissions. In terms of buildings, Singapore is also actively promoting green buildings.

The Green Mark scheme was introduced in 2005 to encourage more environmentally friendly buildings. At present, all new buildings are required to meet minimum Green Mark standards, and it is intended to improve and expand the coverage of the scheme as needed. It is administered by the Building and Construction Authority (BCA).[566] These are elaborated on below.

I. CDM Projects

245. The Clean Development Mechanism (CDM) of the Kyoto Protocol allows GHG emission reductions from projects implemented in non-Annex I countries, such as Singapore, to be used to offset emissions of Annex I countries, such as Japan and the EU. NEA has been appointed as Singapore's Designated National Authority (DNA) for CDM projects under the Kyoto Protocol.[567] NEA's role is to issue a Letter of Approval (LoA) to CDM projects that meet Singapore's sustainable development criteria. This LoA supports the registration of the project by the UNFCCC CDM Executive Board (EB). In the LoA application to the DNA, the Project Idea

565. *See* A.T.K. Yee, Richard T. Corlett, S.C. Liew and Hugh T.W. Tan 'The Vegetation of Singapore – An Updated Map' (2011) Gardens' Bulletin Singapore 63(1 & 2): 205–212. 2011 .
566. *See* https://www1.bca.gov.sg/buildsg/sustainability/green-mark-certification-scheme. *See also* https://www.nccs.gov.sg/singapores-climate-action/buildings/.
567. *See* 'Clean Development Mechanism' at https://www.nea.gov.sg/programmes-grants/schemes/clean-development-mechanism.

Note (PIN) must be submitted with the Project Design Document (PDD) that will be (or has been) provided to the designated operational entity for validation. The PIN must demonstrate how the project meets Singapore's sustainable development criteria. As of December 2020, Singapore has six registered CDM projects covering projects such as thermal energy recovery, dehydration of sewage sludge, biomass and wood recycling, and biogas plants for treatment of poultry waste.

246. The sustainability criteria for Singapore are as follows:

a. Environmental Sustainability:
   i. Project meets NEA's Environmental Protection requirements, standards and regulations.
   ii. Project produces real and measurable reductions in GHG emissions.
b. Economic Sustainability:
   i. Project utilises more efficient and/or environment-friendly technology than common industrial practice.
c. Social Sustainability:
   i. Project helps to improve quality of life by creating opportunities for jobs, job enhancement, etc.

247. NEA also administers the CDM Documentation Grant, which is a co-funding scheme to encourage companies to develop CDM projects in Singapore.[568]

§3. Carbon Pricing

248. The Carbon Pricing Act 2018 (CPA) and its accompanying Regulations came into operation on 1 January 2019.[569] There are two main categories of obligations under the CPA:

a. Reporting of emissions only for a Reportable Facility.
b. Reporting of emissions and payment of carbon tax for a Taxable Facility.

A Reportable Facility is any industrial facility that emits direct GHG emissions equal to or above 2,000 tCO2e annually. Such a facility would have to register as a reportable facility and submit an annual Emissions Report. A Taxable Facility is any industrial facility that emits direct GHG emissions equal to or above 25,000 tCO2e annually. Such facility would have to register as a taxable facility and submit a Monitoring Plan and Emission Report annually.

568. Details of the grant can be found at https://www.nea.gov.sg/programmes-grants/schemes/clean-development-mechanism.

569. Act 23 of 2018. *See* – Carbon Pricing (Registration and General Matters) Regulations GN S 858/2018; CP (Measurement, Reporting and Verification) Regulations 2018 GN S 857/2018; CP (Composition of Offences) Regulations GN S859/2018); CP (Carbon Tax and Carbon Registry) Regulations GN S 330/2020; CP (Appeals) Regulations GN S 532/2020.

The carbon tax is applicable to all Taxable Facilities for reckonable GHG emissions. The initial carbon tax was set at a rate of SGD 5 per tonne of GHG emissions (tCO2e) from 2019 to 2023, providing a transition period for business to adjust. The carbon tax is slated to be raised as follows:[570]

- SGD 25 per tonne in 2024 and 2025
- SGD 45 per tonne in 2026 and 2027
- between SGD 50 and SGD 80 per tonne by 2030.

The carbon tax revenue collected is used to support decarbonisation efforts, the transition to a green economy, and to cushion the impact on businesses and households.

249. Taxable Facilities are allowed to use high-quality International Carbon Credits (ICC) to offset up to 5% of their taxable emissions. For Voluntary Carbon Credits to qualify as ICCs, they must meet Singapore's Eligibility Criteria, as prescribed in the Carbon Pricing (Carbon Tax and Carbon Credits Registry) (Amendment) Regulations 2023. Next, the underlying project producing the carbon credits needs to be on the Eligibility List, which differs by host countries, as it is bilaterally agreed upon between Singapore and the respective host country. This initiative reflects Singapore's broader ambition to become a leading carbon services and trading hub. The National Climate Change Secretariat has said that Singapore is in a good position to support the development of an internationally trusted carbon services and trading ecosystem in Asia due to its robust legislative framework and position as an established professional services, trading, and financial hub.[571]

§4. Energy Conservation Act (ECA), 2012

250. To help Singapore achieve the target of a 35% improvement in energy intensity by 2030, from 2005 levels, as well as to improve the energy performance of companies and make them more competitive in the global economy, new energy policies had to be instituted.

251. The Energy Conservation Act 2012 (ECA) was passed by Parliament on 9 April 2012[572] and came into effect on 1 July 2012[573] 'to mandate energy efficiency

570. *See* https://www.nea.gov.sg/our-services/climate-change-energy-efficiency/climate-change/carbon-tax.

571. Other initiatives in Singapore include the launch of a digital platform that allows businesses to buy and sell carbon credits by Singapore-based carbon exchange Climate Impact X (CIX) in 2022 and Singapore's National Climate Change Secretariat's (NCCS) collaboration with Gold Standard and Verra's Verified Carbon Standard (VCS) Programme to support countries to better leverage and utilise carbon crediting programs to achieve their Nationally Determined Contributions (NDCs) under the Paris Agreement in 2023.

572. Act 11 of 2012, 2020 Rev Ed.; amended by Act 30/2015, Act 24/2017, Act 23/2018. *See* https://www.nea.gov.sg/our-services/climate-change-energy-efficiency/energy-efficiency/industrial-sector/mandatory-energy-management-practices-for-existing-industrial-facilities.

requirements and energy management practices, to promote energy conservation, improve energy efficiency and reduce environmental impact ...'. It is jointly administered by the Ministry of Sustainability and the Environment (MSE) and the Ministry of Transport (MOT). MSE will oversee industry and household-related measures, while MOT will oversee measures for the transport sector. With effect from 22 April 2013, energy-intensive companies in the industrial and transport sectors are required under the ECA to register with the NEA and to implement mandatory energy management practices. These are large energy users which consume energy at or above the specified threshold (15 GWh or 54 TJ of energy each year. These corporations will need to be registered and will need to appoint an energy manager, monitor and report energy use and GHG emissions, as well as submit an Energy Efficiency Improvement Plan.

252. Part III on energy conservation measures for domestic and industry sectors (other than transport) regulates specific goods by registration, energy labelling, minimum performance standards, energy management practices, penalties and powers of enforcement. Part IV relates to the transport industry. It requires fuel economy labelling for motor vehicles, energy management practices for transport facility operators, and specifies penalties and powers of enforcement.

253. The NEA held consultations with industry from March to June 2012, and gave a briefing in March 2013 to update on the key feedback from consultants, as well as on the final requirements in the subsidiary legislation and key amendments, as well as the initiatives to assist industry to comply with the ECA requirements. The Act was amended in 2014 and later enhanced in 2017. The latest enhancements came into effect from 2018 and included strengthening measurement and reporting requirements for GHGs, requiring companies to undertake regular energy efficiency opportunity assessments and introducing minimum energy performance standards for common industrial equipment and systems. Additionally, GHG reporting will be enhanced as larger industrial facilities are required to submit monitoring plans and enhanced GHG reports for NEA's approval. Companies investing in new industrial facilities and expansions will also be required to review their new facility design for energy efficiency.[574]

254. In March 2017, NEA consolidated all its existing incentive schemes and grants to promote adoption of industrial energy efficiency measures into a single fund known as the Energy Efficiency Fund (E2F).[575] The fund supports efforts of businesses with industrial facilities to improve energy efficiency. Components of the grant include:

– Resource Efficient Design of New Facilities or Major Expansions.
– Energy Assessment of Existing Facilities.

---

573. ECA (Commencement No. 1) Regulations GN S. 305/2012, ECA (Commencement No. 2) Regulations GN S. 306/2012; GN S 771/2021 (Amendment of Schedule) Order.
574. *See* https://www.nea.gov.sg/media/news/news/index/enhancements-to-the-energy-conservation-act.
575. *See* https://www.nea.gov.sg/programmes-grants/grants-and-awards/energy-efficiency-fund.

– Adoption of Energy-efficient Technologies.
– Implementation of Energy Management Information System.
– Adoption of Water-cooled Chillers using Low-GWP Refrigerants.

§5. Energy and Resource Efficiency

255. Since 2000, Singapore has significantly reduced its emissions by switching from fuel oil to natural gas, which is a much cleaner fossil fuel for power generation.[576] Natural gas made up around 95% of Singapore's fuel generation mix in 2023, compared to around 18% in 2000.[577] In line with Singapore's 2009 Copenhagen pledge, Singapore is currently working to reduce emissions by 16% below 2020 Business As Usual (BAU) levels.[578] So, in April 2009, the Inter-Ministerial Committee on Sustainable Development launched the Sustainable Singapore Blueprint (SSB) following extensive private, people and public consultation. The SSB details the measures that Singapore intends to take to achieve this goal. In 2015, building on its earlier commitment, Singapore pledged to reduce its Emissions Intensity by 36% from 2005 levels by 2030, and to stabilise emissions with the aim of peaking around 2030.

256. A key pillar of the strategy to mitigate GHG emissions is to improve energy efficiency across different sectors of its economy. This is because Singapore's small size, geographical location, and other physical characteristics pose considerable difficulties in switching easily to clean, renewable alternative energy sources such as wind, hydro, and geothermal. Given its location in the tropics, solar has some potential, but the current state of technology is not adequate for solar to meet its needs on a sufficient scale. Singapore's leaders have emphasised that as an open economy without natural resources, Singapore will need to achieve energy efficiency in a manner that addresses its international competitiveness and cost of living considerations, i.e., it must be cost-effective. Thus, the Government has identified the following areas as part of a comprehensive energy efficiency strategy for Singapore:[579]

1. Promoting adoption of energy-efficient measures and technologies by addressing market barriers to energy efficiency.
2. Building capability to sustain and drive energy efficiency efforts and to develop the local knowledge base and expertise in energy management.
3. Raising awareness to reach out to the public and businesses so as to stimulate energy-efficient behaviour and practices.

---

576. By increasing the share of natural gas used in electricity generation, from only 19% in 2000 to about 96% today, Singapore has substantially reduced its emissions growth over the last ten years.
577. *See* https://www.ema.gov.sg/Vision_Mission_Values.aspx, and https://www.ema.gov.sg/singapore-energy-statistics/Ch02/index2.
578. *See* https://www.nea.gov.sg/our-services/climate-change-energy-efficiency/climate-change/singapore's-efforts-in-addressing-climate-change.
579. *See* https://www.nccs.gov.sg/docs/default-source/default-document-library/singapore's-fourth-national-communication-and-third-biennial-update-repo.pdf.

4. Supporting research and development to enhance Singapore's capability in energy-efficient technologies.

As part of its energy transition and other initiatives under the Singapore Green Plan 2030, Singapore aims to tap into low-carbon energy sources across its economy. To further decarbonise the power sector, Singapore will harness and tap on four switches to transform its energy supply: solar, regional power grids, emerging low-carbon alternatives (such as ammonia and advanced geothermal systems), and natural gas.[580] The Energy Market Authority's latest emissions standards require new fossil fuel generation units to be at least 30% hydrogen-ready by volume, with the ability to be retrofitted to become 100% hydrogen-ready in future. This will enable Singapore to further reduce its power sector emissions when hydrogen becomes more commercially viable. While Singapore has not made a decision whether to deploy nuclear energy, it has been building its capabilities in nuclear science and technology to better understand it.

257. The *Energy-Efficient Programme Office (E2PO)* was established to drive energy efficiency improvements in the various sectors of the economy.[581] The E2PO is a multi-agency committee co-led by the National Environment Agency (NEA) and the Energy Market Authority (EMA). The Government has implemented various policies and measures across different sectors to improve energy efficiency and reduce GHG emissions.

I. Power Generation

258. The power sector is a major source of emissions and contributes to about 40% of total emissions. The decision to liberalise the electricity market in 2000 has driven Singapore's overall power generation efficiency to about 48% as of 2023, with total energy input at 10,275 ktoe and total gross energy generated correspondingly at 4,934 ktoe.[582] This was brought about by the change in power generation fuel mix from fuel oil to natural gas, a cleaner form of fossil fuel for power generation. Since 2000, the percentage of natural gas used in electricity generation has increased from 19% to 95%.[583] Singapore has diversified its supply of natural gas with the development of a liquefied natural gas (LNG) terminal on Jurong Island.[584] Operations commenced on 7 May 2013. Plans to develop a second LNG terminal were announced on 23 October 2024, which is expected to be operational by 2030. Together with the existing terminal on Jurong Island, the second LNG terminal is expected to increase Singapore's combined LNG regasification capacity from 10

580. https://www.nccs.gov.sg/singapores-climate-action/power-generation/.
581. *See E2 Singapore* at https://www.e2singapore.gov.sg/who-we-are/about-us. *See also* https://www.nea.gov.sg/our-services/climate-change-energy-efficiency/energy-efficiency/energy-efficient-singapore.
582. *See* https://www.ema.gov.sg/singapore-energy-statistics/Ch02/index2.
583. *See* https://www.nccs.gov.sg/singapores-climate-action/power-generation/.
584. https://www.ema.gov.sg/Gas_Terminal_Development.aspx.

million tonnes to 15 million tonnes on a yearly basis.[585] This will supply more gas for meeting Singapore's electricity demand and enable us to diversify its natural gas sources for energy security. There are other non-fossil fuel sources of energy in Singapore. Waste-to-incineration plants contribute to about 3% of our generation capacity. The number of solar installations in Singapore has also grown steadily from virtually none in 2008 to 210 MWp in 2018, and 1,348 MWp in June 2024.[586] It is now on track to meet its target of 2 GWp by 2030, with solar eventually allowing Singapore to meet 10% of its projected electricity demand in 2050.[587] As of March 2021, Combined Cycle Gas Turbine Co-Generation and Tri-Generation plants collectively accounted for 80% of the total generation capacity in Singapore. Steam Turbines, Solar PVs, Waste-to-Energy and Open Cycle Gas Turbines contributed to the remaining share of 6%, 7%, 3% and 1% respectively.[588]

259. Energy Reset Targets under the 2030 Green Plan are as follows:[589]

- Increase solar energy five-fold, to at least 2 GWp, which can meet around 3% of the projected 2030 energy demand, and generate enough electricity to power more than 350,000 households a year (1.5 GWp by 2025, to meet around 2% of the projected 2025 energy demand, enough to power 260,000 households a year).
- 200 MW of energy storage systems deployment beyond 2025, which can power more than 16,000 households a day.
- Best-in-class generation technology that meets heat-rate/emissions standards and reduces carbon emissions.
- Diversified electricity support with clean electricity imports.

II. Industry

260. There are various schemes in place to help businesses reduce their carbon footprint, lower operational costs, and increase business competitiveness. These schemes include the Energy Efficiency Grant (EEG), which co-funds investment in energy-efficient equipment,[590] the Resource Efficiency Grant for Emissions (REG(E) which encourages manufacturing companies and data centres to invest in

585. *See* https://www.ema.gov.sg/cmsmedia/Newsletter/2014/04/spotlight-on/singapores-first-lng-terminal-launched.html. *See also* https://www.seatrade-maritime.com/asia/singapore-plans-build-second-lng-terminal; https://www.straitstimes.com/business/development-of-s-pore-s-second-lng-terminal-to-begin.
586. *See* https://www.ema.gov.sg/resources/singapore-energy-statistics/chapter6.
587. https://www.ema.gov.sg/our-energy-story/energy-supply/solar#:~:text=Located%20near%20the%20equator%2C%20Singapore,costs%20or%20even%20earn%20revenue.
588. https://www.ema.gov.sg/singapore-energy-statistics/Ch02/index2.
589. https://www.greenplan.gov.sg/.
590. https://www.nea.gov.sg/programmes-grants/grants-and-awards/energy-efficiency-grant.

projects that improve energy efficiency,[591] and the Investment Allowance for Emissions Reduction,[592] which is granted on capital expenditure incurred for energy-efficient or green data centre projects. The government also supports local enterprises, particularly Small and Medium Enterprises (SMEs), in building long-term capabilities in sustainability and capturing green growth opportunities through the Enterprise Sustainability Programme.[593]

261. Additionally, there are other initiatives to improve industrial energy efficiency, which include the Energy Services Company (ESCO) Accreditation Scheme and Singapore Certified Energy Manager (SCEM) Programme to help grow technical and professional capabilities in Singapore, and the Energy Efficiency National Partnership (EENP), which comprises industry players to encourage industries to share best practices on energy efficiency.[594]

III. Transport

262. Singaporeans are also encouraged to use public transport, which is the most efficient and sustainable form of motorised transport. Singapore targets to achieve a public transport modal shift of 75% in the morning peak period by 2030, up from 67% in 2019.[595] To achieve this, the Government is making significant improvements to the public transport system – new lines and extensions and the rail network will be increased to 360 km in 2030 from 260 km in 2024. The network is projected to have eight in ten households within a ten-minute walk of a train station by 2030. This will enhance the coverage and connectivity of the rail network. Capacity on existing lines will also be enhanced.[596] Other measures include the Mandatory Fuel Economy Labelling Scheme[597] for new passenger cars and light goods vehicles to provide buyers with fuel economy information. In 2018, the Fuel Economy Labels for cars were replaced. In its place, the NEA and the Land Transport Authority (LTA) introduced the new Vehicular Emissions Label, which displays the emissions bands of five pollutants, resultant Vehicular Emissions Scheme

591. https://www.edb.gov.sg/en/incentives-and-programmes/incentives-and-facilitation-programmes.html.
592. https://www.edb.gov.sg/en/our-industries/sustainability.html.
593. https://www.enterprisesg.gov.sg/grow-your-business/boost-capabilities/sustainability/enterprise-sustainability-programme.
594. *See* https://www.nea.gov.sg/our-services/climate-change-energy-efficiency/energy-efficiency/industrial-sector/energy-efficiency-national-partnership.
595. *See* https://www.mot.gov.sg/about-mot/land-transport/public-transport.
596. For information on initiatives on transport measures, *see* https://www.mot.gov.sg/About-MOT/Land-Transport/Public-Transport/Trains/.
597. Since 1 Jan. 2008, registrable goods must carry energy labels under the Environmental Protection and Management Act, (EPMA) 1999. From 1 Apr. 2009, passenger cars and light goods vehicles that are sold in Singapore must be affixed with the Fuel Economy Label under the mandatory Fuel Economy Labelling Scheme (FELS). The scheme has been administered by the NEA. From 1 Jul. 2012, the Land Transport Authority (LTA) has taken over the administration of FELS under the Energy Conservation Act, 2012. *See* Energy Conservation (Fuel Economy and Vehicular Emissions Labelling) Regulations 2012 (GN S307/2012), amended S 775/2017, S 428/2018, S 878/2018, S 649/2020, S 212/2021.

rebate or surcharge and the fuel economy of the car. The new label will have to be affixed on showroom cars displayed for sale with effect from 1 January 2018.[598] Additionally, to support the transition and adoption of electric vehicles, there are policies to reduce the cost of buying and owning an electric vehicle. This includes the EV Early Adoption Incentive (EEAI), Enhanced Vehicular Emissions Scheme (VES),[599] Additional Registration Fee (ARF) floor reduction and revision of road tax framework for electric cars.

IV. Buildings

263. The BCA's Green Mark Scheme encourages developers and owners to build and maintain greener buildings. This initiative promotes sustainability in the built environment and raises environmental awareness among developers, designers and builders. New buildings and existing buildings undergoing major retrofitting are also required to meet minimum requirements on environmental sustainability equivalent to Green Mark standards. Key criteria include: climate-responsive design, building energy performance, resource stewardship, smart and healthy building and advance green efforts.[600] Depending on the level of building performance and Green Mark Score, the building development will be certified as one of the following four ratings: BCA Green Mark Certified, Gold, GoldPlus or Platinum.[601] Singapore's first eco-precinct, Treelodge@Punggol, was completed in December 2010. It is the first public housing project to be awarded the Green Mark Platinum Award and to incorporate green technologies and innovations such as centralised recyclable refuse chutes, rainwater harvesting system, green roofs, LED lighting and elevator energy regenerative systems.[602] The 2030 Green Plan pushes for the adoption of super-low-energy buildings and seeks to green 80% of Singapore's buildings by Gross Floor Area (GFA) by 2030.

264. Efforts are also made to make public housing estates more resource-efficient. As part of the HDB's island-wide test-bed of solar technology in public housing precincts, the SolarNova Programme was launched in 2014 to accelerate deployment of solar photovoltaic (PV) systems to supply electricity to common areas and lifts. Today, the SolarNova programme is a Whole-of-Government effort led by the EDB and HDB. Having achieved its earlier solar target of 220 MWp by

598. *See* https://www.lta.gov.sg/content/ltagov/en/newsroom/2017/12/2/joint-media-release-by-the-land-transport-authority-lta-nea---new-vehicular-emissions-label-from-1-january-2018.html.
599. https://onemotoring.lta.gov.sg/content/onemotoring/home/buying/upfront-vehicle-costs/emissions-charges.html#EnhancedVES_At_a_glance.
600. *See* https://www1.bca.gov.sg/buildsg/sustainability/green-mark-certification-scheme.
601. *See* https://www1.bca.gov.sg/docs/default-source/docs-corp-buildsg/sustainability/gm_certification_std.pdf.
602. *See* https://www.nccs.gov.sg/singapores-climate-action/test-bedding/; Lye Lin Heng 'Public Housing in Singapore: A Success Story in Sustainable Development' in *The Impact of Environmental Law – Stories of the World We Want,* Eisma-Osorio, R-L., Kirk, E., and Albin, J. (eds) The IUCN Academy of Environmental Law Series, Edward Elgar Publishing.

2020, HDB announced a new solar target of 540 MWp by 2030.[603] In addition, the 2030 Green Plan targets for sustainable towns and districts include the reduction of energy consumption in existing HDB towns by 15%. It also plans for new and greener HDB town concepts, e.g., Tengah will have the first car-free HDB town centre. Roads are planned to run beneath the town centre, freeing up space at the ground level for retail and recreational use. The first batch of flats in Tengah was launched for sale in August 2020.

V. Households

265. The bulk of energy consumption for the households sector is used for air-conditioners and refrigerators, followed by appliances such as consumer electronics (e.g., TVs, DVD players, computers), lighting and water heating. The Mandatory Energy Labelling Scheme (MELS)[604] keeps consumers informed of the energy efficiency of an appliance, helping them choose a more energy-efficient model. From January 2008, all household air-conditioners and refrigerators, which together account for about 50% of the average household electricity bill, sold in Singapore are required to carry an energy label. The scheme was extended to household clothes dryers from April 2009. In 2014, the NEA enhanced its MELS by recalibrating the energy rating scheme. Under the new system, the most efficient models are awarded five ticks, while one-tick products are the lowest efficiency band. The energy label design was also updated to boost readability. Further, Singapore implemented a Minimum Energy Performance Standard (MEPS) for household air-conditioners and refrigerators in 2011 to raise the average energy efficiency of regulated goods in the market.[605] In 2014, MEPS was extended to include more appliances – namely, clothes dryers and general lighting. The NEA is looking into progressively tightening MEPS levels and extending MEPS to other appliances so as to further encourage suppliers to continually bring in even more energy-efficient household appliances.[606]

266. In March 2020, mitigation measures were announced to reduce Singapore's GHG emissions arising from the use of hydrofluorocarbons (HFCs) in the refrigeration and air-conditioning (RAC) sector.[607] Hydrofluorocarbons (HFCs) are chemicals commonly used as refrigerants in refrigeration and air-conditioning

603. *See* https://www.hdb.gov.sg/about-us/news-and-publications/press-releases/06042023-HDB-Launches-Largest-Solar-Leasing-Tender-Under-SolarNova-Programme.
604. *See* https://www.nea.gov.sg/our-services/climate-change-energy-efficiency/energy-efficiency/household-sector/about-mandatory-energy-labelling-and-minimum-energy-performance-standards.
605. *Ibid.*
606. *See* https://www.todayonline.com/singapore/energy-labels-be-revised-sept-1?singlepage=true (11 Mar. 2014). *See also* https://www.nea.gov.sg/our-services/climate-change-energy-efficiency/energy-efficiency/household-sector/minimum-energy-performance-standards. See paras 88, 265–267 *supra*.
607. https://www.nea.gov.sg/media/news/news/index/nea-introduces-measures-to-reduce-greenhouse-gas-emissions-from-refrigeration-air-conditioning.

(RAC) equipment. HFCs were adopted to replace previous refrigerants such as chlorofluorocarbons (CFCs), which were phased out for contributing to ozone depletion and global warming. While not as harmful as CFCs, HFCs are still highly potent greenhouse gases (often far higher than carbon dioxide) that contribute significantly to global warming.[608] To reduce greenhouse gas (GHG) emissions from the use of HFC refrigerants, NEA introduced a raft of mitigation measures. First, a climate-friendly label was introduced for household refrigerators and air-conditioners that use refrigerants with a lower global warming potential (GWP). This is a voluntary initiative to enable consumers to identify and select air-conditioner and refrigerator models that use climate-friendly refrigerants.

NEA will also be progressively phasing out RAC equipment that uses high-GWP refrigerants. A number of electric appliances are regulated; suppliers must register themselves and their regulated goods before supplying the regulated goods in Singapore.[609] Since 2022, certain RAC equipment using high-GWP refrigerants cannot be supplied in Singapore: water-cooled chillers and household air-conditioners and refrigerators must use refrigerants with GWP below specified limits.[610]

267. NEA is working with the Institute of Technical Education (ITE) and Temasek Polytechnic to introduce training courses for household air-conditioner technicians and chiller technicians to ensure that they will be able to effectively handle these refrigerants. From 2022 onwards, companies that carry out the installation, maintenance or decommissioning of chillers will be required to employ at least one certified chiller technician. From July 2021, the Resource Sustainability Act 2019 will mandate the recovery and reclamation or destruction of spent refrigerants in decommissioned RAC equipment. E-waste recyclers, who take in household air-conditioners and refrigerators for recycling, and certified chiller technicians will be required to recover refrigerants from decommissioned RAC equipment. Refrigerant treatment facilities and e-waste recyclers that handle the reclamation and destruction of spent refrigerants will have to obtain a Toxic Industrial Waste Collector (TIWC) licence from NEA. Recovered refrigerants that are passed to the licensed refrigerant treatment facilities can be either reclaimed and reintroduced into the market to service RAC equipment or destroyed using established destruction technologies to ensure environmentally sound management of the spent refrigerants. These HFC mitigation measures would help reduce Singapore's HFC consumption and contribute towards meeting Singapore's 2030 pledge under the Paris Agreement.

608. https://www.nea.gov.sg/our-services/climate-change-energy-efficiency/climate-change/reducing-ghg-emissions-from-the-use-of-refrigerants-in-rac-sector.
609. EPMA ss 40B–40D; EPM (Regulated Goods and Registered Suppliers) Regulations 2022.
610. EPM (Regulated Goods and Registered Suppliers) Regulations 2022 First Schedule.

§6. Environmental Technology and Research

268. The NEA's Environment Technology and Industry Development Division (ETIDD) oversees NEA's overall research and development plans and project portfolio, which entails operations-technology visioning, technology master planning, project pipelining and providing oversight of fund allocation. ETIDD is also responsible for providing oversight of NEA's plans and projects for leveraging science and technology across NEA, so as to achieve operations-technology integration and enhance NEA's operational effectiveness.[611]

269. Some research funds and opportunities administered by NEA pertaining to technology and research are:

– Environmental Robotics Programme (ERP).

270. NEA Innovation Calls under the National Innovation Challenges.
The ERP is an R&D funding initiative that was launched alongside the Environmental Services Industry Transformation Map (ES-ITM) in December 2017. As part of NEA's strategy to leverage robotics technology to transform Singapore's environmental services sector, the ERP was developed. The funding initiative aims to: (a) enable productivity gains, (b) enable sustainable manpower stream, and (c) enhance current capabilities and enable new ones – all through the research about and use of robotic technology, particularly for NEA's work areas of cleaning public spaces, waste management, inspection, monitoring and sampling for pest and pollution control.[612]
The National Innovation Challenges are periodic open innovation calls to academia and industry to work together with government agencies to develop practical, impactful solutions to large and complex problems facing Singapore. By bringing together industry partners, government agencies, and innovators to work on the identified challenges, these calls seek to harness Singapore's formidable research and innovation capabilities to develop innovative technological solutions to sustain our long-term growth and resilience. Past challenges include calls such as: Innovation Call for Pollution Monitoring Solutions.[613]

271. Additionally, NEA has established a regulatory sandbox under the Environmental Services Industry Transformation Map to create an environment for experimentation, to promote innovation in Singapore's environmental services industry.[614] It allows interested parties to apply to experiment with innovative environmental services-related technologies and solutions in a controlled environment, before allowing the regulator to assess the impact of these new technologies to

611. *See* https://www.nea.gov.sg/corporate-functions/who-we-are/groups-and-divisions/policy-corporate-and-technology-groups-and-divisions.
612. *See* https://www.nea.gov.sg/programmes-grants/grants-and-awards/environmental-robotics-programme.
613. *See* https://www.nea.gov.sg/programmes-grants/grants-and-awards/nea-innovation-calls.
614. *See* https://www.nea.gov.sg/industry-transformation-map/intensify-innovation-and-technology-adoption/regulatory-sandbox.

determine the appropriate regulatory adjustments. NEA also runs the Innovating and Curating Better Automation and Technologies for Environmental Services (INCUBATE) Programme, where NEA partners with technology and service providers as well as premises owners to address challenges in environmental services by conducting trials of technologies and innovations.[615]

272. In 2021, under the Low-Carbon Energy Research Funding Initiative (LCER FI), the Singapore Government awarded SGD 55 million to support twelve research, development and demonstration projects on low-carbon energy technology solutions such as hydrogen, and carbon capture, utilisation and storage.[616]

615. *See* https://www.nea.gov.sg/industry-transformation-map/intensify-innovation-and-technology-adoption/incubate.

616. *See* https://www.ema.gov.sg/news-events/news/media-releases/2021/12-projects-awarded-55-million-to-accelerate-decarbonisation-in-singapore.

Chapter 11. The Marine Environment

§1. Introduction and MARPOL

273. Singapore is one of the world's busiest ports in terms of shipping tonnage. The Straits of Singapore and the Straits of Malacca are extremely busy waterways, rendering Singapore very vulnerable to pollution from discharges from ships as well as pollution resulting from collisions at sea, particularly involving bulk carriers. Pollution of the seas can be caused by vessels as well as by land-based activities. Pollution from land-based activities is regulated by the NEA and the Public Utilities Board (PUB) under the laws just considered, which prevent dumping of raw sewage and untreated trade effluent into open drains and seas. Pollution of marine waters is the province of the Marine and Port Authority of Singapore (MPA), established under the Maritime and Port Authority of Singapore Act (Cap. 170A). Singapore is party to the International Convention for the Prevention of Pollution from Ships (MARPOL 73/78),[617] as well as to the UN Convention on the Law of the Sea (UNCLOS).[618] UNCLOS calls on states to adopt laws and regulations to prevent pollution from land-based sources (Article 207).

274. The Prevention of Pollution of the Sea Act, 1990 (PPSA),[619] was passed to implement MARPOL and prescribes measures to prevent pollution of Singapore waters, from both land-based sources and apparatus, as well as from dumping from ships. The Act also gives the MPA power to take preventive measures to prevent pollution, including denying entry or detaining ships. Regulations have been passed[620] relating to Oil,[621] Oil Pollution Preparedness, Response and Cooperation,[622] Hazardous and Noxious Substances Pollution Preparedness, Response and Cooperation,[623] Noxious Liquid Substances in Bulk,[624] Reporting of Pollution

---

617. International Convention for the Prevention of Pollution from Ships, 1973, as modified by the Protocol of 1978 relating thereto (MARPOL 73/78).
618. *See* Alan Khee-Jin Tan, Vessel Source Marine Pollution – The Law and Politics of International Regulation (Cambridge University Press, 2006).
619. Act 18 of 1990, 2020 Rev. Ed.; amended by Act 7/1996, Act 8/1999, Act 26/2017.
620. There are eight subsidiary laws, *see* full list of subsidiary legislation at https://www.mpa.gov.sg/web/portal/home/port-of-singapore/maritime-legislation-of-singapore/prevention-of-pollution-of%20the-sea-act.
621. PPS (Oil) Regulations, 2006 (GN S 685/06); amended by GN S 393/2007, GN S 792/2010, GN S 867/2014, GN S 800/2015, GN S 666/2016, GN 805/2020.
622. PPS (Oil Pollution Preparedness, Response and Cooperation) Regulations, GN S 271/99, RG. 5; amended by S 479/2016.
623. PPS (Hazardous and Noxious Substances Pollution Preparedness, Response and Cooperation) 2004, GN S 120/2004 ; amended by GN S689/2006 and GN S 478/2016.
624. PPS (Noxious Liquid Substances in Bulk) Regulations, 2006 (GN S 686/2006), with effect from 1 Jan. 2007; amended by S 470/2013, GN S 868/2014, GN S 667/2016,GN S 1021/2020.

Incidents,[625] Reception Facilities and Garbage Facilities,[626] Composition of Offences,[627] Air,[628] Sewage[629] and Harmful Anti-Fouling Agents,[630] Garbage[631] and Ballast Water Management.[632]

The Act is administered by the MPA. There are also laws relating to dangerous goods, petroleum and explosives that are carried into Singapore waters.[633]

275. Under the PPS (Oil Pollution Preparedness, Response and Cooperation) Regulations, every oil tanker of 150 gross tonnage and above, and any other ship of 400 gross tonnage and above, must be surveyed and issued with an International Oil Pollution Prevention Certificate. There are detailed provisions relating to the control of operational pollution. Every owner of bulk handling facilities is required to keep 10,000 litres of readily usable dispersants and every tug boat owner must keep 400 litres of such dispersants. They are also required to keep minimum items of equipment as specified in the Second and Third Schedules to ensure their readiness for emergencies. In the event of an incident, they must render such assistance and service as is required by the MPA, but may be reimbursed for costs.

276. Through the years, an efficient emergency response plan has been instituted to deal with such incidents. The concerted actions of the NEA, PUB, the MPA and the Singapore Civil Defence Force (SCDF) ensure that oil and other spills are dealt with quickly to limit and contain the environmental pollution that arises.[634] One of the latest and most major oil spills affecting Singapore was in 2024, when a dredging boat hit a stationary cargo tanker at Pasir Panjang Terminal, causing 400

625. PPS (Reporting of Pollution Incidents) Regulations, GN S 60/1991, RG. 3, amended by GN S 71/1991 and GN S 391/1997.
626. PPS (Reception Facilities and Garbage Facilities) Regulations, GN S. 61/1991 (RG. 4), amended by GN S72/1991, GN S/364/1999, GN S 687/2006, GN S 502/2017.
627. PPS (Composition of Offences) Regulations, GN S 63/1991, (RG. 6), amended by S 63/1991, S 73/1991, S 272/1999, S 365/1999.
628. PPS (Air) Regulations, 2005 (GN S134/2005), amended S 620/2006, S 331/2010, S 398/2011, S 21/2012, S 467/2013, S 376/2015, S 78/2016, S 492/2017, S 113/2018, S 904/2018, S 563/2019, S 117/2022, S 209/2022.
629. PPS (Sewage) Regulations, 2005 (GN S 135/2005) amended by GN S 394/2007, GN S 467/2008, GN S 662/2012, GN S 468/2013, GN S 801/2015, GN S 665/2016, GN S 493/2017.
630. PPS (Harmful Anti-Fouling) Regulations, 2010, GN S 198/2010.
631. PPS (Garbage) Regulations 2012, GN S 663/2012, amended by GN S 471/2013, GN S668/2016, GN S 114/2018, GN S 807/2020.
632. GN S 504 of 2017, amended by S 685/2019.
633. Maritime and Port Authority of Singapore (Dangerous Goods, Petroleum and Explosives) Regulations, GN S 24/2005.
634. The worst oil spill in Singapore waters occurred on 15 Oct. 1997. A collision between two oil tankers, the 'Evoikos' and the 'Orapin Global' in the Singapore Straits resulted in the spillage of 28,500 tonnes of heavy marine fuel oil only 2 km from Singapore's southern shores. The concerted action of '16 ministries/agencies, oil terminals, salvage companies, oil spill response companies and one foreign agency, led by MPA, and some 80 craft and 650 personnel, implementing the Marine Emergency Action Procedure (MEAP)' resulted in a successful clean-up within three weeks. *See* Capt. Mark Heah Eng Siang, MPA 'Prevention and Combat of Oil Pollution in Singapore and the 'Evoikos' Oil Spill Incident on 15 October 1997' presented at PAJ Oil Spill Symposium 1998, Tokyo, Japan at http://www.pcs.gr.jp/doc/esymposium/12172/98_mark-heau-e.pdf. *See also* the response of Semco at http://www.pcs.gr.jp/doc/esymposium/12172/98_chris-richard-e.pdf.

tonnes of low-sulphur fuel oil in the cargo tanker to flow into the sea. This resulted in the Southern coastline turning black, affecting the water quality at Labrador Nature Reserve, Sentosa, East Coast Park, the Southern Islands and Changi.[635]

277. The oil companies also have their emergency response plans, as does Jurong Island. The MPA has held biennial Joint Oil Spill Exercise (JOSE) since 1998, to test inter-agency and industry coordination and response to oil spills. On 11 October 2024, the 16th JOSE was held, and a 'spill' exercise was conducted with more than 100 officials from 18 government agencies and companies taking part.[636] In this exercise, many new technologies were explored, such as the hyperspectral cameras, which have the potential to detect oil slicks below the water surface, laser cleaning machine that uses intense light beams to break down and vaporise oil stains, and an oil recovery robot that can separate oil from water in shallow waters.[637] MPA also strengthens oil spill response and coordination with its neighbouring countries. On 11 Feb 2025, MPA conducted a table-top exercise (TTX) with Indonesia and Malaysia to improve coordination procedures between the littoral States during an oil spill incident, ensure rapid deployment of oil spill response assets by the littoral States, and facilitate collaboration between government agencies and oil spill response companies to optimise oil spill response resources.[638]

§2. Bulk Oil Tankers

278. Pollution by bulk oil tankers is governed by the Merchant Shipping (Civil Liability and Compensation for Oil Pollution) Act, 2008.[639] It provides for civil liability for oil pollution by merchant ships and gives effect to the International Convention on Civil Liability for Oil Pollution Damage 1992, and the International Convention for the Establishment of an International Fund for Compensation for Oil Pollution Damage, 1992. Section 3 imposes liability on the ship owner where any oil is discharged or escapes from a ship and causes damage by contamination outside the ship in the territory of Singapore. The ship owner is also liable for the cost of any measures reasonably taken after the discharge or escape for the purpose of preventing or reducing any damage so caused in the territory of Singapore. However, such liability may be limited under section 6 and the ship owner may apply to the court for a determination of the limitation of that liability (section 7). The Act requires all ships carrying a cargo of more than 1,000 tons of oil to be compulsorily insured to satisfy the requirements of Article VII of the Liability Convention before they are allowed to enter Singapore waters. The MPA is empowered to arrest and

---

635. *See* https://www.straitstimes.com/multimedia/graphics/2024/06/oil-spill-singapore-clean-up/index.html (June 2024).
636. *See* https://www.mpa.gov.sg/media-centre/details/biennial-oil-spill-exercise-tests-operating-procedures-and-new-oil-spill-response-technologies.
637. *See* https://www.straitstimes.com/singapore/transport/mpa-holds-routine-joint-oil-spill-exercise-about-four-months-after-pasir-panjang-incident.
638. *See* https://www.mpa.gov.sg/media-centre/details/singapore-strengthens-oil-spill-response-and-coordination-with-indonesia-and-malaysia-in-table-top-exercise.
639. Act 24 of 2008, 2020 Rev. Ed., amended by Act 40/ 2019 and Act 25/2021.

detain the ship as well as any person who is believed to have committed an offence under the Act. Where any fine imposed has not been paid, the Court may direct a distress sale of the ship.

279. A Code of Practice for Bunkering for Bunker Barges/Tankers – Singapore Bunkering Procedure (CP 60/1996) was implemented in June 1997, as a Singapore National Standard Code, administered by the Standards, Productivity and Innovations Board (SPRING Singapore). This was replaced by the 2004 version (CP 60/2004). The latest edition is the 2022 edition, Singapore Standard (SS 600/ 2022).[640]

§3. Tanker Cleaning and the Disposal of Sludge and Slop Oil

280. Since 4 April 1993, Singapore has implemented a system to tighten control on tanker cleaning activities and the disposal of sludge and slop oil generated from tanker cleaning activities. The MPA will only issue permits to registered tanker cleaning contractors. These contractors must be registered with the NEA to carry out tanker cleaning activities in designated areas. To qualify for registration with the NEA, tanker cleaning contractors must undertake to dispose of all tanker sludge and slop oil at approved facilities.[641] Proper reception facilities have been established.[642]

§4. Offences

281. The following are the main offences for marine pollution under the PPSA:

- Throwing any pollutants into Singapore waters – persons who do so are liable to a fine of up to SGD 20,000 or imprisonment up to six months, or both.[643]
- Discharging of any refuse, garbage, wastes, effluents, plastics and dangerous effluents from a ship onto Singapore waters. The master, owner and ship's agent shall each be guilty of the offence, which carries a maximum fine of SGD 20,000 or imprisonment of up to six months, or both.[644]

640. *See* https://www.singaporestandardseshop.sg/Product/SSPdtDetail/d22e4e2e-c4a9-449f-b894-0a20 3c0e37a4.

641. https://www.mpa.gov.sg/web/portal/home/port-of-singapore/circulars-and-notices/port-marine-cir culars/detail/pc08-16 – Port Marine Circular on Procedures to Control Tank Cleaning and Disposal of Sludge and Slop.

642. *See* PPS (Reception Facilitiesand Garbage Facilities) Regulations, GN S. 61/1991 (Reg. 4).

643. Section 5, PPSA (2017 Rev Ed). *See Jupiter Shipping Pte Ltd v. Public Prosecutor* [1993] 2 SLR 69 – ship receiving bunker oil, sudden overflow resulted in oil slick covering 1,500m; CA Held that a fine of SGD 10,000 was not manifestly excessive. *See also Ventura Navigation Inc v. Port of Singapore Authority and Another* [1989] SLR 626 – grounding of ship (not an oil tanker) ruptured its tanks and spilled oil onto Singapore's waters. Plaintiffs (PSA) sought to recover damages for the clean-up under the PPSA. Ship owners tried to limit liability under Merchant Shipping (Civil Liability for Oil Pollution) Act. This was disallowed as it was not an oil tanker.

644. Sections 6, 7, 8, PPSA.

- Discharging any oil or oily mixture from a vessel into Singapore waters. The master, owner and ship's agent shall each be guilty of the offence, which carries a fine of SGD 1,000 to SGD 1,000,000 or imprisonment of up to two years or both fine and imprisonment.[645]
- Discharging noxious liquid substances from ships. The master, owner and agent of the ship are each liable to a fine up to SGD 20,000 or imprisonment up to six months, or both fine and imprisonment.[646]
- Throwing or discharging of any ash, solid ballast or any matter into Singapore waters without permission from the Port of Singapore Authority (PSA).[647]
- Emitting smoke, soot, ash, grit or oil from a vessel in such quantity or density as may, in the opinion of the MPA, be a nuisance or an annoyance.[648]
- Failure to report discharges of oil, oily mixtures and substances from land or apparatus – a fine of up to SGD 5,000 may be imposed on the occupier of the place on land or the person in charge of the apparatus, as the case may be.[649]

282. A maximum fine of SGD 1,000,000 is imposed whenever oil or any oily mixture is discharged from a ship into Singapore waters, or from a Singapore ship into any part of the sea; otherwise, the fines can range from SGD 1,000 to SGD 20,000 with a daily fine of up to SGD 1,000, and imprisonment for a term not exceeding two years. Certain offences may be compounded for a sum not exceeding SGD 2,000.[650] Cases may be heard by the Magistrates' or the District Courts.[651] The ship owner is liable for costs incurred in clean-up operations.[652] Inspectors are given wide powers, including power to seize the ship and apply for distress. A court may order that the ship be sold and the proceeds applied towards payment of the fines. All fines are paid to the funds of the MPA.[653]

283. The Prevention of Pollution of the Sea (Garbage) Regulations 2012 have replaced the earlier Garbage regulations. Annex V of the MARPOL Convention now applies to Singapore via the Schedule.

645. Section 3, PPSA.
646. Section 10 PPSA.
647. *See* r. 65 – pollution of port waters, Maritime and Port Authority (MPA) of Singapore (Port) Regulations, Rg 7, GN S 187/1997, amended by S 518/2017.It should be noted that garbage from vessels in Singapore waters is collected daily by barges and brought on-shore for incineration. The ash is then brought via barges to the off-shore island sanitary landfill, Pulau Semakau. *See* https://www.nea.gov.sg/corporate-functions/resources/publications/books-journals-and-magazines/envision-lite/june-july-2020/semakau-landfill-20th-anniversary.
648. *See* r. 66, *ibid.*
649. Section 16 PPSA.
650. Section 33 PPSA.
651. Section 32 PPSA.
652. Sections 17–21 PPSA.
653. Section 33A PPSA.

§5. Carriage of Dangerous Goods

284. The MPA (Dangerous Goods, Petroleum and Explosives) Regulations, 2005,[654] govern the carriage of petroleum within the port, covering matters such as tests for different classes of petroleum, loading and discharging of petroleum, restrictions on tanker cleaning, conditions of discharge, and prohibitions on handling at night. General safety provisions are detailed in the Regulations, which also govern the carriage of dangerous goods and arms and explosives, covering matters such as their delivery, handling, loading and unloading and safety precautions.

Breaches of these Regulations entail a penalty of a fine not exceeding SGD 5,000 and a further fine not exceeding SGD 1,000 for each day the offence continues after conviction.[655] Responsibility for compliance is placed on the 'owner, agent or master of a vessel … in so far as they relate to the vessel'.[656] Some offences may be compounded in accordance with section 102 of the Act.[657]

654. GN S 24/2005, amended by GN S 587/2007, GN S 649/2009, GN S 795/2015 and GN 907/2021.
655. *Ibid.*, para. 78.
656. *Ibid.*, para. 77.
657. Maritime and Port Authority of Singapore (Composition of Offences) Regulations, GN S 778/2021.

Part II. Conservation and Management of Heritage Sites and Nature

Chapter 1. Monuments and Landscapes

§1. The Man-Made Landscape/Environment

I. Conservation of the Built Environment

285. As urban renewal was the focus of Singapore's early years as an independent nation, conservation was often overlooked.[658] The celebrations of the 150th Anniversary of Singapore in 1969 compelled a re-examination of its roots.[659] It was realised that the destruction of the historical landscape made Singapore a sterile and less attractive place to tourists. It also deprived younger Singaporeans of their 'roots' and this was unwise in 'nation-building'. As a result, conservation started in the 1970s and more than 7,000 buildings have been conserved since then. The URA shares that conserving the built heritage is an important part of Singapore's development as it adds variety to our urban fabric and helps rejuvenate dilapidated areas into thriving districts.

A. *National Monuments*

286. The Institute of Architects and the Historical Association of Singapore held a public meeting to discuss the creation of a civic organisation to preserve historic buildings. Thus was born the Preservation of Monuments Board (PMB) in 1971, with the passing of the Preservation of Monuments Act, 1971 (PMA), 'to preserve for the benefit of the nation, monuments of historic, traditional, archaeological, architectural or artistic interest'.[660] The Board came under the wing of the URA. The 1971 Act was repealed in 2009 with the passing of a new Preservation of Monuments Act, 2009,[661] to merge the PMB with the National Heritage Board (NHB)

658. It should be noted that the 1958 Master Plan contained a list of 30 structures proposed for preservation.
659. 'Urban conservation and heritage management' Chapter 9 in Martin Perry, Lily Kong and Brenda Yeoh, *Singapore – A Developmental City State,* World Cities Series, John Wiley & Sons, 1997, at p. 258.
660. *See* https://eresources.nlb.gov.sg/history/events/a3be461e-c6a1-4fe0-8740-f7ec29baa8ef.
661. Act 16 of 2009, 2020 Rev. Ed, amended by Act 40/2019 and Act 36/2021.

(section 24)[662] and provide for the appointment of a Director of National Monuments (section 8) as well as Monument Inspectors (section 9) and a National Monuments Advisory Committee (section 7). Subsequently, a revised version of the Act came into operation from 31 December 2011.[663] The URA identifies and recommends buildings of historical, architectural and cultural merit for conservation. It produces manuals and guidelines on conservation[664] (after seeking the views of the private sector), initiates private projects to demonstrate appropriate restoration techniques, and releases conservation buildings to the private sector for restoration. To date, more than 7,000 buildings have been conserved. Buildings and structures in Singapore that have specific historic, traditional, archaeological or artistic value can be preserved by the National Heritage Board. They are monuments and sites that are accorded the highest level of protection in Singapore. The Board can also promote research and public interest in the monuments.[665] To date, some seventy-five buildings and structures have been gazetted as national monuments.[666] To encourage landowners to conserve their buildings, rent control legislation was revoked, in stages.[667] Other incentives include waiver of development charges and parking requirements, as well as government assistance in the relocation of elderly tenants to public housing.

287. Section 4 of the PMA provides that the functions of the NHB shall include :

a. to identify monuments that are of such historic, cultural, traditional, archaeological, architectural, artistic or symbolic significance and national importance as to be worthy of preservation, and to make recommendations to the Minister for their preservation;
b. to undertake, commission, sponsor or facilitate research on monuments which have been identified for preservation or which are being preserved under this Act;
c. to determine standards and issue guidelines for the restoration and preservation of monuments under this Act and for the proper control, management and use of such monuments;
d. to determine the best method for the preservation of any national monument, and to cause or facilitate the preservation of such national monument in accordance with such method;

662. The National Heritage Board Act, 1993 was passed to transfer to the Board the National Museum, the National Archives and Records Centre and the Oral History Department and for matters connected therewith.
663. 2020 Rev Ed, amended by Act 16/2009 and Act 30/2021.
664. *See* Conservation Guidelines https://www.ura.gov.sg/Corporate/Guidelines/Conservation/Conservation-Guidelines.
665. Examples include the Raffles Hotel and Goodwood Park Hotel, the National Museum, City Hall, Parliament House, Convent of the Holy Infant Jesus and St Joseph Institution.
666. *See* https://www.roots.gov.sg/nhb/monuments; *see also* https://en.wikipedia.org/wiki/National_monuments_of_Singapore.
667. *See* Lye Lin Heng, 'De-control', Chapter 12, *Landlord and Tenant Law*, Singapore Law Series, 1990, Malaya Law Review & Butterworths. [Chapter 12 has been removed from the 2nd edition of this book (2021) as Rent Control was abolished in Singapore as of 1 Apr. 2001].

e. to protect national monuments;
f. to promote and stimulate public interest and support in the preservation of monuments, and public knowledge, appreciation and understanding of national monuments;
g. to record, preserve and disseminate information relating to national monuments; and
h. to advise the Government in respect of matters relating to the preservation of monuments.

288. Section 11 empowers the Minister of National Development, after consulting the Board, to make an order (called a 'Preservation Order') to place any monument under the protection of the Board – the order must be gazetted in the Government Gazette (S.11(4)(a)). A copy of the Preservation Order together with a notice stating the effect thereof shall be served upon the owner or occupier of the monument (S.11(5)). The Act requires that before the Minister makes, amends or revokes a preservation order, the Board shall give written notice of the Minister's intention to do so to the owner and occupier of the monument and any affected adjacent land, and in such notice, specify a reasonable period within which such owner and occupier may submit to the Board their objections (if any) to the order. The Board must consider every objection received and make its recommendations to the Minister in relation thereto (S. 11(7)(c)). A preservation order 'shall bind all subsequent owners and occupiers of the land which is the site of the monument and shall operate as a statutory obligation under section 142 of the Land Titles Act, 1993 (S. 11(8))'. There are duties on the landowner or occupier to maintain the national monument (section 13).

B. Conservation Areas

289. The Urban Redevelopment Authority (URA) identifies buildings and areas for conservation. These are selected for conservation based on their historical and architectural significance, rarity in terms of building types, styles, and their contribution to the overall environment. Section 9 of the Planning Act, 1998,[668] empowers the Minister of National Development to approve a proposal to amend the Master Plan to designate an area as a 'conservation area' if it is 'of special architectural, historic, traditional or aesthetic interest'. A conservation area may comprise an area, a single building or a group of buildings. Section 11 also authorises the URA to issue guidelines on conservation.[669] The map of conservation areas and buildings is accessible via the URA website.[670] As of 2025, the conservation areas are as follows:

668. Act 3 of 1998, 2020 Rev. Ed, amended by Act 17/2001, Act 30/ 2003, GN S 657/2004, Act 16/ 2009, Act 7/ 2017, GN S 339/2017, Act 40/ 2019 and Act 25/2021.
669. These can be found in their website at https://www.ura.gov.sg/Corporate/Guidelines/Conservation /Conservation-Guidelines.
670. *See* https://www.ura.gov.sg/maps/?service=CONSERVATION.

- Historic Districts: Boat Quay, Chinatown, Kampong Glam, Little India.[671]
- Residential Historic Districts: Blair Plain, Cairnhill, Emerald Hill.[672]
- Secondary Settlements: Balestier, Beach Road, Geylang, Jalan Besar, Jalan Jurong Kechil, Joo Chiat, Mount Sophia, River Valley, Tanjong Katong, Upper Circular Road and Tiong Bahru.[673]

§2. Landscape Protection

290. There is no definition of 'landscape' in Singapore's laws.[674] Section 16 of the Parks and Trees Act, 2005,[675] enables the Minister of National Development, after consultation with the National Board, to conserve the flora or vegetation in any area in Singapore (not within any national park or nature reserve) as important elements of the surrounding streetscape or landscape. This is done by publishing an Order in the Government Gazette designating it a 'heritage road green buffer':

a. any green verge (whether within or outside a tree conservation area); or
b. any other area located along or on land fronting, adjoining or abutting any street (whether within or outside a tree conservation area).

291. To date, five roads have been so gazetted – they are Mount Pleasant Road, South Buona Vista Road, Lim Chu Kang Road, Arcadia Road, and Mandai Road.[676] It is the duty of the Board to manage and maintain these areas (section 17). No tree or plant within these buffers can be cut or damaged without the permission of the Board (section 18). The penalty is a maximum fine of SGD 50,000.

---

671. https://www.ura.gov.sg/Corporate/Guidelines/Conservation/Conservation-Guidelines/Part-2-Planning-Parameters-and-Restoration-Guidelines/Historic-Districts_1.
672. https://www.ura.gov.sg/Corporate/Guidelines/Conservation/Conservation-Guidelines/Part-2-Planning-Parameters-and-Restoration-Guidelines/Residential-Historic-Districts.
673. https://www.ura.gov.sg/Corporate/Guidelines/Conservation/Conservation-Guidelines/Part-2-Planning-Parameters-and-Restoration-Guidelines/Secondary-Settlement.
674. *See* Lye Lin Heng, 'Landscape Protection Laws in the Evolution of Modern Singapore' chapter in *Landscape, Nature and Law – A Tribute to Alexander Kiss*, Antonio Herman Benjamin, ed., Law for a Green Planet Institute, Brazil, June 2005, 119–134. *See also* Lye Lin Heng, 'Land Use Planning, Environmental Management and the Garden City as an Urban Development Approach in Singapore' Chapter 21, *Land Use for Sustainable Development Series*: IUCN Academy of Environmental Law Research Studies, Vol. 2, Nathalie Chalifour, John Nolon, Lye Lin-Heng; Patricia Kameri-Mbote, eds. (New York: Cambridge University Press, 2007) pp. 374–396.
675. Act 4 of 2005, 2020 Rev. Ed.
676. Section 15, PTA, Parks and Trees (Heritage Road Green Buffers) Order, GN S 287/2006.

Chapter 2. Nature Conservation

§1. Overview

292. Laws to protect Singapore's wild flora and fauna were passed over a hundred years ago.[677] Today, almost all wild fauna are protected in Singapore. There are also laws protecting trees and other plants. The extent of protection depends on their precise location in this island-state, as different laws and regulations apply. The greatest protection for nature is in nature reserves and national parks, where breaches of the laws will entail a fine of up to SGD 50,000 or imprisonment of up to six months or both fine and imprisonment under the Parks and Trees Act 2005. Flora and fauna in public parks are protected to a lesser extent under the Parks and Trees Act. Separate laws protect parks in Sentosa Island, and parks administered by the Jurong Town Corporation (JTC) and the Public Utilities Board (PUB). Lastly, there are laws governing particular areas in Singapore, such as tree conservation areas and heritage roads.

As with other cities, one of the biggest challenges for Singapore is allowing for development while conserving its natural environment. The lack of physical space brings development into confrontation with conservation. The first Singapore Green Plan (SGP), which lasted for ten years, pledged to set aside 5% of the land for nature conservation. This was closely followed by its Action Programmes, which identified nineteen nature sites and four coral reefs as worthy of conservation.[678] Under the 2015 Sustainable Singapore Blueprint,[679] which followed after Singapore's 2012 Green Plan and set even higher goals, 9% of the land was pledged for Nature Reserves and Parks by 2020. Today, some 4.5% of the nature sites have legal protection, under the National Parks Act – with the four Nature Reserves accounting for 3,300 hectares of land. Singapore also declared its first and only marine park in 2014. This is the Sisters' Island Marine Park, a 40-hectare area around Sisters Islands and along the Western Reefs of both St John's Island and Pulau Tekukor.[680]

Singapore continues to strive to increase and enhance its greenery as well as its freshwater ecosystems and indeed has achieved considerable success through its National Parks Board (NParks). NParks initiated the Cities Biodiversity Index, which was adopted at the Convention on Biological Diversity (CBD)'s Conference

677. *See* Lye Lin Heng, 'Wildlife Protection Laws in Singapore' (1991) SJLS 287–319; Lye Lin Heng, 'Legal Protection of the Natural Environment', *State of the Natural Environment in Singapore*, Clive Briffett & Ho Hua Chew eds., Nature Society Singapore, June 1999; Joseph Chun, 'Wildlife Law in Singapore: Protecting Wildlife in the 'Garden City'' in *Wildlife Law: A Global Perspective* (ABA Publishing, 2008); Joseph Chun 'Enhancing the Garden City: Towards a Deeper Shade of Green' (2006) Singapore Academy of Law Journal. *See also* Melissa BN Tan and Hugh TW Tan, *The Laws Relating to Biodiversity in Singapore* (2013) Raffles Museum of Biodiversity Research, National University of Singapore; Joseph Chun, 'The Protection of Nature Reserves under the Parks and Trees Act – a Deep Dive', APCEL working paper – https://papers.ssrn.com/sol3/papers.cfm?abstract_id=3506421 (19 Dec. 2019).
678. *See* Lye Lin Heng, 'Legal Protection of the Natural Environment', *supra* n. 677.
679. https://www.clc.gov.sg/docs/default-source/urban-solutions/urb-sol-iss-7-pdfs/illustration-sustainable-singapore-blueprint.pdf.
680. https://www.straitstimes.com/singapore/environment/5-things-about-the-sisters-islands-singapores-first-marine-park (16 Jul. 2015).

of the Parties in Nagoya in 2010.[681] The Singapore Index comprises three components: (1) Biodiversity in the City, (2) Ecosystem Services provided by the Native Biodiversity in the City, and (3) Governance and Management of Biodiversity in the City. In this form, it would function as a monitoring tool.[682]

293. Singapore's commitment to biodiversity conservation is embodied in the National Biodiversity Strategy and Action Plan (NBSAP), titled 'Conserving Our Biodiversity', which was launched by NParks in 2009 and updated in 2019. The NBSAP provides a framework to guide efforts to conserve Singapore's rich biodiversity, keeping in mind the challenges of achieving this within a densely populated city-state and the need to balance development with conservation. It consists of five strategies:

- safeguard biodiversity;
- consider biodiversity issues in policy and decision-making;
- improve knowledge of biodiversity and the natural environment;
- enhance education and public awareness;
- strengthen partnerships with all stakeholders and promote international collaboration.

294. Singapore's 2015 Sustainable Blueprint[683] sets six targets under the goal of 'More Green and Blue Spaces':

1. 9% of land for Nature reserves and parks.
2. 9 in 10 homes to be within a ten-minute walk of a park.
3. 400 km of park connectors.
4. Enhanced ecological connectivity with 180 km of Nature Ways.
5. Over 100 potential ABC Waters projects identified for implementation island-wide.
6. 200 ha of skyrise greenery, equivalent to about 650 school fields.

295. The 2030 Green Plan aims to transform Singapore into 'A City in Nature'. Its targets include:

- the planting of 1 million trees across Singapore by 2030;
- increase land for nature park networks, which buffer nature reserves from impacts of urbanisation, by over 50% from the 2020 baseline;
- naturalise gardens and parks near homes;
- every household must be within a ten-minute walk from a park; and
- enhancing vet care and animal management.

681. *See* https://www.nparks.gov.sg/biodiversity/urban-biodiversity/the-singapore-index-on-cities-biodiversity. *See also* https://www.cbd.int/article/2021-singapore-index.

682. *See* draft Users Manual on the CDB website at http://www.cbd.int/doc/groups/cities/cities-draft-user-manual-singapore-index-2009-07-01-en.pdf. (29 Jun. 2009).

683. *See* https://www.clc.gov.sg/docs/default-source/books/ssbcombined-cover-text.pdf. *See also* https://www.clc.gov.sg/docs/default-source/urban-solutions/urb-sol-iss-7-pdfs/illustration-sustainable-singapore-blueprint.pdf.

I. Protection of Flora and Fauna in National Parks and Nature Reserves

296. The greatest protection for nature is found in the laws that govern Singapore's nature reserves and national parks – infringements will entail a fine of up to SGD 50,000 or imprisonment of up to six months or both fine and imprisonment under the Parks and Trees Act, 2005.

297. Singapore has four nature reserves and two national parks. The nature reserves are: Bukit Timah Nature Reserve, Central Catchment Nature Reserve, Labrador Nature Reserve and the Sungei Buloh Wetland Reserve.[684] The national parks are the Singapore Botanic Gardens and Fort Canning Park. All are protected under the Parks and Trees Act, 2005.[685] This was passed on 1 August 2005, 'to provide for the planting, maintenance and conservation of trees and plants within national parks, nature reserves, tree conservation areas, heritage road green buffers and other specified areas, and for matters connected therewith'.

298. Section 7 provides that national parks and nature reserves are set aside for all or any of the following purposes:

a. the propagation, protection and conservation of the trees, plants, animals and other organisms of Singapore, whether indigenous or otherwise;
b. the study, research and preservation of objects and places of aesthetic, historical or scientific interest;
c. the study, research and dissemination of knowledge in botany, horticulture, biotechnology, or natural and local history; and
d. recreational and educational use by the public.

A. *Protection for Animals in National Parks and Nature Reserves*

299. Section 9, Parks and Trees Act, 2005, makes it an offence to:

a. capture, displace or feed any animal;
b. disturb or take the nest of any animal;
c. collect, remove or wilfully displace any other organism;
d. use any animal, firearm, explosive, net, trap, hunting device or instrument or means, whatever for the purpose of capturing any animal; or
e. carry or have in the person's possession any explosive, net, trap or hunting device.

Subsection (2) makes it an offence for any person to carry out any activity within any national park or nature reserve which he knows or ought reasonably to know

684. Sungei Buloh and the Bukit Timah Nature Reserve are also ASEAN Heritage Parks – declared on 18 Dec. 2003 and 19 Oct. 2011 respectively.
685. Act 4 of 2005, 2020 Rev Ed, amended by Act 15/ 2010, Act 9/ 2017, Act 10/ 2019 and Act 40/2019.

causes or may cause injury to, or the death of, any animal or any other organism within the national park or nature reserve. Subsection (3) makes it an offence to release any animal into a nature reserve or to allow a domestic animal to stray into a nature reserve. The penalty is a fine of up to SGD 50,000, or imprisonment up to six months or both fine and imprisonment, and a daily fine of SGD 500. Finally, section 10 makes it an offence to wilfully or negligently destroy, damage or deface 'any object of zoological, botanical, geological, ethnological, scientific or aesthetic interest'. The penalty is a fine of up to SGD 20,000.

300. Some offences may be compounded where the offender pleads guilty – he is fined a lesser amount (section 51(1)).[686] The term 'animal' is given a very wide definition in section 2, to mean 'any mammal (other than man), bird, reptile, amphibian, fish (including shellfish), insect or any other living creature, vertebrate or invertebrate, and includes any egg or young thereof'.[687]

B. Protection for Trees and Plants in National Parks and Nature Reserves

301. The Parks and Trees Regulations provide for the management, care and control of nature reserves, national parks, as well as public parks. It prohibits smoking within a nature reserve, national park and public park, unless the area has been designated as a smoking facility.[688] The penalty is a fine of SGD 2,000.[689]

302. Section 2 of the Parks and Trees Act, 2005, defines 'plant' to mean 'any member of the plantae, protista, monera or fungi kingdom, and includes any angiosperm, gymnosperm, pteridophyte, bryophyte, algae, lichen or fungus'. Section 8(1) of the Parks and Trees Act makes it an offence to cut, collect or displace any tree or plant or any part thereof within a nature reserve or national park. Section 8(2) prohibits any person from carrying out 'any activity within any national park or nature reserve which he knows or ought reasonably to know causes or may cause alteration, damage or destruction to any property, tree or plant within the national park or nature reserve'.

303. Again, contravention of these laws constitutes an offence carrying a penalty of a fine up to SGD 50,000 or imprisonment for a term not exceeding six months or to both fine and imprisonment and, in the case of a continuing offence, to a further daily fine of SGD 500 so long as the offence continues after conviction.

---

686. *See also* Parks and Trees (Composition of Offences) Regulations, GN S 520/2005 RG 2.
687. Compare this definition with that in the Wildlife Act, 1965, (2020 Rev. Ed) which defines 'animal' in s. 2 to 'include any mammal, bird, reptile, amphibian, fish or invertebrate, whether of a wild nature or otherwise.'
688. *See* r. 6, Parks and Trees Regulations, GN S 519/2005, RG 1.
689. *See* r. 23 above.

II. Protection of Flora and Fauna Within a Public Park

304. A 'public park' is defined under the Parks and Trees Act (section 2) to mean 'any State land, any land belonging to the NParks or any other land, which is:

a. utilised as a public park, recreation ground, playground, garden, public open space, walk, park connector or green verge; and
b. managed or maintained by the Board'.

A. Protection of Animals in Public Parks

305. Regulation 5, Parks & Trees Regulations[690] prohibits any person from carrying on any activity in any public park 'which he knows or ought reasonably to know … (b) causes or may cause injury to, or the death of, any animal or any other organism within the public park'. The penalty is a maximum fine of SGD 5,000 under Regulation 23(b). It is also an offence under Regulation 8(2) to '(f) capture, displace or feed any animal; (g) disturb or take the nest of any animal; (h) collect, remove or wilfully displace any other organism; (i) use any animal, firearm, explosive, net, trap, hunting device or instrument or means whatever for the purpose of capturing any animal; (j) carry or have in the person's possession any explosive, net, trap or hunting device'.

306. Regulation 10 contains restrictions on the bringing of animals (other than a pet or guide dog) into a national park or public park. It is an offence to 'leave, abandon or release any animal in a national park or public park', or to allow the animal to enter any lake, reservoir, pond, stream or fountain in any national park or public park. The penalty is a maximum fine of SGD 2,000 under Regulation 23(a).

B. Protection of Trees and Plants in Public Parks

307. Under Regulation 5, no person is allowed to carry out any activity within any public park 'which he knows or ought reasonably to know (a) causes or may cause alteration, damage or destruction to any property, tree or plant within the public park'. The penalty is a maximum fine of SGD 5,000 under Regulation 23(b). Regulation 8(2) contains many prohibitions in relation to a public park. In the context of plants, it is an offence to '(a) cut, collect or displace any tree or plant or any part thereof; (c) clear, break up, dig or cultivate any land'. The penalty is a maximum fine of SGD 2,000 under regulation 23(a).

---

690. GN S 519/2005 (RG 1) with effect from 1 Aug. 2005.

III. Protection of Flora and Fauna in Other Parks in Singapore

308. Specific laws have been enacted to protect the flora and fauna in the parks managed by the Jurong Town Corporation (JTC), Sentosa Development Corporation (SDC), and the Public Utilities Board (PUB).

A. *Jurong Town Corporation (JTC) Parks*

309. The JTC manages several parks, including the Chinese Garden and Japanese Garden. The JTC (Parks) Regulations[691] define 'parks' to include '... any walk, recreation ground, playground, lake, open space, traffic island and garden maintained by the Manager'.[692] Regulation 4 makes it an offence to commit the following acts in a JTC park:

1. remove, cut or displace any soil, turf, plant or tree;
2. pick any part of any tree, shrub or plant;
3. throw or discharge any missile in any manner likely to cause or which causes damage to any soil, turf, plant or tree;
4. bathe, wade or wash in any lake, ornamental lake, fountain, pond or stream, or foul or pollute any water thereof;
5. capture, injure or destroy or attempt to capture, injure or destroy any fish or waterfowl in any such lake, ornamental lake, pond or stream, except in certain areas designed by the Manager for persons to bathe, wade or fish by a notice affixed or set up in some position at or near to each of the areas;
6. displace, disturb, injure, destroy or take away any bird's nest or egg;
7. capture, injure or destroy any bird, butterfly or other insect, or spread, use or set any net, snare or other instrument for the capture, injury or destruction of any bird, butterfly or other insect;
8. enter any flower-bed or any part of the park which is being prepared as a flower-bed or for other planting;
9. release any animal;
10. throw or discharge any stone or missile to the danger of any person, animal, bird, fish, reptile or insect.

310. There are also restrictions on the bringing in of dogs and other animals to JTC parks. Failure to comply constitutes an offence entailing a fine of up to SGD 500 and the offender may be arrested by the manager or any member of the Singapore Police Force, the Auxiliary Police Force or the Vigilante Corps.[693]

---

691. GN S 285/88 Rg 2, with effect from 15 Oct. 1988.
692. *Ibid.*, r. 2; 'Manager' refers to the Parks and Recreation Manager.
693. *Ibid.*, rr 11 and 12.

B. Sentosa Development Corporation Parks

311. The Sentosa Development Corporation Regulations[694] apply to Sentosa Island as well as eleven other smaller islands. Regulation 7 lists various acts that are prohibited on these islands. In particular, it states that 'No person in Sentosa or the other islands shall:

a. wilfully damage or remove any tree or plant;
b. remove earth or soil from any property belonging to the Corporation;
c. kill, hunt, shoot or capture any animal, bird or insect or do any act which may cause injury or destruction to any animal, bird or insect or the eggs and young thereof;
d. have with him:
   i. any dog that is not on a lead and under proper control; or
   ii. any other animal that is not under proper control.
e. release any animal in Sentosa or the other islands.
f. fish in any place where fishing is prohibited.'

Regulation 8 specifies that '... No person in Sentosa or the other islands shall, without the prior approval in writing of the Corporation:

a. collect any bird's egg or nest;
b. remove or cut any plant or tree or any part thereof ... .'

The penalty is a fine of up to SGD 2,000.[695]

C. Catchment Area Parks

312. The Public Utilities (Reservoirs, Catchment Areas and Waterways) Regulations were passed in 2006.[696] Catchment area parks are defined in the First Schedule. The Second Schedule specifies the 'central water catchment area'. Section 6 lists various prohibited activities in Catchment Area Parks. These are much the same as in JTC and Sentosa Island parks, particularly prohibiting the damaging of any flora and the killing, hunting, shooting or trapping of any animal or the doing of any act which causes injury to the fauna, releasing any animal or allowing any animal to stray into a catchment area park. Prior approval is needed to enter or fish in any reservoir or stream; collect any bird's egg or nest; or remove or cut any plant, shrub or tree. Additional offences include using any part of the Central Water Catchment Area or Catchment Area Park as a location for the shooting of a film or the setting

694. GN S 454/97, 3 Oct. 1997, 1998 Rev Ed.
695. *Ibid.*, r. 57.
696. S 401/2006, formerly Public Utilities (Catchment Area Parks) Regulations (GN S 48/89). Amended by GN, GN S 70/2015 and GN S 166/2018.

of a play; using any live bait for fishing; drawing water from any reservoir or stream; or feeding any marine animal with any kind of food. The penalty is a maximum fine of SGD 3,000.

IV. Tree Conservation Areas

313. There are two tree conservation areas (outside national parks or nature reserves) in Singapore, established by the Parks and Trees (Preservation of Trees) Order.[697] Part IV of the Parks and Trees Act (sections 13–15) applies to tree conservation areas. Trees with a girth of more than one metre measured a half-metre from the ground, growing on tree conservation areas or on growing on vacant land (whether within or outside a tree conservation area) cannot be cut down without the permission of the Commissioner of Parks and Recreation.[698] The penalty on conviction is a fine of SGD 50,000.[699]

314. The Commissioner may protect a large tree or group of large trees (girth of at least one metre) by serving a Tree Conservation Notice under section 15, Parks and Trees Act. However, this can be done only if the tree is either in a tree conservation area or is growing on vacant land. This Notice can be revoked at any time.

V. Heritage Road Green Buffers

315. The Parks and Trees Act, 2005 (section 16), allows the Minister, after consultation with the NParks, to conserve roadside greenery along the verges of roads with mature trees and greenery, by designating the green verges of these roads as Heritage Road Green Buffers. To date, five roads have been so gazetted – they are Mount Pleasant Road, South Buona Vista Road, Lim Chu Kang Road, Arcadia Road, and Mandai Road.[700] It is the duty of NParks to manage and maintain these areas (section 17). No tree or plant within these buffers can be cut or damaged without the permission of the Board (section 18). The penalty of a maximum fine of SGD 50,000 applies.

697. Cap. 216, Order 1, 2 Aug. 1999. 1998 Rev Ed, amended by S 661/2017. The two tree conservation areas are: (1) The area bounded by Dunearn Road, Whitley Road, Mt. Pleasant Road, Thomson Road, Lornie Road, Pan Island Expressway, Clementi Road, Pasir Panjang Road, Telok Blangah Road, Lower Delta Road, Ayer Rajah Expressway, Alexandra Road, River Valley Road, Fort Canning Road and Selegie Road. (2) The area bounded by Netheravon Road, Cranwell Road, Loyang Avenue, Loyang Way, Upper Changi Road North and Changi Village Road.

698. Parks and Trees (Preservation of Trees) Order 1991, GN S 327/91, amended GN S 661/2017.

699. It is noted that s. 54 Parks and Trees Act (PTA) provides certain presumptions and defences.

700. Section 15, Parks and Trees Act, Parks and Trees (Heritage Road Green Buffers) Order, GN 287/2006.

VI. Heritage Trees

316. The National Parks Board (NParks) has established a Heritage Trees Scheme 'to identify, recognise and conserve majestic individual trees in our landscape'. The Scheme was announced on 17 August 2001 with the objectives to conserve and to educate the community on the importance of protecting our mature trees.[701] The scheme is open to the public and members of the public are invited to nominate these heritage trees via an online Heritage Tree nomination form. The list of nominated trees will be inspected by NParks arborists before being submitted to the Heritage Tree Panel. Only trees endorsed by the Heritage Trees Panel would be accepted as Heritage Trees. Heritage Trees are typically (dependent on species) more than five metres in girth, and are noted because of their rarity of species, aesthetics and growth form, historical significance, cultural reasons, social and educational value. However, it does not appear that trees designated as 'Heritage Trees' have legal protection per se. To date, there are some 260 trees, located all over the island, each specifically mentioned in 'Singapore's Heritage Trees Register', kept by the NParks.[702] All of these are of native, indigenous species.

VII. Planting Areas and Streetscapes

317. Part V Division I (sections 22–27) of the Parks and Trees Act 2005 enable the Commissioner of Building Control, where building works are being carried out, to require that the area be surrounded by a 'planting area' of certain dimensions. The Minister may also, for the purpose of enhancing greenery and promoting the use of trees and plants as important elements of streetscapes and landscapes, by notification in the *Gazette*, prescribe different dimensions (including the location and site specifications) of planting areas for different classes or descriptions of premises. It is an offence to carry out building works within these planting areas – section 24 (fine SGD 30,000 and a daily fine of SGD 500 for continuing offence) or to interfere with these planting areas. There is a duty on the occupier of the premises within which any planting area has been made up to maintain the planting area (section 25). The Commissioner is also empowered under section 27 to require that the occupier of any premises fronting, adjoining or abutting any public street, plant or replant any tree or plant within the green margin and provide for their maintenance and protection, and even clear the area of weeds or cut the grass. The law also provides for the provision of open spaces as public parks, in premises where building works are being undertaken (section 28). Such open spaces may be vested in the government (section 29) and protect green verges on public streets (sections 30 and 31).

701. https://www.nparks.gov.sg/gardens-parks-and-nature/heritage-trees.
702. *Ibid.*

VIII. Cutting Down Trees

318. The Commissioner of Parks and Recreation is empowered to order that any plant or tree be cut down where it obstructs traffic or poses an imminent danger to life or property.[703]

IX. Taking of Timber and Other Natural Resources

319. An old statute, the State Lands Encroachment Act, 1883, prohibits the digging or taking from any State land 'any live or dead timber, or other vegetable product, or any beeswax, guano, mineral, gravel, stone, coral, shell, sand, loam, brick-earth or other product' as well as the 'cutting, removal, or sale of any timber or produce lying or being on State land or stripping or removal of bark from any tree in any State land', unless there is a permit from the Land Office.[704] Breach of this provision constitutes an offence carrying a penalty of a fine of up to SGD 2,000.

703. Sections 37 and 38, PTA.
704. Cap. 315, 2020 Rev. Ed (Ordinance 10 of 1883), s. 14.

Chapter 3. Wildlife Protection

§1. General Protection for Wild Animals and Birds

320. Laws to protect Singapore's wild fauna were enacted as far back as 1884 (Wild Birds Protection Ordinance).[705] The modern equivalent is the Wild Animals and Birds Act (WABA), passed in 1965. In 2020, the Wild Animals and Birds (Amendment) Act was passed on 25 March, and it has renamed WABA as the Wildlife Act (WA).[706] Its preamble states that it is 'An Act for the protection, preservation and management of wildlife for the purposes of maintaining a healthy ecosystem and safeguarding public safety and health, and for related matters.' The WA and its subsidiary laws used to be administered by the Agri-Food and Veterinary Authority (AVA) but are now administered by NParks.[707] It requires NParks to appoint a Director-General, Wildlife Management (section 4). The term 'wildlife species' is defined in section 2 of the Wildlife Act to 'mean any species of animals and birds of a wild nature, but does not include domestic dogs and cats, cattle, sheep, horses, goats, domestic pigs and poultry'. 'Wildlife' is defined in section 2 to 'mean an animal that belongs to a wildlife species, and includes the young or egg of the animal'. The new Wildlife (Protected Species) Rules[708] contain a list of 'Protected Wildlife Species' comprising eleven mammals, six birds, nine reptiles, three fishes, and eight invertebrates. However, some wildlife species are not protected. These are listed in the Wildlife (Exemption) Order[709] – four species of mammals (rats and mice), four species of birds, five species of reptiles, and all invertebrates other than those specially protected under the Wildlife (Protected Species) Rules.

321. The Wild Animals (Licensing) Order allowed the keeping of specific species of wild fauna with a licence from AVA. But in practice, it would appear that AVA had not issued licences for the keeping of any wild animal for many years.[710] This Order was revoked on 1 June 2020.[711]

322. The Wildlife Act prohibits the 'intentional' feeding of wildlife (section 5A), the 'intentional' release of wildlife (section 5B) without written approval, entailing a maximum fine of SGD 5,000 and in the case of a second offence under section 5A, a fine of SGD 10,000. Section 5C prohibits the intentional 'killing, trapping, taking or keeping of wildlife'. Breach of section 5C entails a SGD 50,000 fine or

705. *See* Lye Lin Heng, 'Wildlife Protection Laws in Singapore', [1991] SJLS 287–319. *See also* Melissa BN Tan and Hugh TW Tan, *The Laws Relating to Biodiversity in Singapore* (2013) Raffles Museum of Biodiversity Research, National University of Singapore, https://lkcnhm.nus.edu.sg/wp-content/uploads/sites/10/app/uploads/2017/04/biodlawsgp.pdf.

706. Cap. 351, 2000 Rev Ed (Ordinance 5 of 1965), amended by Act 10 of 2019 and Act 18 of 2020. *See* Joseph Chun 'The Wild Animals and Birds (Amendment) Act (Act 16 of 2020' APCEL working paper, at https://law.nus.edu.sg/apcel/publications/.

707. Wildlife (Revocation) Rules 2020, S 413/2020.

708. S 411/2020 with effect from 1 Jun. 2020.

709. S 414/2020.

710. S. 55/75. 1990 Rev. Ed, amended by S 169/1998, S 103/2000, Act 16 of 2000, S 158/2004, S 460/2006, S 230/2019 and S 413/2020.

711. Wildlife (Revocation) Rules 2020, *supra* n. 707.

imprisonment of up to two years or both, if the animal is a protected species and if the person is in an 'animal-related business' which is defined in the Act. Where the wildlife is not a protected species, the fine is SGD 20,000 or imprisonment for up to one year or both fine and imprisonment. In all other cases, the fine for a first offence is SGD 10,000, or imprisonment up to six months, or both fine and imprisonment.

323. The Wild Animals and Birds (Bird Sanctuaries) Order has also been revoked as of 1 June 2020.[712] It is clear that it is no longer necessary, as the new Wildlife Act protects all species of wildlife, including birds, except those listed in the Wildlife (Exemption) Order.

324. In 2022, NParks opened a Centre for Wildlife Rehabilitation (CWR), which provides veterinary care and rehabilitation for wild animals in Singapore and builds NParks' expertise in the rescue, treatment and release of wildlife. It complements the work and expertise of our wildlife rescue partners such as ACRES and Mandai Wildlife Group, and strengthens collaboration with the wildlife management industry. It also enhances NParks' biosurveillance and wildlife population research capabilities and is key to our community and science-based approach to wildlife management and conservation.[713] In the same year, Nparks opened the Centre for Animal Rehabilitation, Singapore's first dedicated facility for animal behavioural rehabilitation.[714] The opening of the centre supports the existing nationwide Trap-Neuter-Release-Manage (TNRM) programme, which aims to rehome as many free-roaming dogs and cats as possible.[715] TNRM is a holistic, humane, and science-based approach to managing the community cat and dog population, as well as the potential inconveniences or concerns that these animals may cause in the community.

§2. The Protection of Marine Life

325. The Sungei Buloh Wetland Reserve is protected under the Parks and Trees Act. Although four coral reefs were identified for conservation under the Singapore Green Plan (SGP) in 1992, only one marine park exists – the Sisters Island Marine Park, established in 2014. To date, there are no laws specifically protecting a particular marine area or ecosystem. The only laws that apply to marine areas are:

---

712. *Ibid.*
713. https://www.nparks.gov.sg/news/news-detail/nparks-opens-centre-for-wildlife-rehabilitation-to-provide-veterinary-care-and-rehabilitation-for-wildlife.
714. https://www.mnd.gov.sg/newsroom/speeches/view/opening-remarks-by-mos-tan-kiat-how-at-the-opening-of-centre-for-animal-rehabilitation.
715. *See* https://www.nparks.gov.sg/avs/animals/animal-management/living-with-community-animals-in-your-neighbourhood/tnrm-programme-for-free-roaming-dogs#:~:text=The%20Trap%2DNeuter%2DRehome/Release%2DManage%20(TNRM)%20program%20is%20a%20five%2Dyear,the%20free%2Droaming%20dog%20population%20within%20five%20years; and https://www.nparks.gov.sg/avs/pets/cat-management-framework/cat-management-framework/tnrm-programme-for-community-cats#:~:text=Under%20TNRM%2C%20free%2Droaming%20dogs,with%20community%20cat%20caregiver%20networks.

- The State Lands (Encroachment) Act, 1883[716] – Section 14 prohibits the digging or taking from any State land '… any mineral, gravel, stone, coral, shell, sand, loam, brick-earth or other product' without a permit from the Land Office. The penalty is a fine of SGD 2,000. In practice, permission for the collection of corals is only granted for scientific, educational or conservation purposes.
- The Fisheries Act, 1966[717] and its regulations– these provide considerable control over the fishing industry. It is administered by the Singapore Food Agency (SFA), which replaced the Agri-Veterinary Authority (AVA) in 2019. The term 'fish' is defined to 'include any of the varieties of marine, brackish water or fresh water fishes, crustacea, aquatic mollusca, turtles, marine sponges, trepang and any other form of aquatic life and the young and eggs thereof'. These laws require persons who use fishing gear to obtain a licence. Fishing vessels plying at any port in Singapore also require a licence. The trapping of fish by explosives or poisons, and the use of trawl nets, are prohibited. Penalties include a fine of up to SGD 10,000 and/or imprisonment of up to twelve months. There may be a daily fine of SGD 50, and where the offence continues for a period exceeding ten days after conviction, the offender shall be liable to a term of imprisonment not exceeding six months. It is an offence to keep dangerous fish such as the piranha, and the penalty is a fine of up to SGD 50,000 and/or imprisonment up to twelve months.[718]

326. Apart from these, no laws exist to specifically protect Singapore's marine life, either as individual specimens or species or as an entire ecosystem; although in the context of the Singapore Green Plan 1992, it was stated that the four coral reefs will come under the control of the NParks. While one site (the Sisters Islands Marine Park) has been declared a Marine Nature Area[719] by the Urban Redevelopment Authority (URA), it was unclear what this means. It was identified in the 2015 Sustainable Singapore Blueprint to be a platform for outreach, educational, conservation and research activities related to native marine biodiversity. This was made clearer in 2017 when the definition of a 'public park' under the Parks & Trees Act 2005 (PTA) was amended to include 'land used as a marine park' and 'marine park' is defined to mean 'any area of the sea or seabed that is set aside for conservation of marine organisms and is designated in Part III of the Schedule'.[720] In 2021, the Big Sister's Island underwent upgrading works to make it more visitor-friendly and to serve as a place for people to learn more about Singapore's marine life, which is often invisible to the city dweller, and was finally reopened to the public in 2024. It is the first marine park that protects the country's coral reefs and marine life and promotes marine-related education, research and conservation activities.[721] There are further plans to designate the southern part of Lazarus Island and the reef off

---

716. *See ibid.*
717. Act 14 of 1966, 2020 Rev. Ed.; amended by Act 30/1973, Act 12/1994, Act 5/1999, Act 16/2000, Act 10/2002, Act 11/2019, Act 15/2019. (formerly the Fisheries Ordinance, 1905).
718. Animals and Birds (Piranha) Rules 2019, GN S 210/19.
719. This is the site of the twin islands, called 'Sisters Island'.
720. Act 4 of 2005, 2020 Rev. Ed.
721. *See* https://www.straitstimes.com/singapore/sisters-islands-marine-park-reopens-visitors-can-hike-a-coastal-trail-and-see-corals-up-close.

Kusu Island as Singapore's second marine park.[722] Another site identified under the Green Plan (Pulau Semakau) has since been turned into an offshore dump-site, but it has received considerable accolades for its greenery and flora and fauna.[723]

327. It is still unclear which government agency is responsible for marine conservation in general. The Singapore Land Authority (SLA) is responsible for issuing licences for removal of the substrate (sand, rock, coral) but not for living organisms on the substrate or in the water column. NParks is assuming increasing responsibility for surveys and data collection on marine life, protection and rehabilitation projects. Additionally, it has put up more signs and stepped-up patrols to prevent beachgoers from mandling marine creatures.[724] It would appear that with the 2017 amendment to the PTA, at least in the case of a marine park (and so far there is only one, the Sisters Island Marine Park), the responsibility for its protection falls on NParks. The Singapore Food Agency (SFA) is responsible for the Fisheries Act – these provisions mostly relate to the fishing industry, but it is laudable that the use of explosives and poisons is prohibited.

§3. Trade in Endangered Species: CITES

328. Singapore ratified the Convention on International Trade in Endangered Species of Wild Flora and Fauna (CITES) in 1986 and passed the Endangered Species (Import and Export) Act (ESA)[725] into implementation. The Act was repealed in 2006 and replaced with a new Endangered Species (Import and Export) Act, 2006.[726] It prohibits trade in endangered animals, plants and their by-products, unless with a permit from the National Parks Board (NParks) (this used to be implemented by the now defunct Agri-Food and Veterinary Authority (AVA)). The subsidiary laws prohibit the sale of parts and derivatives of tigers and rhinoceros[727] and exempt artificially propagated plants with proper permits.[728] The penalties for illegal trade in the scheduled specified are severe. For offences committed in relation to species specified in Appendix I of the Schedule, the maximum fine is SGD 100,000 for each scheduled species (but not to exceed in the aggregate SGD 500,000) or imprisonment for a term not exceeding six years or to both fine and imprisonment. For offences committed in relation to species specified in Appendix II or III of the Schedule, the maximum fine is SGD 50,000 for each scheduled species (but not to exceed in the aggregate SGD 500,000) or to imprisonment for a term

722. *See* https://www.straitstimes.com/singapore/s-pore-s-proposed-second-marine-park-in-lazarus-south-kusu-is-home-to-rare-rocky-shore-coral-habitat.
723. *See* http://www.wildsingapore.com/places/semakau.htm. *See also* https://www.nea.gov.sg/corporate-functions/resources/publications/books-journals-and-magazines/semakau-landfill-story.
724. *See* https://www.straitstimes.com/singapore/environment/nparks-taking-steps-to-stop-manhandling-of-marine-life.
725. Cap. 92A, 2000 Rev. Ed.
726. Act 5 of 2006, 2020 Rev. Ed. . Amended many times – *see* Legislative History (https://sso.agc.gov.sg/Act/ESIEA2006?ProvIds=xv-#xv-) with the latest amendments being GN S 93/2021 and GN S 380/2021.
727. GN S 100/2006.
728. GN S 98/2006.

not exceeding four years or to both fine and imprisonment.[729] Officers from AVA have wide powers of enforcement, including powers to investigate and powers of entry, search and seizure.[730] Infringements have declined substantially since the passing of this new Act.

At the ASEAN level, a Wildlife Enforcement Network (ASEAN-WEN) was established in 2006 to combat transnational crime in endangered wildlife. It is the world's largest wildlife law enforcement network involving the police, customs and environment agencies of all ten ASEAN countries, with an office in Bangkok, Thailand.[731] Together with the ASEAN Member States, ASEAN-WEN was supported by its Program Coordination Unit (PCU), and its Partner Organisations: the USAID ARREST *(Asia's Regional Response to Endangered Species Trafficking)* programme, implemented by FREELAND foundation; TRAFFIC Southeast Asia; and TRACE Forensics Network. The ARREST programme is a five-year programme funded by the US Agency for International Development (USAID) and implemented by the FREELAND Foundation aimed at fighting the trafficking of illegal wildlife in Asia in three ways: reducing consumer demand; strengthening law enforcement; and strengthening regional cooperation and anti-trafficking network. ARREST unites the efforts of the Member States of ASEAN, China and South Asia, NGOs, and private sector organisations. Additionally, the Law Enforcement Extension Office (LEEO) of the ASEAN-WEN PCU was created in 2008 to support and coordinate operational law enforcement matters and transnational wildlife investigations. LEEO also leads the PCU's partnership building with other international organisations such as INTERPOL, the World Customs Organisation (WCO) and other agencies.[732] In 2016, ASEAN-WEN was merged with the ASEAN Expert Group on CITES to form the ASEAN Working Group on CITES and Wildlife Enforcement.[733]

---

729. https://sso.agc.gov.sg/Act/ESIEA2006?ValidDate=20250207&ProvIds=P12-#pr4-.
730. *Public Prosecutor v. Sustrisno Alkaf* [2006] SGDC 182 – An Indonesian boat captain transiting in Singapore was found to have 2,520 heads of live South Asian Box Turtles (Cuora amboinensis), without a valid CITES permit. He was sentenced to a fine of SGD 20,000 (the turtles were worth SGD 10,000), and five months imprisonment. In *PP v. Wong Wee Keong* [2019] SGCA 21, a case that was appealed to the Court of Appeal, the applicants were charged with importing some 30,000 logs of Madagascan rosewood into Singapore – a scheduled species under the ESA and CITES without a permit. The defence was that the rosewood was in transit in Singapore and thus did not require an import permit. The High Court found that the rosewood was 'imported' and thus an offence had been committed as an import permit had not been obtained. However, this was overturned by the Court of Appeal, which held that the rosewood was in transit in Singapore within s 2(2)(c) of the ESA. *See* Burton Ong, Lye Lin Heng & Joseph Chun, 'Regulating International Trade in Endangered Species – Transshipments of *CITES*-Listed Species in Singapore' (2016) SingJLS 277–306. This article examines the decision, and argues for a purposive construction of these provisions that furthers Singapore's implementation of its obligations as a Party to *CITES*. This is particularly pertinent considering Singapore's role as a significant transshipment hub for endangered species in combatting the illegal wildlife trade. It also calls for greater international cooperation and coordination between *CITES* Parties in the design and implementation of their respective national legal frameworks.
731. *See* https://cites.org/eng/news/sundry/2005/ASEAN-WEN.shtml.
732. ASEAN-WEN and its partners have worked with the NUS Law Faculty's Asia-Pacific Centre for Environmental Law (APCEL). A seminar was held in the Law School, NUS, on 'Strengthening ASEAN Wildlife Enforcement Network (ASEAN-WEN) through Public-Private Partnerships in Legal Cooperation', 30 May 2012. This was jointly organised by APCEL/ASEAN-WEN/

§4. PROTECTION OF BIOLOGICAL DIVERSITY

329. Singapore signed the Convention on Biological Diversity (CBD) on 10 March 1993, and ratified the Convention on 21 December 1995. The main features of the CBD are that under Article 15 (Access to Genetic Resources), States have sovereign rights over their natural resources; access to genetic resources is to be determined by national laws; and each party 'shall endeavour to create conditions to facilitate access to genetic resources for environmentally sound uses by other contracting parties and not to impose restrictions that run counter to the objectives' of the Convention. Under Article 15(4), 'Access, where granted, shall be on mutually agreed terms', and Article 15(5) provides that access to genetic resources shall be subject to the 'prior informed consent' of the party providing the resources. Article 15(6) states that contracting parties are to endeavour to develop and carry out scientific research based on genetic resources provided by other contracting parties with the full participation of the contracting parties. The objectives are 'to share in a fair and equitable way', the results of research and development and the benefits arising from the commercial use of genetic resources with the party providing the resources. Such sharing shall be on mutually agreed terms.

330. Some steps have been taken towards implementing this framework Convention, although specific laws have not been passed for its implementation.[734] Indeed, specific laws may not be necessary as the existing framework of laws to protect biodiversity, wildlife and ecosystems is largely adequate.[735] Surveys have been done of the biodiversity resources in Singapore. NParks has devised an application form which requires all persons conducting Taxonomic/Ecological Research to seek prior written permission from the Board. However, this applies only to research on organisms within areas under the control or management of the Board. The form requires the applicant to state the purpose for this research, the methodology (including duration and frequency of intended field survey or schedule of field

---

ARREST, FREELAND Foundation and Centre for International Law, NUS. In 2016, the *ASEAN Legal Handbook on Legal Cooperation to Combat Wildlife Crime* was developed with the support of USAID, Freeland and APCEL and is broadly endorsed by ASEAN-WEN and its member agencies.

733. http://awgciteswe.org/.

734. An inventory of Singapore's biodiversity was taken in 1994 (*see The Singapore Red Data Book – Threatened Plants & Animals of Singapore,* Nature Society, Singapore, June 1994) and in 2008, *See* https://www.nparks.gov.sg/biodiversity/resources-and-research-permits/singapore-biodiversity-information. NParks has also released some endangered native fauna into the forest reserves. Efforts have also been made towards afforestation with appropriate saplings. The wild boar population has surged and some have to be culled, while the endangered hornbill has been successfully bred.

735. *See* Lye Lin Heng, 'Nature Conservation Laws – The Legal Protection of Flora and Fauna in Singapore', *The Singapore Red Data Book – Threatened Plants & Animals of Singapore,* 2d ed. Nature Society, September 2008 pp. 5–13, GWH Davison, PKL Ng, HC Ho, eds.; Melissa BN Tan and Hugh TW Tan, *The Laws Relating to Biodiversity in Singapore* (2013) Raffles Museum of Biodiversity Research, National University of Singapore, https://lkcnhm.nus.edu.sg/wp-content/uploads/sites/10/app/uploads/2017/04/biodlawsgp.pdf. *See also* B Ong, Lye LH & J Chun, 'Biological Conservation Laws in Southeast Asia and Singapore: A Regional Approach in Pursuit of the UN Sustainable Development Goals?' (2016) 19 APJEL 105–138.

trips), the logistics and field requirements (equipment, manpower, field survey locations, permanent traps/plots, marking, etc.). It also requests details on the collection of specimens – the applicant is to indicate type/number/amount/collection frequency required, specimen collection type (e.g., whether whole plant, animal, or part), and the field or locality of research. The application requires a minimum of two weeks' processing time. As for marine species, the application must be made to the Land Office for permission. There does not appear to be any prescribed form.[736]

331. The Research Permit devised by NParks contains various conditions. These include the following: The researcher must give prior notice to NParks before he proceeds to the field; he must take into account the delicate ecosystem of the field venue, observing minimum clearance and disturbance to surroundings; he must keep the team small and not schedule trips during high-peak hours such as school vacations and public holidays; all maps/data/field sites are confidential and specific for the researchers' own use – they must not be circulated, used or accessed after completion of work; the researcher must submit half-yearly and annual reports to the Biodiversity Centre as well as a copy of the field data recorded or list of specimens collected and other field observations – to be submitted after each field visit; drafts for papers resulting from the study must be forwarded to the Biodiversity Centre for review prior to publication. Two copies of the publication must be given to the Centre. A primary set of materials should be deposited with the Singapore Botanic Gardens Herbarium (if it relates to flora) or the Raffles Museum of Biodiversity Research (if it relates to fauna).[737]

§5. The Development Versus Conservation Dilemma

332. Singapore faces the dilemma that confronts all cities – the choice between conservation (be it of natural or man-made areas) and development. The problem is exacerbated as Singapore's laws do not provide for mandatory environmental impact assessments (EIAs) for projects that may have an adverse impact on the environment. The nearest statutory equivalents to the EIA are found in sections 26 and 36 of the Environmental Protection and Management Act (EPMA), both of which relate to impact assessments in relation to environmental pollution and hazardous installations. In reality, EIAs are done on an ad hoc basis, but increasingly, access has been given to non-government organisations (NGOs) such as the Nature Society, as the authorities and responsible NGOs[738] work at achieving a workable partnership in caring for the environment.

736. *See* Lye Lin-Heng & Rose-Liza Eisma-Osorio, 'Regulatory Measures on Access & Benefit Sharing for Biological and Genetic Resources – National & Regional Perspectives from the Philippines, Singapore & ASEAN', Chapter 13, Charles M McManis & Burton Ong (2017) *Routledge Handbook of Biodiversity and the Law.*

737. For information on research permits *see* https://www.nparks.gov.sg/biodiversity/resources-and-research-permits.

738. These include the Nature Society Singapore (NSS), Singapore Environment Council (SEC), the Blue Water Volunteers (BWV), WWF Singapore. *See also* https://www.towardszerowaste.gov.sg/green-groups-in-singapore/.

There have been calls for the concept of the public trust to be applied, the government being viewed as holding all lands not in private ownership, on trust for its citizens, who are the beneficiaries. It therefore follows that as beneficiaries, they should be consulted on any project that may adversely affect their interests – this ties in with the right to public participation advocated in the Rio Declaration and in Agenda 21.[739] However, it does not appear that an EIA law will be passed in the near future.

333. In October 2020, however, sweeping changes were made to the existing EIA framework. Three key changes were made:[740]

1. Introduction of biodiversity impact assessment guidelines developed by NParks in consultation with experts.[741] Guidelines will ensure consultants assessing sites marked for development have a set of standards to follow.
2. Transparency of environmental studies to be enhanced with the URA spelling out on its website the circumstances under which studies must be done – for instance, if development works are located close to an area of ecological significance, such as nature reserves.
3. With the exception of reports containing sensitive information (such as security considerations), all environmental study reports will be published online by developers and links made available on the URA website.

The Ministry of National Development (MND) suggests that while changes to the framework may not be officially codified in an EIA law, it still has regulatory teeth.

334. In February 2021, the framework was reviewed again in three particular areas:

1. developing a more comprehensive picture of Singapore's nature areas and how they connect to one another;
2. whether it is better to centralise the management of environmental impact assessment consultants instead of having individual developers manage their own; and
3. the use of technology in the built environment sector and see how it can be applied to project management.

From 2023 onwards, following the review, the EIAs were eventually centralised. Environmental consultants who assess the impact of development works on an area's plant and animal life will be managed by NParks instead of the developers

---

739. *See* Joseph Chun, 'Reclaiming the Public Trust in Singapore: (2005) SAcLJ 717–746; Lye Lin Heng, 'Land Law and the Environment – Re-examining the Concept of Ownership and Forging New Rights and Obligations in a Changed World' (2010) SAcLJ 189–229.

740. *See* https://www.straitstimes.com/singapore/environment/development-works-in-singapore-to-be-more-sensitive-to-wildlife-under-changes (25 Oct. 2020).

741. *See* https://www.nparks.gov.sg/biodiversity/urban-biodiversity/biodiversity-impact-assessment-guidelines.

themselves. This move to centralise EIAs will enable NParks to work more closely with the consultants to raise the quality and rigour of their work and ensure urban developments are carried out in a sustainable manner.

Chapter 4. Subsoil and Minerals

335. Singapore has no mineral deposits worthy of commercial exploitation. There are deposits of granite which have, from time to time, been mined. Under the State Lands Act, 1886,[742] a condition is implied in all State grants and leases after 1907 (unless the contrary is expressed), that the State has the right to search for and take any mineral oil found on any lands (section 4(2)). It is also provided that (unless other stated), the grantee or lessee, their successors and assigns shall not work the land for any oil, mines, minerals, quarries, laterite, clay, gravel or sand without the written approval of the President. Instead, they have a duty to preserve all these items. Should these deposits be worked, the State reserves a royalty of 10% of the gross produce (section 7(1)(a)).

336. The State also has an implied right to take without compensation, earth, clay, gravel, sand, stone and other materials which may be required for the building of roads, public buildings and other public purposes, so long as such removal will not affect the dwelling houses or gardens on the land. (section 7(1)(b)).[743]

337. Section 14 of the State Lands (Encroachment) Act prohibits the digging or taking from any State land of '… any mineral, gravel, stone, coral, shell, sand, loam, brick-earth or other product' without a permit from the Land Office. The penalty is a fine of SGD 2,000. It has been mentioned that in regard to the collecting of corals, permission is only granted for scientific, educational or conservation purposes.

742. Ordinance 2 of 1886, Cap. 314, 1996 Rev. Ed.
743. *See* Tang Hang Wu and Kelvin FK Loh, *Tan Sook Yee's Principles of Singapore Land Law,* 4th ed. Lexis Nexis (2019) Chapter 23 'Planning and Development'.

Chapter 5. Zoning and Land-Use Planning

§1. History

338. Land-use planning started soon after Singapore was founded by Sir Stamford Raffles of the East India Company in 1819, when he realised its potential as a trading port for England.[744] The early laws relating to buildings were aimed at ensuring adequate ventilation and proper disposal of garbage for reasons of public health. There was no comprehensive planning legislation until 1927, with the establishment of the Singapore Improvement Trust, which proposed a General Improvement Plan for Singapore. However, these controls were very limited. The Japanese invasion in the Second World War created severe housing needs, as the city had to be rebuilt. In 1947, the Singapore Housing Committee recommended that a master development plan be developed for the whole island. It can be said that modern land-use planning started in 1955 with the completion of the Master Plan, which was introduced in the Planning Ordinance, passed in 1959.

I. The Master Plan

339. Based closely on the UK Town and Country Planning Act, 1947,[745] the 1958 Master Plan[746] emphasised comprehensive development through physical planning. Land use was controlled by zoning and density/plot ratios. All land was (and still is) zoned for a particular use. Land owners who wish to change the use of their land or to develop their land had to comply with the requirements of the Master Plan.[747] The planning authority was given extensive powers to control all developments and subdivisions of land. Written permission from the authority had to be obtained before any land could be developed or subdivided. The Ordinance provided the machinery for the Planning Authority to plan, prepare and review the Master Plan every five years.

340. When Singapore became a Republic on 9 August 1965, this began a period of remarkable growth and development, transforming Singapore into 'one of the

744. Singapore was founded on 30 Jan. 1819, when Sir Stamford Raffles, made an agreement with the Temenggong of Johore for the establishment of a British outpost in Singapore and for exclusive jurisdiction over it. Raffles was Lieutenant-Governor of Java from 1813 to 1816 and was knighted in 1816 by the Prince Regent on his return to England. *See* http://www.nndb.com/people/709/000104397/;http://www.britannica.com/eb/article-9062451/Sir-Stamford-Raffles.
745. No. 12 of 1959.
746. The Master Plan as originally conceived, comprised four component maps, namely, the Central Area Map, Town Map, Island Map and Additional Planning Area Map, accompanied by a Written Statement and a Report of Survey. The maps show the various zones for particular or intended use, while the Written Statement gave guidance by describing the zoning categories and the maximum intensities of development. It was the first comprehensive development plan for Singapore.
747. The Ordinance was soon amended to allow the imposition of a development charge in 1964, and to impose a two year time limit for the carrying out of any development.

most intensively – and successfully – planned cities in the world'.[748] Faced with the urgent task of creating economic opportunities and employment, as well as the need to build housing for the masses, land-use planning was especially important. It was essential that the utilisation of land resources be carefully planned and executed.

341. The Master Plan, drawn up during the early years of transition, when Singapore was just emerging from colonial rule, was soon found wanting. Based on traditional planning concepts, it was static and inadequate for a city embarking on dynamic growth through industrial development. The five-yearly reviews merely served to update the Plan by incorporating all ad hoc alterations in the interim.[749] A new form of planning was needed – a Plan that would conceptualise future developments and thus enable the authorities to plan for it. The Concept Plan was developed to fill this void – it is a strategic land-use plan that will guide Singapore's development for the next forty to fifty years. It is reviewed every ten years to ensure there is sufficient land to meet long-term population and economic growth while providing a good quality living environment. The Concept Plan looks at all land-use needs such as housing, business, transport, infrastructure, recreation and community needs; seeking to balance the different demands for land and ensuring there is sufficient land for future generations.

II. The Concept Plans

A. *Concept Plan 1971*

342. This was initiated with the assistance of the United Nations Development Program (UNDP). It laid the broad guidelines for long-range physical development, including the building of a new international airport, as well as environmental infrastructure for waste management and pollution control. It also identified development constraints and major land uses that affect the environment, such as areas for highly pollutive and hazardous industries, airport zones, and live-firing areas for military training. It projected land needs for environmental infrastructure such as sewage treatment plants and refuse disposal facilities (dump sites and incinerators), as well as transportation and communication needs. It also identified ecologically sensitive areas for nature conservation and for the protection of water catchments.

---

748. Malcolm Grant, Singapore Planning Law – Commentary on the Planning Act 1989 at p. 7. *See also* Nat Khublall & Belinda Yuen, Development Control and Planning Law in Singapore, 199, Chapter 1; Tang Hang Wu & Kelvin FK Loh, Tan Sook Yee's Principles of Singapore Land Law, 3rd ed. Lexis Nexis (2009), 4th ed. Lexis Nexis (2019) Chapter 23. *See also* Heng Chye Kiang ed. 50 Years of Urban Planning in Singapore (2017) World Scientific.

749. Reviews were conducted in 1965, 1970, 1975, 1980, 1985, 1991 and 1997. A thorough review was made in 1997, culminating in the passing of the new Planning Act in 1998 (Act 3 of 1998). It preserved the old provisions that require the Master Plan to be reviewed 'at least once in every five years' – *see* Malcolm Grant's Commentary on this New Act, above.

B. The 1991 Revised Concept Plan: 'A Tropical City of Excellence'

343. The 1971 Concept Plan was revised twenty years later. The Revised Concept Plan 1991 focused on sustaining economic growth and providing a good quality of life, with Singapore as a 'Tropical City of Excellence, an exotic island and an international investment hub.'[750] It was based on a time frame projected to the Year X, an unspecified year beyond 2010, where the population is anticipated to reach 4 million. This day came sooner than expected, at the turn of the new millennium, necessitating the Plan's review. The Plan was reviewed with considerable public discussion. While the public approved of more intensive building, they also wanted more greenery and nature areas, and the preservation of a sense of identity. The government announced a nature conservation policy that promised to set aside 5% of the total land area to be preserved as nature sites.[751] Nineteen nature sites were identified to be monitored by the NParks. However, not all these sites were legally protected.

C. Concept Plan 2001 'Towards a Thriving World-Class City'

344. Concept Plan 2001 entitled 'Towards a Thriving World-Class City in 2001' was drafted after taking into account public feedback.[752] It emphasised a 'live-work-play environment, a dynamic city for business, leisure and entertainment', and 'the cultivation of a deep sense of identity by creating a distinctive and delightful city where people can fondly call home'.[753] It looked at creating a thriving world-class city for the next forty to fifty years in the twenty-first century, for a projected population of 5.5 million. It promised new homes in familiar places, high-rise city living, more choices for recreation, greater flexibility for businesses, a global business centre, an extensive rail network, and a focus on identity.

345. A Parks and Waterbodies Plan[754] was drawn up by the Urban Redevelopment Authority (URA) and the National Parks Board (NParks) to guide the development of parks and waterbodies for the next fifteen years. After extensive public consultation,[755] NParks also commissioned the Singapore Institute of Architects to develop a Streetscape Greenery Master Plan to guide the greening and landscape of Singapore's streets. Development control guidelines have also been relaxed to encourage 'skyrise greenery', including landscaped sky terraces and roof gardens, and landscaped balconies and bridges.

---

750. *Living the Next Lap,* 1991, Urban Redevelopment Authority; *see also* Martin Perry, Lily Kong & Brenda Yeoh, *Singapore: A Developmental City-State,* 1997.
751. *Singapore – A Sustainable City,* Ministry of the Environment, 2002 at p. 21.
752. 'URA Releases Concept Plan 2001 After Extensive Consultations', 20 Jul. 2001, http://www.ura.gov.sg/pr/text/pr01-34.html.
753. http://www.ura.gov.sg/conceptplan2001/index.html.
754. http://www.ura.gov.sg/pwbid/.
755. *See* Speech by Dr Vivian Balakrishna, 'More than 35,000 people visited the exhibition, and we received about 4,500 feedback replies.' at http://www.ura.gov.sg/pr/text/pr03-04.html; Carol Lim, 'Ideas for parks and identity come full circle', *Skyline,* January/February 2003, 7.

346. The Identity Plan identified various areas in Singapore that are worthy of conservation, recognising areas that have 'colour and vibrancy', recognising that 'community life, streetscape and activities are unique anchors that contribute to the character, colour and identity of a place … and that the social history of an area is an important component of its sense of place'.[756]

III. Development Guide Plans (DGPs)

347. As the Concept Plans are only strategic plans, more detailed plans are required. These take the form of Development Guide Plans (DGPs), which detail planning and development at the local level. DGPs show the permissible land use and density for every parcel of land in Singapore. They contain detailed development guidelines on land use, including plot ratios, building height, urban design, urban conservation and road networks. Each DGP area is envisaged to have a population of 150,000, served by a town centre.[757] Presently, there are fifty-five DGPs for the entire Republic, including eleven in the Central Area. Each DGP that is completed is gazetted and replaces the corresponding part of the Master Plan.[758]

348. Thus, while the Concept Plans lay down the directions for the development of Singapore, the DGPs show the permissible land use for each plot of land through the use of zoning. Land development is strictly regulated. No person may develop any land without the written permission of the competent authority.[759] Subdivisions of land are also prohibited unless with written approval.

Zoning and conservation are now acknowledged as part of the whole planning process. Indeed, the Code of Practice on Pollution Control starts with a chapter on the 'Judicious Siting of Industries'.

IV. The Current Master Plan (2019) and Concept Plan (2011)

349. The 2011 Concept Plan Review began in 2009 and a public consultation for its review was launched in 2010. This was the Concept Plan 2011 Review Public Consultation exercise. Two focus groups were appointed to discuss four issues identified – the first, to look into quality of life and ageing issues; and the second to examine issues of sustainability and identity. Each focus group comprised about thirty-five members with a good balance of members from professional organisations, NGOs, academics, community leaders and youth to represent a broad

756. *See* https://www.ura.gov.sg/Corporate/Resources/Ideas-and-Trends/Focusing-On-Identity.
757. John Keung 'Planning for Sustainable Urban Development: The Singapore Approach', in Yuen, *supra* n. 748, p. 17.
758. *See* the Master Plan Written Statement 2001 – http://www.ura.gov.sg/ppd/gazettedmp2003/pdf/Written-Statement%202003.pdf.
759. Section 12(1) and (2), Planning Act. The Minister has designated the Chief Planner as the competent authority.

spectrum of the population. In addition, the public was able to give their feedback through an online survey on the URA website. Findings from the online survey were also given to the focus groups to facilitate deliberations. The Concept Plan 2011 charted Singapore's long-term growth to achieve the following key objectives:[760]

- Economic growth opportunities.
- Good quality living environment.
- Inclusive society where needs of various sectors of the population are taken care of.
- A sustainable Singapore that balances growth with responsible environmental management.
- An endearing home where people have a strong sense of belonging to Singapore.

The 2011 Concept Plan was complemented by the findings of the Population White Paper released in January 2013 and the Land-Use Plan in that same month. The Land-Use Plan contained broad strategies and proposals to provide physical capacity to sustain a high-quality living environment for a possible population range of 6.5 to 6.9 million by 2030, as well as setting aside land to provide options beyond 2030.[761]

350. The 2019 Master Plan[762] was gazetted on 27 November 2019 and focuses on planning for inclusive, sustainable and green neighbourhoods with community spaces and amenities for all to enjoy.[763] It is to be read with its Written Statement, 2019.[764] It also includes strategies that plan for rejuvenation of familiar places and creation of capacity to meet future needs. Preparation of and the review process for the 2019 Master Plan involved much public engagement – URA reached out to multiple groups of stakeholders through many forms such as public exhibitions, focus group sessions, community workshops and stakeholder meetings. The 2019 Master Plan covers five key themes:

1. Liveable and inclusive communities.
2. Local hubs, global gateways.
3. Rejuvenating familiar places.
4. A sustainable and resilient city of the future.
5. Convenient and sustainable mobility.

760. *See* URA News Release 2010 'URA Launches Public Consultation for the Review of Concept Plan 2011' (23 Jan. 2010) at http://habitatnews.nus.edu.sg/pdf/20100127-URA%20CP2011%20Media%20Release.pdf.
761. *See* https://www.ura.gov.sg/Corporate/Planning/Concept-Plan/Land-Use-Plan.
762. *See* https://www.ura.gov.sg/Corporate/Planning/Master-Plan.
763. https://www.ura.gov.sg/Corporate/Planning/Master-Plan/Introduction.
764. https://www.ura.gov.sg/-/media/Corporate/Planning/Master-Plan/MP19writtenstatement.pdf?la=en.

V. The Draft Master Plan (2025) and Long-Term Plan Review (2021)

351. In 2021, the Concept Plan was renamed to Long-Term Plan. Public engagement for the review was conducted from July 2021 to August 2022, engaging over 15,000 people from all walks of life, through a variety of platforms:[765]

– More than 5,600 through an online poll.
– More than 1,200 through in-depth workshops and facilitated discussions.
– More than 7,000 through participatory segments in webinars.
– About 1,200 youths through partnership with the National Youth Council (NYC).[766]

The engagements were designed to first understand Singaporeans' hopes, aspirations and concerns for Singapore's future, to develop a collective vision and shared values for Singapore in the next fifty years and beyond.

A set of planning principles and strategies was subsequently developed based on trends and challenges Singapore faces in the future, as well as ideas and feedback collected over the course of the public engagement. In developing them, URA also considered the need to balance various trade-offs, such as the diverse feedback received from Singaporeans and stakeholders, potential implications of each strategy, as well as the wide spectrum of competing needs for our limited land.

352. The Draft Master Plan 2025 (DMP2025) was launched in June 2025. Since October 2023, URA has engaged almost 220,000 people for their feedback on development plans of varying scales in the DMP2025, shaped around four themes:

– shaping a happy, healthy city where all can live well, play delightfully and move efficiently;
– enabling sustainable growth with a vibrant economy that provides quality work opportunities;
– strengthening urban resilience to combat climate change and optimise limited land use resources; and
– stewarding nature and heritage to enhance natural capital and built heritage.

This was the most extensive public engagement effort to date, to ensure that the DMP2025 balances diverse priorities at the national, community and individual levels.[767]

765. *See* https://www.ura.gov.sg/-/media/Corporate/Planning/LTPR21/Annex_C_publicfeedbackresponses.pdf.
766. *See* https://www.ura.gov.sg/-/media/Corporate/Media-Room/2022/Jun/pr22-25a.pdf.
767. https://www.ura.gov.sg/Corporate/Media-Room/Media-Releases/pr25-32.

Chapter 6. The Future: Building Capacity in Environmental Law and Management and the Challenges of Climate Change

353. While few local law firms have expertise in environmental law, the situation is changing as several law firms open practice groups focused on environmental, social, and governance (ESG) law, and more students study environmental law.[768] Judges do not have special training in environmental law, nor are there special environmental courts. Special courts are not necessary as a good environmental management system (EMS) is in place and there are not many cases that involve environmental law.[769]

§1. Environmental Education

354. Efforts to build capacity in environmental law began in the Law Faculty, National University of Singapore (NUS) in 1994. The Faculty established the Asia-Pacific Centre for Environmental Law (APCEL)[770] in 1996, in close cooperation and collaboration with the IUCN-Commission on Environmental Law and the United Nations Environment Programme (UNEP). APCEL is a founding member of the IUCN Academy of Environmental Law.[771] The Faculty now offers several courses on environmental law and APCEL seeks to help build local and regional capacity in teaching and research in environmental law.

355. In 2001, NUS started a multi-disciplinary graduate programme on environmental management, the Master of Science in Environmental Management (MEM), hosted by the School of Design and Environment (SDE).[772] Half of the students in this programme are from abroad, mostly from developing countries in Asia. NUS has also launched a multi-disciplinary undergraduate programme in environmental studies, the Bachelor in Environmental Studies (BES), in 2011, jointly hosted by the Geography Department in the Faculty of Arts & Social Sciences (FASS), and the Department of Biological Sciences, Faculty of Science.[773] For Graduates, NUS has launched a Master of Science in Climate Change and Sustainability, one year single-degree coursework MSc programme based in the Department of Geography in

768. *See* https://www.straitstimes.com/singapore/trio-of-big-firms-take-the-lead-in-esg-law.
769. *See* Lye Lin Heng 'The Judiciary and Environmental Governance in Singapore', *Journal of Court Innovation: The Role of the Environmental Judiciary (NY)*, Vol. 3 No. 1, Winter 2010, pp. 133–155.
770. *See* http://www.law.nus.edu.sg/apcel/.
771. *See* http://www.iucnael.org/.
772. This programme commenced in 2001 and involves the collaboration of nine faculties/schools in NUS. Environmental Law is a core module, taught by professors from the Law Faculty's APCEL. The SDE has recently merged with the Faculty of Engineering to form the College of Design and Engineering. *See* the MEM programme at https://cde.nus.edu.sg/mem/.
773. *See* http://www.envstudies.nus.edu.sg/. This programme commenced in 2010 following the success of the MEM programme, and involves the collaboration of the same nine faculties and schools in NUS.

2024.[774] The Yale-NUS Liberal Arts programme also had environmental studies as one of its majors for students admitted from 2022 onwards. A student may also pursue a minor in Environmental Studies by completing five Environmental Studies courses, on top of their major. Additionally, for the eco-curious, most Environmental Studies modules are open to students from all fields of study at Yale-NUS.[775] However, the Yale-NUS collaboration came to an end in 2025. NUS has also established a Centre for Nature-based Climate Solutions based on the Faculty of Science.[776] In 2025, NTU launched the NTU Centre for Climate Change and Environmental Health.[777]

§2. Climate Change

356. As a small island-state, Singapore is particularly vulnerable to the effects of climate change.[778] Singapore is especially concerned with impacts such as rising sea levels and temperatures, and the likelihood of more intense storms leading to floods that will threaten its freshwater management as well as its food security, and bring increased vector-borne diseases. Singapore's main climate change strategy is energy efficiency. Its key adaptation measures include coastline protection, addressing flood risks, food security and managing the availability of fresh water. The challenges of climate change and Singapore's response have been discussed. They form an important part of Singapore's Green Plan 2030.

§3. The Singapore Green Plan 2030

357. The Singapore government announced its Singapore Green Plan 2030 on 10 February 2021, calling for a 'whole-of-nation movement' to advance the national agenda on sustainable development. The plan, spearheaded by five ministries (the Ministry of Education (MOE), the Ministry of National Development (MND), the Ministry of Sustainability and the Environment (MSE), the Ministry of Trade and Industry (MTI) and the Ministry of Transport (MOT)), charts Singapore's green targets over the next ten years. It also strengthens Singapore's commitments under the United Nations' 2030 Sustainable Development Agenda and Paris Agreement. There are six areas of focus:

1. City in Nature
2. Sustainable Living
3. Energy Reset

774. *See* https://nus.edu.sg/nusgiving/news-article/2024/08/05/nurturing-natures-guardians-environmental-education-at-nus.
775. *See* https://envs.yale-nus.edu.sg/programme-2/.
776. *See* https://www.nus.edu.sg/cncs/.
777. *See* https://www.ntu.edu.sg/news/detail/new-research-centre-tackles-climate-change-health-risks-in-the-tropics.
778. *See* https://www.mfa.gov.sg/SINGAPORES-FOREIGN-POLICY/International-Issues/Climate-Change.

4. Green Economy
5. Green Government
6. Resilient Future.

The details can be found on this website[779] and on the websites of the five government agencies that are part of this laudable effort. Laws will have to be passed together with soft laws, such as Guidelines and implemented accordingly. It suffices to summarise the main targets:

1. City in Nature
   – the planting of 1 million trees across Singapore by 2030;
   – increased land for nature parks by over 50% from the 2020 baseline;
   – every household to be within a ten-minute walk from a park.
2. Sustainable Living
   – Green schools: Reduction of two-thirds of net carbon emissions from schools by 2030; at least 20% of schools to be carbon neutral from 2030;
   – Green commutes: 75% of trips during peak periods to be on mass public transport by 2030; existing cycling paths to be tripled by 2030; rail networks to be expanded from 230 km in 2021 to 360 km by 2030;
   – Green Citizenry: reduce waste to landfill per capita per day by 20% by 2026 and by 30% by 2030; reduce household water consumption to 130 litres a day.[780]
3. Energy Reset Targets
   – *Cleaner energy vehicles*: stop registration of new diesel cars and taxis from 2025; from 2030, all new cars and taxis must be of cleaner-energy models; road tax for electric cars to be lowered; 60,000 electric vehicle (EV) charging points by 2030, with 8 EV-ready towns by 2025
   – *Greener infrastructure and buildings:*
      i. Green 80% of buildings (by Gross Floor Area (GFA) by 2030; 80% of new buildings (by GFA) to be super-low-energy buildings by 2030;
      ii. Sustainable towns and districts – the reduction of energy consumption in existing HDB towns by 15%;
      iii. Green energy – quadruple energy consumption in HDB towns by 15% by 2025; diversify electricity support with clean electricity imports; increase R&D on renewable energy and emerging low-carbon technologies.

   By 2021, PUB should generate sufficient solar energy from floating solar panels to power 100% of Singapore's waterworks; By 2025, energy consumption for desalination should be reduced from the current 3.5 kWh/m^3 to 2 kWh/m^3 and Singapore's first integrated used water treatment facility at Tuas Nexus should be 100% energy sufficient; 2030 & beyond – reduce energy desalination

779. https://www.greenplan.gov.sg/.
780. This was 141 litres per household per day in 2018. *See* https://www.pub.gov.sg/watersupply/singaporewaterstory.

to 1 kWh/m^3. This will be done through investments in desalination and used water technologies, e.g., electro-chemical desalination and step-feed membrane technology.

4. Green Economy – this aims to seek new investments to be among the best-in-class in energy/carbon efficiency, and view sustainability as a new engine for jobs and growth. This includes establishing Singapore as a leading centre for green finance, a carbon services and trading hub in Asia, and a leading regional centre for developing new sustainability solutions.
5. Resilient Future – this focuses on safeguarding our coastlines against rising sea levels, as well as safeguarding food security and keeping temperatures down.
   - SGD 5 billion will be dedicated to coastal and drainage flood protection measures.
   - Formulation of coastal protection plans.
   - Produce 30% of food locally and sustainably by 2030.
   - Moderate temperature rise by increasing urban greenery.

Conclusion

358. Environmental law in Singapore is informed not only by broader environmental principles but also by its size, industry profile, legal and political systems, geography, and future ambitions. Its laws and policies to address the environmental issues it faces – pollution control, management of hazardous substances and waste, climate change, marine conservation, nature conservation, and wildlife protection – are constantly refined to stay consistent with these contexts as they evolve. Singapore's international obligations will also continue influencing and shaping the content of its environmental laws.

359. As we continue to face the 'triple planetary crisis' of climate change, biodiversity loss, and pollution,[781] it is clear that the environment will be at the forefront of public and private interests. By extension, it ought to continue being a focus for teaching and research in tertiary and research institutions. This is reinforced by the Singapore Green Plan 2030, which demonstrates that the environment will continue being a major focus for the government, and a 'whole of nation' approach will be taken to address all environmental concerns and challenges.

781. *See* https://unfccc.int/news/what-is-the-triple-planetary-crisis.

Selected Bibliography

Chan H.M., Helena. *The Legal System of Singapore.* Butterworths Asia, 1995.

Chan Sek Keong, *Judicial Review: From Angst to Empathy* (2010) Sing. Acad. LJ 469–489.

Chan Sek Keong, The Courts and the 'Rule of Law' in Singapore (2012) Sing JLS 209.

Chun, Joseph. 'Beyond Real Estate: Sowing the Legal Seeds for an Ethical Public Land Stewardship in Singapore'. *Macquarie J. Int'l. & Comp. Envtl. L.* 3 (2006): 1.

Chun, Joseph. 'Enhancing the Garden City: Towards a Deeper Shade of Green'. *Sing. Ac. L.J.* 18 (2006).

Chun, Joseph. 'Reclaiming the Public Trust in Singapore'. *Sing. Ac. L.J.* 17 (2005): 717.

Foo, K.B., K.L. Koh & L.H. Lye. 'Environmental Protection: The Legal Framework'. In *Environment and the City: Sharing Singapore's Experience and Future Challenges,* edited by Ooi Giok Ling. Singapore: The Institute of Policy Studies/ Times Academic Press, 1995.

Foo, K.B. 'Control of Pollution in Singapore'. *S.Ac. L.J.* 5 (1993).

Foo, K.B. 'Environmental Criminal Law in Singapore'. *S.Ac. L.J.* 9 (1997).

Grant, Malcolm. Singapore Planning Law: Commentary on the Planning Act 1989. Butterworths Asia, 1999.

Hassan, Parvex & Azim Azfar. 'Securing Environmental Rights Through Public Interest Litigation in Southeast Asia'. *Va. Envtl. L.J.* 22 (2003–2004): 215.

Heng Chye Kiang ed. *50 Years of Urban Planning in Singapore* (2017) World Scientific.

Jain, M.P. Administrative Law of Malaysia and Singapore. 3rd ed. MLJ, 1997.

'Judicial Decisions and Alternative Dispute Resolution'. In *Capacity Building for Environmental Law in the Asian and Pacific Region,* edited by Donna Craig, Koh Kheng-Lian & N. Robinson. Vol. 1, Ch. 11. ADB, 2002.

Keung, John. 'Planning for Sustainable Urban Development: The Singapore Approach'. In *Development Control and Planning Law in Singapore*, edited by N. Khublall & Belinda Yuen. Longman, 1999.

Koh Kheng-Lian, ASEAN Environmental Law, Policy and Governance: Selected Documents, Vol. I (2009) and II (2012), World Scientific.

Koh, Kheng-Lian, Robinson, Nicholas A, Lye, LH 'ASEAN Environmental Legal Integration: Sustainable Goals' (Cambridge University Press: 2016).

Selected Bibliography

Koh, Kheng-Lian, 'The Garden City and Beyond: The Legal Framework'. In *Environment and the City: Sharing Singapore's Experience and Future Challenges*, edited by Ooi Giok Ling. Ch. 6. Singapore: Institute of Policy Studies, 1995.

Koh, Kheng-Lian, 'Singapore: Fashioning Landscape for "the Garden City"'. In *Landscape Conservation Law: Present Trends and Perspectives in International and Comparative Law.* Part II. Proceedings of a Colloquium Commemorating the 50th Anniversary of IUCN, The World Conservation Union, 30 October 1998, Palais du Luxembourg, Paris. IUCN, 2000.

Koh, Kheng-Lian 'Singapore Report'. In *Biodiversity Planning in Asia*, edited by Jeremy Carew-Reid. IUCN, 2002.

Koh, Kheng-Lian, 'Singapore'. In Legislation for the Implementation of the ASEAN Agreement on the Conservation of Nature and Natural Resources: Country Reports. IUCN Environmental Law Programme, 1994.

Koh, Kheng-Lian & N.A. Robinson. 'Regional Environmental Governance "Examining the Association of Southeast Asian Nations (ASEAN)"'. In *Global Environmental Governance: Options & Opportunities*, edited by Daniel C. Esty & Maria H. Ivanova. Yale School of Forestry & Environmental Studies, 2002.

Koh, Kheng-Lian & N.A. Robinson. 'Strengthening Sustainable Development in Regional Inter-governmental Governance: Lessons from the "ASEAN Way"'. *Sing. JICL* 6 (2002).

Koh, Kheng-Lian. 'The Discourse of Environmental Security in the ASEAN Context', Chapter 9 in Jessup B & Rubenstein K. (eds) Environmental Discourses in Public and International Law (Cambridge University Press: 2012), pp 218–237.

Koh Kheng-Lian. 'Transboundary and Global Environmental Issues: The Role of ASEAN in Transnational Environmental Law', Vol 1(1), Transnational Environmental Law, 1, pp 1–16 (Cambridge University Press: 2012).

Lee, Kuan Yew. 'Greening Singapore'. In From Third World to First: The Singapore Story: 1965–2000: Singapore and the Asian Economic Boom. HarperCollins, 2000.

Ling, Sing Kong & Chua Sian Eng. *More than a Garden City.* Singapore: Parks and Recreation Department, Ministry of National Development, 1992.

Lye Lin Heng, 'A Fine City in a Garden – Environmental Law and Governance in Singapore', (2008) SJLS 68–117

Lye Lin Heng, *Country Report – Singapore,* (2015) IUCN Academy of Environmental Law Journal, pp. 360–368.

Lye, Lin Heng. 'De-control'. In *Landlord and Tenant Law*, edited by Lye Lin Heng. Ch. 12. Singapore Law Series. Malaya Law Review/Butterworths, 1990.

Lye, Lin Heng. 'The Enforcement of Environmental Law in Singapore'. *Environmental Law and Policy in Asia: Issues of Enforcement*, edited by Yoshihiro Nomura & Naoyuki Sakumoto. Tokyo: Institute of Developing Economies, March 1997.

Lye, Lin Heng. 'Environmental Law in Singapore'. In *Comparative Environmental Law*, edited by Nicholas Robinson. Oceana Publications, March 1998.

Lye, Lin Heng. *Environmental Law in Singapore.* Tokyo: Institute of Developing Economies, 1996.

Lye, Lin-Heng. 'Environmental Law, Policy, Governance and Management for Cities: Getting it Right for a Sustainable Future – The Singapore Story', Chapter 7 in *Environmental Policies in Asia – Perspectives from Seven Asian Countries*, Jing Huang, Shreekant Gupta, eds. (2014) World Scientific pp. 171–202.

Lye, Lin Heng. 'Environmental Taxation in the Regulation of Traffic and the Control of Vehicular Pollution in Singapore'. In *Critical Issues in Environmental Taxation: International and Comparative Perspectives*, Vol. 1. Oxford University Press, 2003.

Lye, Lin Heng. 'Implementation of the Convention on International Trade in Endangered Species in Singapore'. *Journal of International Wildlife Law & Policy 2*, No. 1 (1999).

Lye, Lin Heng, 'Land Law and the Environment – Re-examining the Concept of Ownership and Forging New Rights and Obligations in a Changed World', (2010) SAcLJ 189–229.

Lye, Lin Heng. 'Landscape Protection Laws in the Evolution of Modern Singapore'. In *Landscape, Nature and Law: A Tribute to Alexander Kiss*, edited by Herman Antonio Benjamin. Sao Paolo, Brazil: Laws for a Green Planet Institute.

Lye, Lin Heng. 'Land-Use Planning, Environmental Management and the Garden City as an Urban Development Approach in Singapore'. In *Land Use Law for Sustainable Development*, edited by N. Chalifour et al. Cambridge University Press, 2007.

Lye, Lin Heng. 'Legal Protection of the Natural Environment'. In *State of the Natural Environment in Singapore*, edited by Clive Briffett, & Chew Ho Hua. Nature Society Singapore, June 1999.

Lye, Lin Heng. 'Nature Conservation Laws – The Legal Protection of Flora and Fauna in Singapore', in *The Singapore Red Data Book – Threatened Plants & Animals of Singapore*, 5–13 (GWH Davison, PKL Ng, HC Ho, eds., 2d ed., Nat. Soc. September 2008).

Lye Lin Heng, 'Public Housing in Singapore: A Success Story in Sustainable Development' in Rose-Lisa Eisma-Osorio, EA Kirk, JA Albin (eds), *The Impact of Environmental Law – Stories of the World We Want* (2020) Edward Elgar, pp. 128–153.

Lye Lin Heng. 'The Judiciary and Environmental Governance in Singapore' (2010) *Journal of Court Innovation: The Role of the Environmental Judiciary*, Vol. 3 No. 1, Winter 2010, pp. 133–155.

Lye Lin-Heng & Rose-Liza Eisma-Osorio. 'Regulatory Measures on Access & Benefit Sharing for Biological and Genetic Resources – National & Regional Perspectives from the Philippines, Singapore & ASEAN', chapter 13, Charles M McManis & Burton Ong (2017) *Routledge Handbook of Biodiversity and the Law.*

Lye, Lin Heng. 'Singapore: Long Term Environmental Policies'. In *Cities of the Pacific Rim: Diversity & Sustainability*, edited by Genevieve Dubois-Taine & Christian Henriot. PECC Sustainable Cities Taskforce, 2001.

Lye, Lin Heng. 'Singapore's New Environmental Law: The Environmental Pollution Control Act, 1999'. SJLS (2000): 1–32.

Lye, Lin Heng. 'Transport-Based Air Pollution Management: The Singapore Experience'. *Asia-Pacific Journal of Environmental Law* 6, Nos 3–4 (2001).

Lye, Lin Heng. 'Wildlife Protection Laws in Singapore'. SJLS (1991): 287–319.

Ministry of the Environment. *The Singapore Green Plan,* 1992.

Selected Bibliography

Ministry of the Environment. The Singapore Green Plan: Action Programmes, 1993.
Ministry of the Environment. *Singapore: My Clean and Green Home,* 1997.
Ministry of the Environment. *Singapore: A Sustainable City,* 2002.
Ministry of the Environment. Singapore's Initial National Communication under the United Nations Framework Convention on Climate Change, August 2000.
Ministry of the Environment and Water Resources. *The Singapore Green Plan 2012,* rev. ed. 2006.
Ministry of the Environment and Water Resources, Singapore. *Annual Reports.*
Ministry of the Environment and Water Resources, Singapore. *Code of Practice on Pollution Control.* 3rd ed. National Environment Agency, February 2004.
Ministry of Sustainability and the Environment, *The Singapore Green Plan 2030.*
Ministry of Environment Climate Action PlanNational Environment Agency, Environmental Protection Division. *Annual Reports.*
National Environment Agency, Singapore. *Annual Reports.*
National Parks Board Conserving our Biodiversity: Singapore's National Biodiversity Strategy and Action Plan NParks Board 2009, updated 2019.
NParks – Nature Conservation Master Plan (NCMP) 2015.
Nparks Biodiversity Impact Guidelines.
Nature Society, Singapore. Proposed Golf Course at Lower Peirce Reservoir: An Environmental Impact Assessment, 1992.
Nature Society, Singapore. The Singapore Red Data Book: Threatened Plants & Animals of Singapore, June 1994.
Perry, Martin, Lily Kong & Brenda Yeoh. *Singapore: A Developmental City State.* World Cities Series. New York: Wiley, 1997.
Perry, Martin, Lily Kong & Brenda Yeoh. 'Urban Conservation and Heritage Management'. In *Singapore: A Developmental City State.* Ch. 9. John Wiley & Sons, 1997.
Robinson, N.A. 'Forest Fires as a Common International Concern: Precedents for the Progressive Development of International Environmental Law'. Pace Env. L.R. 18 (2002–2001).
Shawn, Lum & Ilsa Sharp (eds). *A View from the Summit: The Story of Bukit Timah Nature Reserve.* Singapore: National Parks Board, 1996.
Sumiko, Tan. *Home, Work, Play.* Singapore: Urban Redevelopment Authority, 1999.
Tan Khee-Jin, Alan. 'The ASEAN Agreement on Transboundary Haze Pollution: Prospects for Compliance and Effectiveness in Post-Suharto Indonesia'. NYU Envtl. L.J. 13 (2005): 647.
Tan Khee-Jin, Alan. 'Forest Fires in Indonesia: State Responsibility and International Liability'. Int'l. & Comp. L.Q. 48 (1999): 826.
Tan Khee-Jin, Alan. Vessel Source Marine Pollution: The Law and Politics of International Regulation. Cambridge University Press, 2006.
Tan Sook Yee. *Principles of Singapore Land Law.* 2nd ed. Butterworths, 2001.
Tan Wee Kiat. *Naturally Yours.* National Parks, 1992.
Tan, Kevin Y.L. An Introduction to Singapore's Constitution. Talisman, 2005.
Tan, Kevin Y.L. 'Parliament and the Making of Law in Singapore'. In *The Singapore Legal System,* edited by Kevin Y. L. Tan. 2nd ed., Ch. 4. Singapore University Press, 1999.

Tan, Kevin Y.L. 'A Short Legal and Constitutional History of Singapore'. In *The Singapore Legal System,* edited by Kevin Y.L. Tan. 2nd ed., Ch. 2. Singapore University Press, 1999.

Tang Hang Wu & Kelvin FK Loh, *Tan Sook Yee's Principles of Singapore Land Law,* 4th ed. Lexis Nexis (2019) Chapter 23 'Planning and Development'.

Tay S.C., Simon. 'Southeast Asian Fires: The Challenge for International Environmental Law and Sustainable Development'. Geo. Int'l. Envtl. L. Rev. 11 (1998–1999): 241.

Tookey, Douglas L. 'Singapore's Environmental Management System: Strengths and Weaknesses and Recommendations for the Years Ahead'. Wm & Mary Envtl. L. & Pol'y Rev. 23 (1998).

UNEP. 'Emerging Trends in National Environmental Legislation in Developing Countries'. In UNEP's New Way Forward, Environmental Law and Sustainable Development. Reproduced in Capacity Building for Environmental Law in the Asian and Pacific Region, edited by Donna Craig, Koh Kheng-Lian & N. Robinson. Vol. 1. ADB, 2002.

Urban Redevelopment Authority, Singapore. Living the Next Lap: Towards a Tropical City of Excellence, 1991.

Urban Redevelopment Authority, Singapore. Skyline, Consulting the Community on Singapore's Future: Bringing Life Back to Heritage Buildings, September/October 2000.

Waller, Edmund. *Landscape Planning in Singapore.* Singapore University Press, 2001.

Woon, Walter. 'The Applicability of English Law in Singapore'. In *The Singapore Legal System,* edited by Kevin Y. L. Tan. 2nd ed., Ch. 6. Singapore University Press, 1999.

Woon, Walter. 'The Doctrine of Judicial Precedent'. In *The Singapore Legal System*, edited by Kevin Y. L. Tan. 2nd ed., Ch. 8. Singapore University Press, 1999.

World Bank Report. 'Doing Business 2007: How to Reform'.

A.T.K. Yee, Richard T. Corlett, S.C. Liew and Hugh T.W. Tan 'The Vegetation of Singapore – An Updated Map' (2011) Gardens Bulletin.

Yeo Tiong Min. 'Jurisdiction of the Singapore Courts'. In *The Singapore Legal System*, edited by Kevin Y.L. Tan. 2nd ed., Ch. 7. Singapore University Press, 1999.

Selected Bibliography

Index

The numbers here refer to paragraph numbers.

Green Plan, 14, 15, 26, 39, 41, 115, 116, 157, 199, 256, 259, 263, 264, 292, 295, 325, 326, 356, 357, 359

Index

Made in the USA
Monee, IL
08 November 2026

68136726R20116